Pacifism, Peace and Modern Welsh Writing

WRITING WALES IN ENGLISH

CREW series of Critical and Scholarly Studies
General Editors: Kirsti Bohata and Daniel G. Williams (*CREW*, Swansea University)

This *CREW* series is dedicated to Emyr Humphreys, a major figure in the literary culture of modern Wales, a founding patron of the *Centre for Research into the English Literature and Language of Wales*. Grateful thanks are due to the late Richard Dynevor for making this series possible.

Other titles in the series

Stephen Knight, *A Hundred Years of Fiction* (978-0-7083-1846-1)
Barbara Prys-Williams, *Twentieth-Century Autobiography* (978-0-7083-1891-1)
Kirsti Bohata, *Postcolonialism Revisited* (978-0-7083-1892-8)
Chris Wigginton, *Modernism from the Margins* (978-0-7083-1927-7)
Linden Peach, *Contemporary Irish and Welsh Women's Fiction* (978-0-7083-1998-7)
Sarah Prescott, *Eighteenth-Century Writing from Wales: Bards and Britons* (978-0-7083-2053-2)
Hywel Dix, *After Raymond Williams: Cultural Materialism and the Break-Up of Britain* (978-0-7083-2153-9)
Matthew Jarvis, *Welsh Environments in Contemporary Welsh Poetry* (978-0-7083-2152-2)
Harri Garrod Roberts, *Embodying Identity: Representations of the Body in Welsh Literature* (978-0-7083-2169-0)
Diane Green, *Emyr Humphreys: A Postcolonial Novelist* (978-0-7083-2217-8)
M. Wynn Thomas, *In the Shadow of the Pulpit: Literature and Nonconformist Wales* (978-0-7083-2225-3)
Linden Peach, *The Fiction of Emyr Humphreys: Contemporary Critical Perspectives* (978-0-7083-2216-1)
Daniel Westover, *R. S. Thomas: A Stylistic Biography* (978-0-7083-2413-4)
Jasmine Donahaye, *Whose People? Wales, Israel, Palestine* (978-0-7083-2483-7)
Judy Kendall, *Edward Thomas: The Origins of His Poetry* (978-0-7083-2403-5)
Damian Walford Davies, *Cartographies of Culture: New Geographies of Welsh Writing in English* (978-0-7083-2476-9)
Daniel G. Williams, *Black Skin, Blue Books: African Americans and Wales 1845–1945* (978-0-7083-1987-1)
Andrew Webb, *Edward Thomas and World Literary Studies: Wales, Anglocentrism and English Literature* (978-0-7083-2622-0)
Alyce von Rothkirch, *J. O. Francis, realist drama and ethics: Culture, place and nation* (978-1-7831-6070-9)
Rhian Barfoot, *Liberating Dylan Thomas: Rescuing a Poet from Psycho-Sexual Servitude* (978-1-7831-6184-3)
Daniel G. Williams, *Wales Unchained: Literature, Politics and Identity in the American Century* (978-1-7831-6212-3)
M. Wynn Thomas, *The Nations of Wales 1890–1914* (978-1-78316-837-8)
Richard McLauchlan, *Saturday's Silence: R. S. Thomas and Paschal Reading* (978-1-7831-6920-7)
Bethan M. Jenkins, *Between Wales and England: Anglophone Welsh Writing of the Eighteenth Century* (978-1-7868-3029-6)
M. Wynn Thomas, *All that is Wales: The Collected Essays of M. Wynn Thomas* (978-1-7868-3088-3)
Laura Wainwright, *New Territories in Modernism: Anglophone Welsh Writing, 1930–1949* (978-1-7868-3217-7)
Siriol McAvoy, *Locating Lynette Roberts: 'Always Observant and Slightly Obscure'* (978-1-7868-3382-2)

PACIFISM, PEACE AND MODERN WELSH WRITING

WRITING WALES IN ENGLISH

LINDEN PEACH

UNIVERSITY OF WALES PRESS
2019

www.uwp.co.uk

British Library CIP Data
A catalogue record for this book is available from the British Library.

ISBN: 978-1-78683-402-7 (hardback)
978-1-78683-403-4 (paperback)
e-ISBN: 978-1-78683-404-1

THE ASSOCIATION FOR
WELSH WRITING IN ENGLISH
CYMDEITHAS LÊN SAESNEG CYMRU

The University of Wales Press acknowledges the financial assistance of the Welsh Books Council in publication of this book.

Typeset by Marie Doherty
Printed by CPI Antony Rowe, Melksham

i

Angela, Hedley, Matthew a Kate

ac er cof am fy mam, fy nhad a'm chwaer Cynthia

Contents

Series Editors' Preface

The aim of this series, since its founding in 2004 by Professor M. Wynn Thomas, is to publish scholarly and critical work by established specialists and younger scholars that reflects the richness and variety of the English-language literature of modern Wales. The studies published so far have amply demonstrated that concepts, models and discourses current in the best contemporary studies can illuminate aspects of Welsh culture, and have also foregrounded the potential of the Welsh example to draw attention to themes that are often neglected or marginalised in anglophone cultural studies. The series defines and explores that which distinguishes Wales's anglophone literature, challenges critics to develop methods and approaches adequate to the task of interpreting Welsh culture, and invites its readers to locate the process of writing Wales in English within comparative and transnational contexts.

Professor Kirsti Bohata and Professor Daniel G. Williams

Founding Editor: Professor M. Wynn Thomas (2004–15)

CREW (*Centre for Research into the English Literature and Language of Wales*)
Swansea University

Preface

Pacifism is not passive. It is part of the radicalism of Wales associated with protest, rebellion and insurgency. The popular conviction that there is, or has been, a tradition of pacifism in Wales has been questioned by reputable Welsh historians, who have traced the way in which the peace organisations have waxed and waned in Wales over the nineteenth and twentieth centuries. But the part that pacifism has played in Welsh life is broader and more complex than the fortunes of the peace movement and is linked to an influential Welsh-language, pacifist intelligentsia.

While this study addresses the organisational history of peace movements in Wales, it is primarily concerned with how pacifism has contributed more widely to Welsh culture, and especially its literature. The part that pacifism has played, and still plays, in the political and cultural evolution of modern Wales is a subject which a literary-historical approach is well equipped to examine and this book breaks new ground in exploring pacifism through texts written in Welsh and English. If anything distinguishes Welsh and English pacifism, it is the Welsh language itself and how Welsh pacifism faces challenges and pressures which never confronted English pacifism. In combining, for the first time, an examination of the history of pacifism with pacifist writing, this study argues that Welsh pacifism and campaigns for peace – through Welsh-language periodicals, pamphlets and literary texts – were brought into existence by a Welsh, and primarily Welsh-language, intelligentsia which it did much, in turn, to constitute.

The texts discussed in this book have been published in English or have been published in translation. The latter is not unproblematic for many reasons, not least because Welsh–English translation is inevitably enmeshed in the wider vicissitudes of Welsh social and cultural politics. Inevitably, these come to the fore in the translation of Welsh pacifist writing into English because pacifists, who historically have been in the vanguard of campaigns in support of nationalism and the Welsh language, have often found themselves confronted by a seemingly impermeable anglicised cultural and political establishment. But in discussing Welsh texts in translation, this book has sought to concentrate on how translators have responded to the subtleties of meaning and the richness of the original Welsh, and have displayed sympathy with the pacifist intentions of the work and its breadth of understanding of pacifism. Beginning with the assumption that readers come to a creative work, whether in translation or in the original language, for the enjoyment of words, the emphasis throughout is on the way in which translators have engaged with particular structures, vocabularies and forms of expression.

It is not news that meaning is always the product of difference between words, but it is particularly important to a discussion of 'pacifism' to keep in mind that the meaning of words is never stable and changes over time. Central to this book is how the concepts of 'pacifism', 'peace' and 'war' stand revealed differently in different works and acquire fresh significances in new contexts. In conflating literature and history, context inevitably assumes considerable significance and this study examines how literature opens up history in ways in which historical discourse alone sometimes fails to do, while always recognising that for many Welsh- and English-language writers context is often a site of anxiety.

This study argues that through a literary-historical approach, relying on the original Welsh or on translation, the philosophical depth, social realism, psychological momentum and even the doubt and despair involved in 'coming out' as a pacifist in a non-pacifist society are more convincingly unveiled. The best Welsh pacifist works, or creative works indebted to concepts which have been developed by Welsh pacifists, are among the most innovative in Welsh writing. In them, it is not only customary discourses, beliefs and preoccupations that are challenged but concepts of time, memory, insight, 'knowing' and 'being'. Thus, this study is poised around how pacifist writing unearths a hidden stream of cultural thought, memory and reflection that for the many reasons explored in this study, whether written in English or Welsh, is distinctly Welsh.

This cultural stream is followed through select key texts from the beginning of the twentieth century, when Welsh pacifism was associated primarily with anti-war and no-conscription movements, to the mid-twentieth century, when it evolved into a much broader social ideology concerned with the wider quality of human life, and to the latter half of the twentieth century, when the emphasis within pacifism shifted to anti-nuclear protest and the need to protect and preserve life and the planet itself. The changing nature of pacifism is linked with the evolution of the language of peace and war and an examination, through these varied texts, of where and how they became fixed, albeit temporarily, in wider binaries and hierarchies of meaning. Within this framework, the book explores how the different affiliations which the language of peace and conflict acquired at different times affected the experience of pacifism and conscientious objection.

The experience of conscience, reflection and 'spirituality' constitutes an important part of these texts, many of which are 'religious' in the widest sense. At one level, the failure to recognise this emerges as one of the reasons why Welsh pacifism, beyond a sequence of movements and organisations, has not been fully explored. However, the 'drama' which we find in Welsh pacifism and in many Welsh pacifist texts often lies in the conflict of voice and perspective, the analysis of event and conscience, and the shifting nature of the relationship between the internal and the external. It is the connection between these different levels of insight, reflection, drama and conflict in Welsh pacifist writing that this study begins to explore.

The book also explores how 'pacifism' in Wales came to mean much more than what we might call 'anti-war-ism', and 'peace' itself came to mean not only 'not being at war' but, in the work of some writers, an inner peacefulness. While 'pacifism', which often slips into discussion of opposition to war and violence, and 'peace', where it signifies a peaceful mode of being, are often distinguished from each other and explored as if they are separate spheres, this is not the case in Wales. The work of the key Welsh pacifist-cum-political writers, such as Waldo Williams and D. Gwenallt Jones, reaches out to an external world comprised of a multiplicity of human voices and complex social and communal structures which they seek to transform by their nationalist ambitions and their pacifist values. Even the most 'political' of the Welsh pacifist poets, including T. E. Nicholas, famous for his prison sonnets, and those torn apart by doubt and depression, are motivated by the connection between an innate peacefulness and being human.

ACKNOWLEDGEMENTS

Like all books by teachers in higher education, this work has benefited from discussions with colleagues and students, and I am grateful to all at the Prince's School of Traditional Arts who have contributed to the development of my thoughts and arguments in ways in which some of them may not even be fully aware. In its later stages, the book also benefited from insights and discussions at an international conference on Virginia Woolf and pacifism at the University of Kent, where I delivered a paper on Woolf's influence on the work of one of Wales's leading pacifist writers, Emyr Humphreys.

I have been inspired by scholars and colleagues who have argued for, and have demonstrated in their own works, an interdisciplinary approach to literature, history and geography and by those who have pursued relationships between Welsh- and English-language literature. My own Welsh has provided me with fresh insights into the history and culture of Wales without which this book would not have been possible, and I am indebted to tutors in Welsh at the Open University and Welsh for Adults, Bangor University, for that.

I am grateful, also, for the encouragement and support of the University of Wales Press and especially Dr Llion Wigley (commissioning editor, Welsh Language and Topics) and his colleagues in the production and marketing divisions.

Many authors are indebted to the patience and support of their families who are up to their necks in their own projects, and in my case I must gratefully acknowledge my wife, Angela.

PACIFISM AND PROTEST

1

Mapping Welsh Pacifism

. . . methodd ein hen elyn
Â diffodd y Goleuni Oddi-mewn
Y fflam sy'n oddaith yn ein hydref melyn
A'n troi, er trallod, yn goncwerwyr ewn.

. . . our old enemy failed
To extinguish the Inner Light.
The flame which is ablaze in our yellow autumn
Will turn us, despite sorrow, into bold conquerors.
(Iorwerth C. Peate, 'Diwedd Blwyddyn')

'No nation has produced, in proportion to its population, a greater number of bards, preachers, musicians and rebels.'[1] The fortunes of the Welsh peace movements, important as they have been to the pacifist cause, are only half the story. We must not overlook the wider network of intellectuals, writers, academics, teachers and theologians who have constituted the Welsh, especially the Welsh-language, intelligentsia. Through their individual and collective stand in the name of peace, as well as their contributions to specific peace organisations, a distinctively Welsh pacifism entered Welsh culture. Some of its principal concerns are, and have always been, different from those of English pacifism, and Welsh pacifism can only be understood through the Welsh-language literary platforms and media that have supported it, the forums in which issues have been debated, and the literature – both in Welsh and English – which it directly or indirectly produced.

How pacifism entered Welsh culture, and especially Welsh-language culture, is a complex story that is unique to Wales, as are many of the associations and concerns that it acquired along the way. But through all its twists and turns, what is exciting about Welsh pacifism is that it has always risen to the moment without ever allowing the moment to define it.

WHAT'S IN A WORD?

Pacifism is not something posted on a closed door. It is an ongoing intellectual, moral and spiritual challenge. The term 'pacifism' was coined by Émile Arnaud (1864–1921) at the tenth Universal Peace Congress in 1902. He meant it to mean a 'celebration of peace' rather than simply an 'opposition to war', which he thought of as 'anti-war-ism'.[2] As will emerge in this study, 'Peace' has a broader range of meaning than 'not being at war'. The peace scholars David Cadman and Scherto Gill make a distinction between Western approaches to peace, which, they argue, 'tend to focus on external harmony, accord and respect for citizens, institutions and nations', and Eastern concepts of peace, which 'are more oriented toward personal virtues and inner qualities'.[3] But, as we shall see, particularly as our discussion of the celebrated Welsh pacifist poets Waldo Williams (1904–71) and D. Gwenallt Jones (1899–1968) unfolds, this distinction is not always applicable to Wales.

The meaning of 'pacifism', like peace itself, has proved fluid, acquiring different connotations and emphases at different times and in relation to changing circumstances. It is not necessary to read very far into Welsh pacifist writing before realising that Welsh pacifism is not simply an opposition to war but addresses the structural roots of conflict in society and the social causes of inequalities including gender, class, ethnicity and race, and in doing so supplants them by pro-peace values.

Examining 'pacifism' in a literary-historical context highlights how the meaning of the word, and the different associations which it has acquired, have determined the experiences and the sufferings of those who have declared themselves 'pacifists', often leading to accusations of cowardice, to personal abuse and assault, and to imprisonment and, even, death. A First World War Welsh-language recruiting poster read: 'Anibyniaeth [*sic*] sydd yn Galw am ei Dewraf Dyn.' In calling for the bravest men to volunteer, it immediately set up a stark opposition between those who were the bravest of men and conscientious objectors, which defined not only what was meant by 'conscientious objector' but also by 'dewraf dyn'.

That there is no clear, stable relationship between the word 'pacifist' and what it signifies is a recurring theme of Welsh, particularly

Welsh-language, pacifist writing. At the heart of this concern is the way in which the term relates to other words (or 'signifiers') such as 'coward', 'hero', 'conscience', 'Christian', 'moral', 'saint', 'realist' and 'innocent'; how meaning is culturally constructed; and how this process of constructing meaning engenders binary oppositions and hierarchies, for example 'war hero' and 'conscientious objector', which determine how society sees pacifists. 'Coming out' as a pacifist, for that is what it is, means experiencing one's own language and culture in ways that are not unexpected but nevertheless still shocking. In Welsh writing about pacifism, be it in Welsh or English, the cultural and linguistic divisions within Wales stand more revealed.

One of the most important twentieth-century Welsh pacifists, George M. Ll. Davies (1880–1949), characteristically pulls no punches in his posthumously published collection of reflective essays and meditations, *Pilgrimage of Peace* (1951): 'We are living according to the thought standard of the "herd" and are unconsciously dominated by these subtle and disguised herd instincts.'[4] Davies was a Nonconformist through and through, and, as the literary critic Wynn Thomas says, this meant 'radically dissenting, both in spirit and in actual social practice, from the comfortably established order of things'.[5] In his essay, 'In Forma Pauperis' (1922), Davies argues that from a radical pacifist point of view, language as well as actions have to be 'stripped of its camouflage'.[6] By camouflage he means the political and ideological inferences language acquires. In relation to war, he suggests that this is often 'according to the outlook of victors and vanquished', so there is an ideological difference between 'Guards in red and Red Guards'; 'guards and gun-men' and between how a 'martyr' in Ireland is a 'miscreant' in England (ETP, p. 66). It is an argument that others, such as the Welsh cultural critic Ned Thomas, have taken further. Thomas maintains:

> Languages are very delicate networks of historically accumulated associations . . . [with] innumerable and untraceable connections with the thought of past centuries, with the environment . . . with the moral and emotional terms in which the community has discussed its differences.'[7]

SPECTACLE OF WAR AND PEACE

Much Welsh pacifist writing seeks to undo conventionally accepted systems of classification and hierarchical distinctions. The cultural historian David Gee points out how British and Commonwealth soldiers 'are universally promoted "heroes", as if the cardinal virtue of their profession were heroic choice rather than obedience to orders'.[8] Thus,

> if a roadside bomb blows a soldier into pieces, he has 'made the ultimate sacrifice', as if he had chosen his own death, and his ignominiously eviscerated body joins 'our glorious dead'. However, a soldier on the other side of the war is never heroic, always 'the enemy', always nameless, and not killed but 'neutralised'.[9]

Although the way in which war is presented has changed over the centuries, in our mass media and consumer culture, militarism has become what is often termed a 'spectacle'. Spectacle, as Gee says, is the product of two features of Western consumer culture: 'ideological consumption' and a sense of 'alienation' from the world in which we are consumers, as if we live in a spiritual void. These cultural forces, acting together, have resulted in 'our growing immersion in the "spectacle" at the expense of critical awareness of the world'.[10] Perhaps not surprisingly then, the importance of critical awareness is at the heart of pacifism. Indeed, it is 'critical awareness' which the Peace Pledge Union has promoted since 1934:

> We believe there is no justification for the widespread promotion of the heroic status of military personnel nor the frequent insistence that children should be grateful to the war dead. We believe that the distribution to every school of educationally questionable material which uncritically praises the armed forces by the government and at remembrance time by the British Legion should be challenged and severely restricted.[11]

In his pamphlet *Religion and the Quest for Peace*, George Davies insightfully argues (which many contemporary world leaders would do well to note) that despite 'high pronouncements', war has always failed to deliver 'mankind from want and fear and force'.[12] His focus is not simply on the carnage of war, the subject of works such as 'Gweriniaeth a Rhyfel' (Republicanism and War) (1920) by the pacifist poet Niclas y Glais (T. E. Nicholas, 1879–1971), but on how war fails to stem the tide of 'the moral degeneracy' that he believed brought it about: 'force, fraud, savagery, untruthfulness' (RQP, p. 8). These are brave words, but Davies always associated pacifism with courage, imagination, education and critical awareness.

As an example of how culturally constructed meanings and hierarchies can become periodically fixed in 'spectacle', Gee offers the symbolic red poppy. When it was originally introduced after the First World War, it was meant to signify the 'sentiment of "Never Again"' which 'percolated through the population'.[13] But it has become, Gee argues, an invitation to 'lionise British and Commonwealth fatalities as "The Glorious Dead"', as in the annual remembrance parade in London and the British Legion charity.[14] By contrast, the white poppy has a more inclusive meaning, signifying the 'remembrance of all the victims of wars – whether soldiers or civilians, whether ours or theirs – and declaring a commitment to build a culture of peace'.[15]

The movement to 'lionise' the war dead in British culture has shaped the way in which the spectacle of war has been perceived in Wales as well as in England. The notable Welsh historian Kenneth O. Morgan maintains that the Zulu War generated anxiety over the status of Wales as an imperial power, but this 'paled by comparison with the acclaim won by the South Wales Borderers at Rorke's Drift and Isandhlwana'.[16] However, what Morgan overlooks is the way in which Rorke's Drift became a 'spectacle' of militarism and, linked with the consequent 'rash of Welsh Victoria crosses',[17] fostered an uncritical appraisal of the war.

Many Welsh pacifist writers have addressed the militaristic connotations of national images and symbols and the way in which they have been accepted uncritically. George Davies, for example, unveils the 'historic emblems' of the '[Great] Powers – the American Eagle, the British Lion, the Russian Bear, the Welsh Dragon, and other terrifying animals, [as] symbols of conceptions and methods of barbarism, of Terror as Power' (PP, p. 29). In his work, it is part of a wider analysis, based on his own experience, of the social structures and hierarchies by which pacifists are oppressed. For example, in *Triniaeth Troseddwyr* (Treatment of Criminals), one of the Heddychwyr Cymru (Peacemakers of Wales) pamphlets by Welsh pacifists at the start of the Second World War, his experience of imprisonment causes him to see warders, governors and prisoners alike as 'so many cogs in a vast machine'.[18] In the essay 'Bottom Dogs – II', this time writing as a conscientious objector undertaking enforced work in rural Carmarthenshire, he sees the social structure as a pyramid in which the governor is at the apex, underneath whom are the county council, contractor, timekeeper, ganger and, at the bottom, the conscientious objector as prisoner.[19]

MILITARISM, DISCOURSE AND MASCULINITY

In confronting the militaristic state, the pacifist is faced with discourses embedded in a complex entanglement of state-sanctified ideologies, social structures and symbolism. This is an important motif in Emyr Humphreys's modernist novel *A Toy Epic*, begun when he was working as a conscientious objector on a farm in west Wales in 1941 and completed in 1958.[20] It is a book with which many Welsh readers will be familiar from their school, college or, simply, general reading. Written in the voices of three boys from different Welsh backgrounds and set in the late 1930s, the novel, as I have explained elsewhere,[21] is influenced by Virginia Woolf's *The Waves* (1931). This novel did not come easily to Humphreys, and Woolf's text seems to have helped him resolve some of the difficulties that he was having with it. Like *The Waves*, it is a novel driven by the consciousnesses of a small group of individuals rather than by plot, and how closely Humphreys used Woolf's model is evident in the way he has employed exactly the same phrase as Woolf to signal a change in the speaking voice – '. . . said . . .' (as in, 'The first day I went to school, said Albie, I was escorted by my mother').[22] At the time Humphreys wrote this novel, he was interested in modernist fiction, particularly the work of William Faulkner, and *As I Lay Dying* would have offered him an example of the kind of novel he wanted to write. But it was clearly Woolf who provided him with the most appropriate model because Humphreys was interested not simply in employing different voices but different consciousnesses. The 1930s, in which the novel is set, was not an easy time for pacifists and in Wales they faced challenges which did not trouble pacifists in other parts of the UK, challenges which the consciousness-driven novel enabled Humphreys to explore.

Although Humphreys adapted the model of *The Waves*, the two novels are different in as far as their content is concerned. Humphreys reduced Woolf's six young men and women to three young men, and further developed her concern with the way in which cultural forces and symbolic discourses define and construct masculinity. Since Humphreys's three boys come from different backgrounds, the most obvious interpretation of the novel is that it explores the varied, regional nature of Wales and what constitutes 'Welshness'. But a further reason why the boys come from different parts of Wales may be that Welsh pacifism involved not only people from different backgrounds but depended on particular cultural and geographical contexts within Wales (such as Welsh-speaking, rural, Nonconformist west Wales) more than others.

Given the decades in which *A Toy Epic* was written and set, and the author's commitment to peace as a conscientious objector, it is unsurprising that the novel frequently touches on the subject of pacifism. However, this is a motif which scholars have surprisingly overlooked. Early in the book, Humphreys invokes popular, pacifist stories about the First World War. One of these involves a British soldier who, at the last minute, baulks at the prospect of killing a German who begs him for his life; another concerns two young British and German soldiers, who, on encountering each other, both lower their guns as the German screams: 'What the h— do you want to kill me for, I dont [*sic*] want to kill you.' They end up walking together, with the British soldier sharing his rations.[23] In essence, these stories are similar to Michael's encounter with a bully on his first day at school in *A Toy Epic*:

> I was pushed fiercely by a thick-set boy wearing long trousers. I turned to face him with anger on my lips, but the hot words turned cold on my tongue as I saw his large clenched fist and ugly look, and my face broke into a false engaging smile.
>
> 'All right,' I said, 'let us sit together. We may as well.'
>
> This had a good effect because he, too, smiled and asked my name. (ATE, p. 51)

This story, like the pacifist tales from the First World War, suggests an alternative to a violent response to confrontation. But Humphreys's novel also advocates that pacifism is about more than simply being anti-war; it is part of an alternative lifestyle in a more holistic sense. It must be said that this broader pacifist perspective is not unique to Welsh pacifism and can be found in many of the oral histories of ordinary people documented in the Imperial War Museum, London. For example, one witness observes that pacifism is not just about international issues but 'a horror of violence, disapproving of blood sports, capital punishment, corporal punishment and the whole shooting match'.[24] Nor is this perspective necessarily a defining characteristic of Welsh pacifism. Welsh-language narratives of life in the Welsh countryside, such as D. J. Williams's *Hen Dŷ Ffarm* (1953), are infused with spirituality, respect for others and the value of neighbourliness, but shooting, poaching and killing fish, birds or animals are accepted and acceptable.

In its exploration of how pacifists contend with violent situations and militaristic dispositions, *A Toy Epic* highlights how violence finds expression in day-to-day behaviour and language. For example, in a development of Woolf's concern (primarily through the consciousness of Woolf's Louis) with why people permit themselves to be dominated by others and dominate others in turn, Michael allows himself to be manipulated by another boy who joins the Air Force, Jac, into taking part in increasingly daring exploits which transgress the boundaries of school behaviour. Jac's story is very different from those of the iconic fighter pilots in *The Boy's Own Paper*, and the one event that particularly undermines how pre-war and wartime boys' comics promoted masculine identity is Jac's death in a pilot-training exercise rather than in a dogfight with the German Luftwaffe. However, it is a death which would have had a particular resonance for Welsh readers when this novel was published, two decades after the involvement of Saunders Lewis and other Welsh pacifists in an arson attack on a bomber flying school established in the Llŷn peninsula.

Jac's friends describe him very differently from the comic book heroes who were intended to celebrate what young men of humble origins could 'make of themselves'. He is described as 'wild', an 'animal' and a 'user of bad language', and his story hammers home the reality that boys from humble origins were more likely to face a violent, premature death than a glorious career. In some respects, Jac mirrors the wilder side of the disciplined Louis in Woolf's novel and is Michael's *alter ego*. Louis uses women whom he sees as his social inferiors to bolster his own sense of superiority, as does Michael in having a relationship with Iorwerth's girlfriend. But the most startling difference between the iconic 'masculine' fighter pilots in *The Boy's Own Paper* and Jac is Iorwerth's pacific image of him, very probably derived from *The Waves*, 'gathering bluebells' (ATE, p. 107).[25] There is a suggestion that in studying these flowers, Jac achieves a momentary inner peacefulness aligned with nature and beauty.

As war draws closer in the novel, two of the boys ponder what they will do when hostilities are declared. Michael, who has changed his position from earlier in the novel, now says that he is not a 'pacifist', and that joining the army would provide him with an opportunity to learn about 'discipline and authority' (ATE, p. 110). In this regard, he mirrors Louis's interest in discipline in *The Waves*, how he admired the way in which the boys marched into the school chapel in pairs and felt inspired by the authority of the headmaster. Michael comes to reflect the way in which boys' comics encouraged young people to think about masculinity, militarism and the military in the inter-war years and during the war itself. The extent to which young men were influenced by this culture is expressed clearly by Woolf in a quotation in her short prose piece, 'Thoughts on peace in an air raid':

> To fight against a real enemy, to earn undying honour and glory by shooting total strangers, and to come home with my breast covered with medals and decorations, that was the summit of my hope . . . It was for this that my whole life so far had been dedicated, my education, training, everything . . .[26]

It is ironic that it is Iorwerth, the most sensitive of the three boys (in some respects modelled on Neville in *The Waves*), who buys a copy of *The Boy's Own Paper* (ATE, p. 56). At the end of the novel, he declares himself a pacifist while Michael accepts the moral guidelines of the comic, talking (like Woolf's Louis) of the importance of 'order', 'discipline' and 'authority'. As Adam Riches has argued, through their adventure, fantasy and war stories, boys' comics sought to convey 'the right kind of standards, values and attitudes'.[27] Michael's announcement that he is looking to learn these values from the armed services is not surprising, for *The Boy's Own Paper*, *Champion*, *Tiger*, *Rover* and *Hotspur* were flooded with young male icons, such as Rock-fist Rogan, Paddy Payne, Stormy Winter and Squadron Leader Rudd, who helped determine how young males perceived themselves. From its inception, when it ran the story 'From *Powder Monkey* to *Admiral*' which was later published as an influential children's book, *The Boy's Own Paper* promoted the idea that a boy's destiny was to become a rugged hero.

At the end of the novel, Iorwerth, unlike Michael, rejects the worldview of *The Boy's Own Paper*, admitting that he will probably register as a 'conscientious objector' because he is opposed to the idea of killing another human being (ATE, p. 109). Although conscientious objectors in the Second World War had a less difficult time than those in the First, the social stigma remained. Given the way in which Iorwerth is shaped by the charismatic Welsh Nonconformist preachers, his purchase of *The Boy's Own Paper* is further ironic because at its beginnings, in January 1879, its editor developed the publication in different ways from those sought by the Religious Tract Society that supported it.[28] Indeed, in publishing 'From *Powder Monkey* to

Admiral' as a book, the editor was forced to defend the paper's support for peace, pointing out that the author of this story was 'a lover of peace' and affirming that his paper had no wish to 'offend peaceable folk' or 'encourage the war spirit'.[29] How far Humphreys was aware himself of this particular wrangle is immaterial, for it encapsulates a generic aspect of these comics, and of pre-war and wartime popular culture, of which Humphreys as a pacifist, and eventually a conscientious objector, would certainly have been aware. Through their promotion of a particular type of male hero, these papers made it difficult for young men such as Iorwerth to abstain from war. As Riches observes, *The Boy's Own Paper* was 'shot through with patriotism and national pride'.[30] For some young people in Wales, this posed a further dilemma whether national pride meant 'British' (or indeed 'English') or Welsh national pride. Significantly, at one point in the novel, Michael, as a Welsh nationalist, ponders whether his nationalism would qualify him to register as a conscientious objector (ATE, p. 110).

Woolf, then, provided Humphreys with an example of a novel driven by the consciousness of its characters rather than by external plot, a model which enabled him to explore the different forces pulling young people in different directions in the 1930s. It seems to have inspired Humphreys's interest in how cultural discourse determined the interconnection of masculinity with militarism and heroism. *A Toy Epic* is Humphreys's first psychoanalytic novel, as *The Waves* is the most psychoanalytic of Woolf's novels, in which he explores the reasons why young men should need the order, discipline and authority of the armed services and why some should wish to dominate others or submit to domination. It is a mode of fiction in which Humphreys is also able to pursue Woolf's conviction that war may be as much a product of the turmoil and hostility within individual consciousnesses as external forces.

DEGREES OF PACIFISM

In the first two decades of the twentieth century, debates concerning pacifism revolved around 'conditional' and 'absolute' pacifism. The latter rejected war and every form of violent action as a means of solving disputes whatever the circumstances. But 'conditional' pacifists felt that they had to take particular circumstances, contexts and implications into account. However, in each case, the arguments related to war and not to the state of peaceful existence itself. The peace historian Oliver Richmond points out: 'War is often thought to be the natural state of humanity, peace of any sort being fragile and fleeting' and peace is believed 'to imply an absence of overt violence or war between or sometimes within states'.[31] Welsh pacifism challenges this commonplace assumption, emphasising how peace, as Richmond observes, 'has been at the centre of the human experience, and a sophisticated version of peace has now become widely accepted'.[32]

Wynn Thomas argues that 'fascination with war – and related forms of violence – is an active element in the creed of pacifism'.[33] As we shall see, there is some evidence of this among English-language pacifist writers, such as Glyn Jones (1905–95), and others who are not necessarily card-carrying pacifists but who write about peace, such as the contemporary English-language Welsh poet Tony Curtis. However, while pacifism is opposed to war, the outlook of Welsh pacifism (as is evident, for example, in the work of George Davies, David Gwenallt Jones and Waldo Williams) extends beyond this to a broader concern with how life should be lived, emphasising, for example: the importance of the individual, the need for an educational system that stresses personal and spiritual growth, the promotion of small communities and the importance of neighbourliness. Remembering the inapplicability of the distinction that Cadman and Gill make between Western and Eastern approaches to peace where Wales is concerned, which we noted earlier, 'peace not as something that is imposed from outside, but as a shared human aspiration, rooted in our innate peacefulness', must be added to this list.[34]

If there is a recurring 'fascination with war' in pacifism, it is a concern (as *A Toy Epic* suggests) as much with the discourse as the horror of war. This is evident in Charles E. Raven's Peace Pledge Union pamphlet, *The Starting Point of Pacifism* (1940):

> This is where the practical task for pacifism begins. For pacifism means taking the other man as he is in the whole of him, believing in the best in him, and making the best out of him: it is the opposite of war which is taking the other man at his worst and making the worst out of him.[35]

Raven had a profound influence on Welsh-language pacifist thinkers such as the distinguished scholar and expert in Welsh folk culture Iorwerth Peate (1901–82), who made his mark as a supporter of the Welsh language, Welsh-language culture and Welsh pacifism. One of the first members of Plaid Genedlaethol Cymru, the Welsh Nationalist Party, who served on the editorial board of its newspaper, *Y Ddraig Goch*, Peate joined the Peace Pledge Union and the Fellowship of Reconciliation in the 1930s.[36] His essay 'Anghydffurfiaeth a'r Trefi' (1944), echoing Raven's insistence that pacifism is about valuing the individual, argues that the Christian gospel is preached to people as individual persons, 'mai sylfaen yr Efengyl yw parch at y dyn unigol fel dyn'.[37] Written at a time of crisis for the Nonconformist church, the key phrase here (allowing for the male gender bias of the times) is 'y dyn unigol fel dyn' (the individual man as man). For that reason, Peate concludes that the only way for the Welsh independent church to contribute effectively to society is if it were 'small enough for everyone to know everyone else personally . . . little democracies of neighbours'.[38]

THE WELSH INTELLIGENTSIA

Scholarship on Welsh campaigns for peace in the first half of the twentieth century has usually focused on the various organisations and movements themselves, such as the Peace Society, Peace Pledge Union, Cymdeithas y Cymod (Fellowship of Reconciliation), a Christian society to promote peace, founded at the end of 1914; the Welsh Council of the League of Nations, established in 1922; and the Welsh National Pacifist Society, founded in 1937. Their membership fluctuated and they waxed and waned. But numbers are not everything, and more important was the nature of the membership, drawn from those who exerted considerable cultural influence in Wales.

As suggested at the outset, the term 'intelligentsia' is used in this book to mean a status class of educated people that critique, guide and take a lead in shaping culture and politics. Of the importance of the Welsh intelligentsia, Ned Thomas argues: 'Wales in the twentieth century has had a small and dedicated intelligentsia, mainly writers, and they have not kept out of politics . . . This is where Wales again differs from some other "development areas" in Britain.'[39] Without suggesting that the entire Welsh intelligentsia supported pacifism, which was certainly not the case, its close-knit nature (partly due to the Welsh-language and the size of the principality itself) meant that it proved important to advancing debates around the causes and obscenities of war. What made for an even closer Welsh-language pacifist intelligentsia, as Gwynfor Evans has demonstrated, was the extent of their involvement in the Christian church.[40]

When Morgan argues that anti-war journalists during 1914–18 were able to point to a coherent peace movement in Wales following the Napoleonic Wars, he has in mind the promotion of Christian pacifism in Welsh local newspapers and Nonconformist periodicals such as *Yr Amserau* and *Y Traethodydd*.[41] The Baptist *Seren Cymru*, edited by the peace activist Revd D. Wyre Lewis, proved to exert an important influence as did the Merthyr *Y Darian*. Up to a point, the entire history of Welsh pacifism could be said to turn on how the Welsh-language press provided a useful forum for different pacifist ideas and perspectives. For example, *Y Faner* (*Baner ac Amserau Cymru*), *Yr Herald Cymraeg*, *Y Tyst* and the Methodist *Y Goleuad* provided a platform for opposition to the South African Boer War, and the monthly periodical *Y Deyrnas*, edited by Thomas Rees (1869–1926), principal of Bala Bangor College, served much the same purpose with regard to the First World War. It was this journal which led the Welsh attack on Lloyd George's premiership, and *Y Genedl Gymreig* campaigned against his anti-working-class policies and his use of violence in Ireland.[42]

It wasn't just that the Welsh-language press as such promoted pacifism in Wales; it was the nature and quality of the work which it published and the significance of the writers and intellectuals associated with the Welsh-language print media and with the Welsh peace movement more generally that proved important. For example, early in his career, the notable Welsh-language pacifist poet and academic T. Gwynn Jones (1871–1949) worked on a variety of journals, including *Y Faner*, *Y Cymro*, where he later became an editor, *Papur Pawb*, *Yr Herald Cymraeg*,[43] while *Y Llenor* (1922–51) – founded by the poet, scholar and academic W. J. Gruffydd (1881–1954), who remained its editor until 1945 – provided a place where many of the key Welsh-language writers could publish their work, be reviewed or promote discussion and debate. The radical activist and poet T. E. Nicholas secured a platform for his pacifist and socialist arguments in his weekly column 'O fyd y werin' (The world of the people) in *Y Cymro* and as the editor of *The Merthyr Pioneer*, the newspaper of the Independent Labour Party.

Even small religious publications, like *The Grail* (Y Greal), i.e. the magazine of the Calvinistic Methodist Theological College, Aberystwyth, had a role in publishing Welsh- and English-language short fiction, poetry, non-fiction and short essays by leading pacifists. Typically, a single issue of *The Grail* in 1911 included a short reflective piece in English, 'The heart of a man' by T. Gwynn Jones, two poems in Welsh by T. E. Nicholas and an essay on 'Life and letters' by the writer and journalist E. Morgan Humphreys, writing as the editor of *Y Genedl Gymreig*, in which he argues that contemporary Welsh literature needs to address the social and political issues of the day.[44] Unsurprisingly, there is a recurring interest in *The Grail* in living a peaceful life. In the same issue, a short piece in Welsh by 'W. D.', 'John y Cwm', with an epigraph from a poem by T. Gwynn Jones, describes the closeness of John to flowers and stars, and in his piece in the magazine, T. Gwynn Jones reveals the roots of his pacifism in admitting the pang of remorse he felt 'after a clumsy shot at a hare, which caused the wounded animal to cry like a child in agony'.[45] Another important publication was *Y Gymraes*, the journal of the north Wales temperance union, Undeb Dirwestol Merched Gogledd Cymru, which reappeared in 1896 and, under the editorship of two prominent members of the union, the author Ceridwen Peris (Alice Gray Jones, 1852–1943) and (after 1919) Mair Ogwen, offered women a radical forum concerned with reform in many aspects of women's lives. It was particularly influential in its support for the women's peace movement in the 1920s and 1930s.[46] Moreover, the international outlook which distinguished Welsh pacifism was attributable to key figures such as the Revd Gwilym Davies (1879–1955), who founded the Goodwill Message from the Children of Wales in 1922; David Davies, who established the first Chair in International Politics at the University College of Wales, Aberystwyth; the indefatigable peace activist Gwladys Thoday, honorary secretary of the North Wales Women's Peace Council, who was also a member of the executive of the Women's International League (which became the Women's International League for Peace and Freedom); and Ruth Osburn of the Women's International League for Peace and Freedom, south Wales branch. To encourage support for the 1926 Peace March, the following resolution was discussed throughout north Wales:

> We members and supporters of the Peacemakers' Pilgrimage, believing that law should take the place of war in the settlements of international disputes, urge His Majesty's government to agree to submit all disputes to conciliation and arbitration, and by taking the lead in the proposed

Disarmament Conference of the League of Nations to show that Great Britain does not intend to appeal to force.[47]

The influence of Welsh pacifists and those in sympathy with the peace movements reached deep into Welsh culture until the third quarter of the twentieth century and turned the five decades from the 1930s to the 1980s into a period of great opportunity for Welsh-language writers.[48] One of the reasons for the pervasive nature of Welsh pacifist influence in the twentieth century was that Welsh writers worked across different genres and often worked within different modes of writing within particular genres. This gave Welsh-language writing a character which was distinctive from English-language writing in Wales. For example, the 1930s was an important period for W. J. Gruffydd, not only because under his editorship *Y Llenor* published and/or reviewed most of the leading Welsh-language writers of the day, but also because Gruffydd himself published his best work: *Caniadau* (1932), *Hen Atgofion* (1936) – largely based on articles published in *Y Llenor* (1936–41) and *Y Tro Olaf ac Ysgrifau Eraill* (1939).[49] He also translated into Welsh the anti-war sermons of the pacifist Maude Royden. Saunders Lewis (1893–1985) wrote seventeen plays between 1948 and 1971, and his novel *Merch Gwern Hywel* was published in 1964. The years following the Second World War were particularly fruitful for D. Gwenallt Jones who produced important volumes of poetry in 1951, 1959 and 1969.[50] The scholar, poet, librarian and, eventually, university principal, Thomas Parry (1904–85) published three major contributions to Welsh literary scholarship between 1935 and 1952.[51] The poet, essayist and scholar Thomas Parry-Williams (1887–1975), acknowledged by notables such as Saunders Lewis as 'the most influential Welsh writer of the inter-war period', published prolifically between 1935 and 1966.[52] Although the poet and novelist T. Rowland Hughes (1903–49) did not write pacifist literature as such, as the producer of feature programmes for the BBC he courageously broadcast *Buchedd Garmon* (The life of St Germanus) by Saunders Lewis while Lewis was awaiting trial for the arson attack at the RAF bombing school on the Llŷn peninsula. Despite his having been diagnosed with multiple sclerosis in 1937, the 1940s was a prolific time for him as a novelist, and much of his fiction is concerned with the 'peace' of everyday life and the way in which it is disrupted by external forces.[53]

Each of these writers was directly or indirectly involved in the promotion of peace. Saunders Lewis as Plaid Cymru's president (until 1943) argued that Wales was detached from the quarrel with Germany and should be able to determine its own foreign policy. W. J. Gruffydd, Thomas Parry, T. H. Parry-Williams, Gwenallt Jones and Waldo Williams were all conscientious objectors, and Gwenallt and Waldo served prison terms for their beliefs. Between 1957 and 1960, when Welsh-language poetry represented 15 per cent of sales of Welsh books for adults,[54] the century's outstanding Welsh pacifist book of poetry was published – Waldo Williams's *Dail Pren* (1956).

If, in discussing the various peace organisations in Wales, we focus on the individuals who were responsible for them, or who played a key part in them, a different picture emerges from that presented by scholarship that only approaches them as anonymous institutions. Part of that picture is how connected the Welsh pacificist intelligentsia were. For example, *Cymdeithas y Cymod* (The Fellowship of Reconciliation in Wales) was founded by George M. Ll. Davies and Richard Roberts from Blaenau Ffestiniog; the Welsh Council of the League of Nations was supported financially by David Davies of Llandinam (1880–1944), and its first director was the Revd Gwilym Davies; the National Temple of Peace and Health, too, was financed by David Davies; the first president and secretary of the Welsh National Pacifist Society were George Davies and Gwynfor Evans respectively. George Davies spoke against the bombing school in Penyberth in May 1936 and was also a friend of the pacifist, writer and teacher, D. J. Williams (1885–1970) who actually took part in the arson attack on the site.[55] Waldo Williams himself translated D. J. Williams's account of rural life in west Wales in his parents' and grandparents' times, *Hen Dŷ Ffarm* (1953), into English. T. E. Nicholas's first selection of his prison sonnets, *Llygad y Drws: Sonedau'r Carchar* (Eye of the Door: Prison Sonnets) (1940) was introduced by D. Gwenallt Jones, while the preface of the first selection of his prison poems in English, published in 1948, was written by Iorwerth Peate (these are discussed in more detail in Chapter 2). Daniel Hughes, the principal translator of the prison sonnets, was himself a conscientious objector who was imprisoned in Caernarfon county gaol during the First World War.

Meanwhile, pacifists and writers were brought together by the universities in the northern half of Wales, and the role they played in creating a Welsh-language, pacifist and nationalist intelligentsia must not be overlooked. My own *alma mater*, the University College of Wales, Aberystwyth – often by coincidence rather than by design – provided support in the radicalisation of several key Welsh pacifists in the first part of the twentieth century, including W. J. Gruffydd, T. Gwynn Jones, Iorwerth Peate, Gwenallt Jones and Waldo Williams. But shamefully this was not always the case. In 1918, the college authorities closed *Y Wawr*, the radical magazine that had been set up by the students in 1913. T. H. Parry-Williams, as R. Gerallt Jones points out, ran into difficulties for a time when the university was adamant that those who went to war should not 'be placed at a disadvantage *vis-à-vis* those who had been allowed to stay at home by calling themselves "conchies"'.[56]

So close-knit was the community of pacifism in Wales that some of the interconnections were remarkable. When George Davies was imprisoned in 1917 as a conscientious objector, he was arrested by a serving soldier, Dan Thomas, who had worked under him when he was a bank manager. Thomas later became a pacifist himself and worked with Gwynfor Evans, whom his daughter married and at whose marriage Davies delivered the address, as treasurer of Plaid Cymru for forty years. Such was Welsh pacifism!

However, the key issue is not that the Welsh-language pacifist intelligentsia was close-knit but that communication among members did not function according to a hierarchical model. One factor that has not been explored in scholarship on the Welsh peace movements has been the extent to which influence and communication across the organisations and among individuals flowed in a non-hierarchical fashion. This is important because pacifism frequently stresses how strongly hierarchical societies are more inclined to separation, violence and war than to peace.

CENTRES OF RADICALISM

There is no doubting the cultural influence that the Welsh pacifist intelligentsia exercised, but an important question is, how radical were they? It could be said that Welsh pacifism differs from English pacifism in the extent to which it is associated with centres of radicalism. George Davies himself said of Merthyr, where he preached on peace in 1915: 'Merthyr had been an old hearth-stone for the fire of Peace. Had not Henry Richard and Keir Hardie represented Merthyr in Parliament and preached peace and social righteousness?' (PP, p. 62). T. Gwynn Jones in his pamphlet on Thomas Huws Davies (1882–1940), secretary of the Welsh Church Commission who broadcast highly esteemed talks in Welsh and English, points out that he was brought up in Tregaron 'with its statue of the Peacemaker, Henry Richard, whose fearless face still dares all the demons there be'.[57] It hardly needs pointing out, as John Davies argues, that Nonconformists were proud of the peace-loving tradition of Henry Richard; in 1913 the Union of Welsh Independents declared that 'every war is contrary to the spirit of Christ'.[58]

Not all, of course, but a considerable number of events associated with the deaths of Welsh soldiers in the First World War fuelled the pacifist cause, and not all of these were on the front line. A well-publicised example at the time was the suicide in 1916 of Private David Davies of the Welsh Guards who hanged himself in an outhouse at a farm near Tregaron.[59] Not all the examples of courage on the front line itself lent themselves as support of stereotypical heroic militarism, as in the case of the pacifist and nationalist Ben Owen, who was awarded the Military Medal in the First World War for rescuing a fellow soldier from no man's land, an incident which may have inspired one of the poems in Tony Curtis's *War Voices* which we discuss in Chapter 5.[60] More famously, in 1917 at the Birkenhead Eisteddfod Lloyd George himself 'stage-managed' the highly charged empty-chair ceremony. The Trawsfynydd bard, Hedd Wyn (E. H. Evans, 1887–1917), was unable to take the chair because he had been killed shortly before in Flanders.[61] Draped in black for the rest of the Eisteddfod, the 'Black Chair', as it was soon known, became an anti-war symbol that pacifist writers, such as Williams Parry in a series of *englynion*, were quick to draw upon.[62]

Of particular importance to the establishment of a Welsh socialist and pacifist intelligentsia in south Wales was the Cardiff Workers' Co-operative Garden Village which began in 1912. In *Rhwng Dau Fyd* (Between Two Worlds) (1976), Iorwerth Peate recalls Rhiwbina as 'a vibrant intellectual enclave'.[63] With it seems a hint of regret, he notes that it was an 'ardal ddi-Gymraeg' (a non-Welsh-speaking area), but nevertheless one which provided valuable interaction between Welsh- and English-language intellectuals and professionals.[64] In *Rhwng Dau Fyd*, he remembers the various streets and the intellectuals who came to live on them. The list is almost endless, and although he does not mention the pacifist Lily Tobias, whose novel *Eunice Fleet* is discussed in Chapter 3, it is very unlikely, as Donahaye surmises, that she did not meet some of these.[65] Within the Rhondda enclave, too, there were groups within groups. The theologian, Welsh nationalist and pacifist Pennar Davies (1911–96) was a member of the Cadwgan Group, a small group of intellectuals and avant-garde writers who met at the Rhondda home of Professor J. Gwyn Griffiths, a Classics scholar and Egyptologist.

Given the size of Wales, it is unsurprising that key pacifists and writers frequently came from the same radical area. This was the case for Waldo Williams and Niclas y Glais (T. E. Nicholas), who wrote *Cerddi Rhyddid* (*Songs of Freedom*), which included his anti-war, and in M. Wynn Thomas's opinion 'Whitmanesque, poem written in response to the carnage of WW1, "Gweriniaeth a Rhyfel"/"Republicanism and War", which had a profound influence on the most acclaimed Welsh pacifist poet, Waldo Williams'.[66] James Nicholas reminds us that in the last essay that Waldo wrote, published in 1970, he recalls his father reading Niclas's 'Gweriniaeth a Rhyfel' to his mother in 1916 when he was twelve years old:

> 1916 was a strange and terrible year. The European Governments had become stubborn in their lunacy. Their subjects with rare exception, responded completely to their demands under thick layers of the same self-justification, self-deception and hypocrisy. The curtain was drawn on freedom. Civilization was sinking into the mud – the mud of the Somme. States were sending their sons to fight one another and to die in the mud and on the barbed wire – up to a quarter a million of them at the final count.[67]

Clearly, he had recognised that 'the poem was sensational, something completely new in Welsh Literature'.[68] They both came from an area that was 'noted for a religious and political radicalism which had several times found expression in militant direct action'.[69] As a pacifist and a member of the Independent Labour Party, T. E. Nicholas was an example of what has been called 'y farn annibynnol' (the independent's viewpoint) which Waldo himself valued highly.[70] Exemplifying the kind of independence of mind which characterised the Welsh-language intelligentsia as a whole, he found himself too out of step with his church and national policy in the First World War to remain in post as a Congregational minister.[71]

PRISON AND RADICALISM

Historians have tended to underemphasise the number of political perspectives in British politics that entered into debate with each other from the late nineteenth century onwards. Liberal internationalism and non-interventionism, socialist internationalism, jingoistic forms of imperialism, and nationalism immediately come to mind.[72] Of direct relevance to Welsh pacifists in the first quarter of the twentieth century was the confrontation of two discourses: a conservative, and Conservative, patriotism and a radical patriotism associated with the peace and internationalist movements.[73] As far as pacifism is concerned, the debate and shifting political opinion over the Boer War, even after its conclusion, were less significant than the subsequent attempts to reconstruct patriotism radically as 'a devotion to humanity' itself.[74]

This radical devotion to humanity is reflected in the number of leading pacifists who were imprisoned for their beliefs. In this regard, this section is a brief introduction to Chapter 3, which, in keeping with the literary-historiographical approach of this book as a whole, examines some of the ways in which the prison experiences of conscientious objectors entered Welsh writing in both English and Welsh. George Davies was imprisoned in late December 1917 in Wormwood Scrubs. In the course of his incarceration, he was moved to a CO settlement attached to Dartmoor Prison, then to a camp at Caeo in Carmarthenshire, and towards the end of the war he was sent to the work centre at Knutsford in Cheshire, a much freer regime than at other prisons. Waldo Williams was imprisoned twice for refusing to pay his income tax in protest at the Korean War. In September 1960, he served six months in Swansea and, in February 1961, a further six months in Ashwell Open Prison, Rutland. But whereas Waldo was imprisoned late in his life, Gwenallt Jones, like George Davies, was imprisoned during the First World War as a conscientious objector in Wormwood Scrubs and Princetown work centre (in former Dartmoor prison), experiences which formed the basis of his Welsh-language novel, *Plasau'r Brenin* (1934) which is discussed in Chapter 3.

The imprisonment of Welsh-language intellectuals over matters of conscience kept a radical pacifism to the fore in Wales during both world wars. In the 1920s and 1930s, George Davies became a hero following his imprisonment, inspiring many young men to become conscientious objectors in the Second World War.[75] But he was not the only Welsh pacifist who became an iconic figure as a result of his imprisonment. The school teacher and founder member of the No-Conscription Fellowship, Morgan Jones, on whom one of the central characters in Lily Tobias's *Eunice Fleet* is based, served time in various prisons in England and Wales.[76] Merfyn Turner (1915–91), sentenced to three months' hard labour by a tribunal in Aberystwyth, became a pioneer in the social rehabilitation of ex-prisoners.[77] He proved a key figure in the transition of pacifism from simply an anti-war movement to one advocating wider social and educational reform – writing six important books, two in Welsh, on his social experiments.[78] T. E. Nicholas's poetry based on his prison experiences, which we mentioned earlier, did much to inspire pacifists and political activists and, like the work of Waldo and Gwenallt – as we shall discuss in later chapters – advocated replacing divided and hierarchical societies, inclined towards violence and war, with more harmonious, rural communities inclined towards external and inner peace.

But the radical, pacifist wing of the Welsh intelligentsia suffered for their beliefs in ways other than imprisonment. On being considered for the chair of Welsh at the University College of Wales, Aberystwyth in 1914, T. H. Parry-Williams faced a vociferous campaign against him on account of his pacifism, although he was eventually appointed in 1920.[79] It was Thomas Parry's standing as a conscientious objector that probably cost him the principalship of the University College of North Wales, Bangor.[80] In the Second World War, Iorwerth Peate, registered unconditionally as a conscientious objector by the south Wales tribunal, was dismissed from his post as keeper of the Folk Life Department of the National Museum of Wales. As Morgan says, since criticism of him 'related solely to his views as a member of the Welsh pacifist movement, this action [could] only appear as a senseless act of persecution'.[81] It resulted in a national campaign instigated by W. J. Gruffydd, as the editor of *Y Llenor*, and over 200 motions from cultural, educational, church and local authorities to reinstate him.[82]

The impact which those who were sent to prison for their beliefs in the First World War had on sustaining, if not increasing, support for the peace movement was due in part to *Y Deyrnas* which published accounts of their experiences. Its impact is evidenced in the fact that after the war Morgan Jones won the Caerphilly by-election of 1921 and George Davies was elected as a Christian pacifist to represent the University of Wales in 1923. According to Gwynfor Evans, Davies's election did much to strengthen the Welsh intelligentsia, or in his words, 'proved there was still some backbone left in the graduates of the University of Wales'.[83]

The publication of the prison experiences and sufferings of conscientious objectors undoubtedly contributed, too, to the demise of

Liberal values and disillusionment with Lloyd George. John Davies describes how Lloyd George's 'attitude and that of his government between 1914 and 1922 were at the roots of the disillusionment that was so obvious a feature of life in Wales and Britain in the 1920s'.[84] The disillusionment with Lloyd George and Liberal values was most keenly felt in Wales because he had been so prominent in generating enthusiasm for the war in his own heartland. In poems such as '1914–1918: the young to the old', 'Litani yn Amser Rhyfel' (Litany in Wartime), 'Cathl i'r Yspryd Glân' (Hymn to the Holy Spirit) and 'Sionyn' (Johnnie) from *Caniadau* (Poetry) (1932), W. J. Gruffydd articulated the views of many in the 1920s and helped shape those of even more in the 1930s. One of the most accomplished scholars of Welsh literature of the time, H. Idris Bell, said that he had expressed 'all the pent-up bitterness of a generation sacrificed to the folly of elderly statesmen'.[85]

THE INTER-WAR YEARS

It hardly needs to be said that, from the nineteenth century onwards, Wales underwent fundamental transformations that affected all domains of life: industrialisation, urbanisation, social differentiation, professionalism and a multiplication of voices within Welsh public opinion. Initially, this was most keenly felt in the south and dominated all areas of private and public life including employment, transport, local government, education, religion, public health and welfare. Nor does it need to be pointed out that by the 1920s and 1930s no area of Wales had escaped.

However, it is often overlooked that the radicalism which Welsh pacifism continued to assume in the inter-war years proved another factor which distinguished it from English pacifism. The crux of the challenge which pacifism faced in the late 1920s and 1930s was whether the pacifist voice of rural west and north Nonconformist Wales could be successfully transferred to industrial south Wales. Through its central character, Humphreys's novel *Outside the House of Baal*, as we shall discuss in more detail in Chapter 5, questions how far pacifist idealism could embrace wider ideological concerns and engage with the socio-economic 'realities' of the Welsh industrial belt. Humphreys's novel resists the absolute binary between a Welsh-language, Nonconformist north Wales and an English-speaking, socialist south Wales which we find in one of the most important Welsh-language novels about industrial south Wales, T. Rowland Hughes's *William Jones* (1944). It presents a more complex, and truer, picture where pockets of Welsh-language culture, Nonconformity and pacifism survived in industrial south Wales, supported by men and women who came from the north and the west, not only into mining and the heavy industries themselves but into running the chapels, shops, transport, pubs and schools that developed around them.

Some Welsh historians have suggested that not all political developments in twentieth-century Wales point to a radical intelligentsia. It is an argument often traced to the Labour Party's announcement of its willingness to participate in First World War recruitment campaigns and the election of the pro-war exponent C. B. Stanton (1873–1946) to the Merthyr seat on Keir Hardie's death in 1915. These developments prompted right-wing journalists to claim that 'the [Welsh] working class was casting off the pacific and revolutionary ideas of the ILP [Independent Labour Party]',[86] overlooking the 6,080 votes secured by James Winstone, the Labour Party candidate and the president of the South Wales Miners' Federation, against Stanton's 10,286.

However, there can be no denying that, as the First World War dragged on, the arguments of *Y Deyrnas* found increasing acceptance among Nonconformists in Wales, although this was checked to some extent by the British army successes in 1918.[87] Looking back on the war, W. J. Gruffydd argued that *Y Deyrnas* was 'one of the strongest reasons why Wales did not completely lose its soul at the time of the great madness'.[88] Alongside the eagerness of Welsh men to enlist, urged on by their non-pacifist preachers and politicians like David Lloyd George, it must be remembered that many influential pockets of pacifism endured.

As noted above, one of the first causalities of the sustained success of the peace movements during the First World War was 'Liberal Wales' itself.[89] In the 1930s, a new, socialist pacifism emerged in Wales in which pacifism drew upon an additional radicalism, as it were, which again can be traced to the First World War. W. F. Hay, one of the authors of *The Miners' Next Step*, published an article in *The Welsh Outlook*, urging the colliers of Europe 'to lay down tools and arms for the cause of human fellowship'.[90] Fenner Brockway, the editor of *The Labour Leader*, established the No-Conscription Fellowship to campaign against military conscription. And, as

Davies says, the Fellowship had considerable support in the coalfield, especially in areas like Merthyr and Briton Ferry.[91] The Fellowship cooperated closely with the Quakers and the pacifist Fellowship of Reconciliation established in December 1914 and became synonymous with George Davies. But the No-Conscription Fellowship also contributed substantially to the development of pacifism as a social rather than simply an anti-war movement.

Welsh pacifism's enduring post-First World War faith in a warless world is traceable to a number of iconic events during the war itself and in the decade which followed. These include what came to be known as the 'Battle of the Cory Hall' in Cardiff, which occurred in November 1916. A pacifist meeting which had been called to hear Ramsay MacDonald, who had opposed the First World War and at the time was the leader of the ILP in Parliament, and the suffragette, pacifist and political writer Helena Swanwick, was attacked by a splinter group from a protest by pro-war 'patriots' led by C. B. Stanton. Although the local press took the opportunity to generate banner headlines over the outbreak of mayhem and disorder, the pacifist press saw this event as a moral victory of peacemakers over the advocates of war.

Of more lasting significance, however, was the creation of a petition and memorial for peace in 1924. It encapsulated two of the most important features of Welsh pacifism: its international appeal and its support among the women of Wales. Three notable women, Mrs Hughes Griffiths (president of the Campaign for Peace), Mrs Huw Pritchard (organiser, north Wales) and Miss E. Poole (organiser, south Wales) were behind the petition, which was signed by 60 per cent of the female population in Wales. Meanwhile, the international recognition which Welsh pacifism acquired in the inter-war period was exemplified by the iconic Temple of Peace and Health (1938). It was the brainchild of Lord Davies (David Davies of Llandinam), who having fought in the trenches in the First World War, wanted to bring together the twin ideals of peace and health. In providing a home for the King Edward VII Welsh National Memorial Association (a voluntary organisation founded in 1910 dedicated to the prevention, treatment and eradication of tuberculosis) and serving as a memorial to all those who died in the war, it looked forward to what was to become one of the most significant transformations in inter-war Welsh pacifism, the development of a 'social gospel' of peace to which we will return in a moment. But, with an opening ceremony performed by Mrs Annie Elizabeth James, who lost three of her sons in the First World War, it also recalled the 1924 Petition for Peace.

The Temple of Peace and Health exemplifies how Welsh pacifism between the wars became increasingly concerned with arguing for an international peace. Acknowledging that the thousands of men who lost their lives serving in Welsh regiments named in the Book of Remembrance died on foreign soil, the bronze on the glass casing of the Book of Remembrance is French and the marble pedestal on which it rests is Belgian. Moreover, the Temple served as the home of the League of Nations Welsh Union Council. Established in 1920 as a result of the Paris Peace Conference, the League aimed to prevent wars through collective disarmament, although it supported the use of arms by democratic states to resist attacks upon them. The League was also part of how Europe, through European broadcasting, thought about itself as hospitable and promoting peace through intellectual exchange and discussion. The League of Nations Peace Conference in September 1936 made clear how radio-linked Europe conceived of itself as an instrument of moral disarmament. Thinking of itself, at one level, as part of a radiophonic pact of non-aggression, the League of Nations had much in common with the Welsh National Eisteddfod, which sought to promote global peace through music, poetry and the performing arts. But an important difference between them is that a radio-linked Europe posed problems as, dependent upon transmitters, it tended to support the status quo and did not sufficiently include the small nations that stood on the outside.

A 'SOCIAL GOSPEL' OF PEACE

Despite what pacifists achieved in the inter-war years, the left wing of the Welsh pacifist movement could be said to have struggled. The context of the 1930s was not favourable to pacifism. Although the League achieved much in promoting the ideals of peace and health internationally, it failed to respond to the harbingers of the Second World War – for example, Hitler's remilitarisation of the Rhineland, occupation of the Sudetenland and *Anschluss* of Austria – or to check rearmament among league members. In permitting the use of arms by democratic states to resist aggressive states, the League proved attractive to conditional pacifists, but this also served to deepen the rift between absolute and conditional pacifism, in effect underlining the difficulties which absolute pacifists faced when confronted with events of the 1930s.

Pacifism, especially absolute pacifism, not only faced the challenge of how to respond if the country were invaded by Nazi-led Germany but also how to respond to the challenge posed by the economic suffering and poverty of the Welsh people. While T. Gwynn Jones was a meditative, romantic philosopher-poet, he was also an uncompromising conviction pacifist with 'a passionate hatred of injustice, oppression, and avoidable suffering'.[92] This aspect of his life and work is often overlooked, but he was responsible for one of the most socially aware poems in the Welsh language, the searing sonnet 'Senghenydd', written as a response to the explosion at Senghenydd colliery on 4 October 1913, which killed 439 miners and a rescuer. Important to the development of Welsh-language political poetry, it clearly pointed in a hard, socialist direction which embraced a different strain of 'Welshness' from that expressed in his work on Welsh folk culture. As Ned Thomas says, 'The truth is that our whole industrial civilisation has been based on exploitation – not only the exploitation of workers by owners, and of the countryside for profit, but the exploitation of everything, including ourselves.'[93] The poem helped encourage Gwenallt to extend his pacifist outlook to deaths and injuries from man-made disasters and led eventually to his 'Trychineb Aber-Fan', comparable to 'Senghenydd' in that both deal with horrific mine disasters caused by those responsible cutting corners (to which we will return in Chapter 4). But 'Senghenydd' also anticipates the way in which Welsh pacifism tried to reinvent itself as a 'social gospel' based on a broader understanding of what constituted 'pacifism' and which gave Welsh pacifism in the inter-war years a relevance that was distinctively Welsh.

Although most histories of the twentieth-century peace movements stress the challenges which different types of warfare posed for pacifism, very few of them address how the social misery of the south Wales coalfields threatened the very creed on which Christian pacifism was based. This is encapsulated in T. Rowland Hughes's *William Jones*: 'If God was love . . . Did He see the poverty, the affliction in these dreary valleys?'[94] It was difficult for social pacifism, based on post-Calvinist, Nonconformist interpretations of scripture, to face the Welsh unemployed of the 1930s who felt that God had turned his back on them, as Hughes's novel clearly spells out: 'Then came enmity and mockery, scourging, a crown of thorns and a cross. The father had hidden His face: God was no longer Love.'[95]

However, as we shall see in a discussion of Emyr Humphreys's historical novel *Outside the House of Baal* (1965) in Chapter 5, this development in Welsh pacifism was not without considerable controversy. But at its most positive, it led prominent Welsh pacifists to develop social projects – serving for example the unemployed – which were based on pacifism's principles and its utopian vision. Stressing that 'the witness of the Society of Friends was not limited to their opposition to war', George Davies highlighted 'their remarkable initiative in organising works of mercy and relief' (RQP, p. 25). In Wales, pacifists such as Davies extended the concept of a 'social gospel' to all conflicts including class warfare, racism and gender conflict. Debates over whether war might be opposed conditionally or had to be opposed absolutely were, at least for the time, displaced by arguments over how far pacifism was plausible as a wider social philosophy.

The development of a 'social pacifism', for want of a better term, was due in part to the overlap between pacifist organisations and the labour movement, and to the influence of Marxism and international socialism, especially where the Independent Labour Party worked with other anti-war movements and in the newer coalfield communities. Not only did the labour movement oppose the stockpiling of armaments but the unions and the Labour Party were bound by a resolution passed by the International Socialist Conference in 1907, that 'it was the duty of the members of the working class to prevent the outbreak of war; if they failed, they should make every effort to transform a war between states into a war between classes'.[96]

As Morgan observes, while 'the impact of the anti-war movements in Wales must not be exaggerated', as 'the war helped undermine the older radicalism, it gave impetus and vigour to the new socialism'.[97] In this regard, it would be extremely remiss not to mention the Welsh Jewish writer Lily Tobias. Apart from supporting the No-Conscription Fellowship in Swansea and Cardiff, in her support of the Independent Labour Party and as a socialist and pacifist she exemplified how socialism and pacifism merged in the inter-war years, being described at the time as a 'young, battling, aggressive socialist pacifist'.[98] Or not to acknowledge again one of the foremost social-pacifist exponents T. E. Nicholas, who was indefatigable in his work for both the Independent Labour Party and the anti-war movement, eventually joining the Communist Party.[99] Only ten years after the conclusion of the Second World War, Bell described Nicholas as 'the poet of revolt, the uncompromising pacifist, the rebel against social injustice and inequality, a stormy petrel alike in society and in the Church'.[100]

Hughes's fictional quarryman who moves from a Welsh-language community in north Wales to the south Wales coalfields discovers a strong, primarily English-speaking community with a confident cultural identity built around chapels, choirs and rugby. In areas where pacifism was eradicated rather than reinvigorated by the new socialism, this had as much to do with hard economic realities as pacifist ideologies. Following the impact of the strike of 1921, the long dispute of 1926 and unemployment in the 1930s, vividly recorded in Hughes's novel, the growth of socialism in the coalfields owed much to the increasing number of young miners attracted to the radical Independent Labour Movement after the First World War. But, as Hughes's William Jones also discovers, the south Wales of the 1920s and 1930s was a turbulent place politically. The Communist Party was formed in Wales in 1921, and Marxism spread rapidly across the coalfields, where international radicalism and ideas about syndicalism found a natural home.

The Welsh industrial novel, in English and in Welsh, which evolved from the harsh economic realities of the 1930s and political turbulence of south Wales is too well documented to need further discussion here.[101] But it is worth re-noting that novels such as *William Jones* still carry a punch in their depictions of the workless poor, soup kitchens in the chapels, money collections through choirs and bands, and the scanty unemployment benefit. However, less attention has been paid to the dialectic between socialism and pacifism in areas where the former did not displace the latter, leaving unexplored how the pacifist social gospel managed at times to blur the boundaries between pacifist and non-pacifist socialist ideologies.

WELSH PACIFISM AND GERMANY

Of the controversies around pacifism in the 1930s, one in particular has to be addressed, the controversy generated by the attitude of prominent pacifists to Hitler. Many at the time and since have not seen this as Welsh pacifism's finest hour. Welsh pacifists shared the concerns of many non-pacifists over what was happening in Germany in the 1930s, but they did not necessarily see war as the solution. The

Welsh peace movement supported negotiation with Hitler, believing that Hitler and his policies had been brought about by the way in which Germany had been humiliated by the Treaty of Versailles.[102] How pacifists should respond to Hitler is a subject that recurs in pacifist publications and conversations of all kinds in the 1930s. Emyr Humphreys, writing in the early 1960s, reflects the importance of the topic to the 1930s in *Outside the House of Baal*. Wynne Bannister, married to the sister of the central character, J.T., compares Hitler to Lloyd George:

> This chap Hitler's got some good ideas you know. Work camps for young men. The best of army life without the killing and the snags. Good idea that you know. Clean up the country in no time with a few ideas like that. Probably pinched the idea from Lloyd George. It's a quick way to conquer unemployment you see. That's the man we need, you know, if you ask me. Get Lloyd George back.[103]

Some Welsh nationalists, intrigued by Hitler's nationalism, found themselves thinking about the rights of their own small nation. But, after the outbreak of the Second World War, Iorwerth Peate became concerned to stress the difference between Hitler's nationalist ideologies and nationalism in Wales. In 'Anthropoleg a Phroblemau Cyfoes' (Anthropology and Contemporary Problems) (1940), he maintains that anthropologists could have spoken out more strongly against the racial theories of Hitler's *Mein Kampf*. Hitler's arguments for the distinctiveness of the Germanic race led Peate to ask whether the Welsh people were distinctive, but in other ways. While Hitler thought in terms of race, Peate maintained the importance of thinking about culture. In careful Welsh prose, he ponders: 'A ydym yn wahanol iawn yn y ffordd yr edrychwn ar bethau?' (Are we different in the way we see things?)[104] But he knows the answer. Seizing on the Eisteddfod and the nation's peace movements, he suggests that the way the two are linked defines Welsh culture: 'Er enghraifft, dywedwyd amdanom mai ein dwy nodwedd genedlaethol amlwg yw ein hymlyniad wrth yr Eisteddfod a'r gred mewn heddwch cyd-genedlaethol.'[105] Here, he turns to the evidence provided by the thousands who come to the Eisteddfod field and the numbers who attend the peace meetings.[106] While he acknowledges that the Welsh language is important to the distinctiveness of the Welsh nation, he suggests that it is not only the language itself, but the language as, what he calls, 'y cyfrwng mynegiant',[107] the medium of creative expression in the arts, especially literature and music, that is most significant.

With hindsight, believing that Hitler would be willing to agree to peace may seem (in Densil Morgan's words) 'an incapacity to comprehend the disturbing, the irrational, and the demonic'.[108] Morgan argues that with Mussolini's sacking of Addis Ababa in 1935, 'the chill winds of realism first began to cool Welsh Nonconformist ardour for peaceful change'.[109] However, when 'realism' is employed, as here, to imply that pacifism is not 'realistic', the terms require examination. After all, as Morgan says, no one on either side of the pacifist boundary doubted that 'international disputes could be eliminated without undue recourse to force', that 'governments acting in good faith could curb wars of aggression', or that 'conflicting national interests could be ultimately harmonized'.[110] The philosopher Anthony Grayling observes that it was 'realism' which became 'the dominant theory since 1945 about the causes of war'.[111] But, it was much earlier in the troubled 1930s that 'realism' began to define the public attitude to pacifism. For Grayling, 'realism is a pessimistic view which is never fully persuaded that peacemaking processes will succeed . . . it does not think that in situations of unequal distributions of power internationally, the stronger will inevitably show self-restraint towards the weaker'.[112]

Thus, as Morgan argues, the palpable weaknesses of pacifism became perceived as the failure to understand 'the complexity of evil'; belief in 'an overly optimistic evolutionary view of human nature' and 'a failure to differentiate between personal morality and collective evil'.[113] Nazism and 'the deepening trouble-filled situation throughout Europe' appeared to leave 'the ideals of rational discussion and conciliation' of Welsh Nonconformity teetering on the verge of collapse.[114] By 1940 Denmark, Norway, Belgium, the Netherlands and France had all been invaded and it seemed that there were two apparently incontestable justifications for war, which Grayling summarises as 'self-defence against aggression, and defence of those who cannot defend themselves against aggression'.[115] While Grayling overlooks the fact that many pacifists would, and did, have little difficulty in arguing against the former, the latter proved a more formidable obstacle, which is evident in the higher number of pacifists who changed their allegiance in the Second World War compared to the First World War. The horrors of the Second World War reshaped the worldview of even the most ardent absolutist Welsh pacifist; even Gwynfor Evans, who once argued vociferously for negotiation with Hitler, came to see him as a 'monster'.[116]

Three years into the Second World War, George Davies seized on how Hitler and Mussolini had invoked the *Pax Romana*, the apparent long period of peace and economic stability of Rome under its first emperor Augustus, claiming a 'Germanic succession to the Greco-Roman ideals' (RQP, p. 5). He pointed out that there was an alternative way of looking at Augustus' reign, anticipating David Gee's argument that the occupied peoples experienced 'imperial might as a presence lingering in the shadows, ready to crush the least smattering of dissent'.[117] Gee, in effect, provides a retrospective gloss on Davies's essay, maintaining that 'to the occupying powers, such enforced quietude is experienced as a form of "peace", as in Pax Romana, Pax Britannica, and Pax Americana, but the colonised know it for the violence it is'.[118]

Over 60 percent of those who participated in the peace ballot held by the League of Nations supported negotiating peace with Germany.[119] In order to understand why many in the late 1930s, pacifist and non-pacifist alike, entertained the possibility of peace with Germany, it is important to remember that there is a growing body of evidence that Hitler, at least for a time, was interested in peace. The evidence for this goes beyond Chamberlain's return from Munich declaring 'peace in our time'. Kershaw points out that towards the end of his radio address to the nation on 1 February, 1933, 'Appeal of the Reich Government to the German People', Hitler 'posed for the first time as a man of peace, stating, despite love of the army as the bearer of arms and symbol of Germany's great past, how happy the government would be "if through a restriction of its armaments the world should make an increase of our own weapons never again necessary"'.[120] On the subject of German–Polish relations, as late as August 1939, Viscount Halifax telegraphed Sir H. Kennard (Warsaw) to say, 'I have the impression that Herr Hitler is still undecided, and anxious to avoid war and to hold his hand if he can do so without losing face.'[121] On 23 August, Hitler himself wrote to the Prime Minister: 'Germany was prepared to settle the questions of Danzig and of the Corridor by the method of negotiation on the basis of a proposal of truly unparalleled magnanimity.'[122] In the last paragraph of his communication, he insists:

> The question of the treatment of European problems on a peaceful basis is not [a] decision which rests on Germany but primarily on those who

> since the crime committed by the Versailles [Treaty] dictate have stubbornly and consistently opposed any peaceful revision.[123]

Thus, it is not necessarily correct to associate pacifism in the late 1930s, to re-employ Morgan's words, with a failure to understand 'the complexity of evil' and belief in 'an overly optimistic evolutionary view of human nature'.

PACIFISM AND THE FEAR OF INVASION

Earlier we mentioned that one of the challenges which pacifists faced in the late 1920s and in the 1930s was how to hold on to pacifist beliefs in the face of invasion and conquest. One of the key pacifist poems of the time, T. Gwynn Jones's 'Argoed', linked military invasion and linguistic conquest. It helped raise awareness of the threat which anglicisation posed to the Welsh language but also helped prepare pacifists to meet the challenges posed by the invasion of small countries in Europe by Nazi Germany and, eventually, the very real prospect of the invasion of Britain.

Six years after T. Gwynn Jones's death in 1949, Bell described him as 'perhaps the most prominent and most widely loved literary figure in Wales'.[124] Although he had an affiliation with Nonconformity, where the roots of his pacifism lay, like several other Welsh pacifist poets (most notably Gwenallt), he was attracted to Catholicism[125] – a gravitation possibly connected to the doubt that 'reality' cast on his idealism. The poem 'Mater dolorosa' suggests that the Catholic concept of the Virgin Mary as intermediary between imperfect, suffering humanity and the ideal purity of Christ may have rescued him from despair.

Argoed is an imaginary pastoral community in a remote region of ancient Gaul which retained its ancient traditions. However, the poem has not often been read as the pacifist text it so obviously is. As a pacifist, pastoral community, Argoed clearly evokes rural west Wales, which Waldo Williams and Gwenallt tended to idealise as a Welsh-speaking, pacifist heartland. But another world enters 'Argoed', as it did in west Wales in the Second World War when the nation was required to turn over more land to crop farming. The traditional community of Argoed discovers that Rome has already conquered the greater part of the country, an allegory for the anglicisation of Wales, and finds that over a large swathe of the country a new language is spoken and that their own language is no longer universally understood.

As an allegory, 'Argoed' implies that pacifism had strong links with Welsh-speaking traditional communities, and war with English-speaking, industrial communities which also threatened the Welsh language, culture and traditions. But if that is the intended allegory it is much too simple, for a large number of Welshmen enlisted in the First World War even before the introduction of conscription, just as many in the conquered Roman provinces joined the auxiliaries of the Roman army, established to recruit, or receive conscripts, from among non-Roman citizens. The conquest of Gaul by the Romans and the impending demise of Argoed offer insights into situations which were extensively discussed among Welsh pacifists in the first few decades of the twentieth century. It encourages us to think about how peoples respond to 'invasion' and how life in one way or another carries on in a country which has been defeated militarily.

In the 1930s the Roman empire would have been on many educated people's minds because so many aspects of Nazi-led Germany were based on it and the way Roman emperors consolidated their personal power. In their grand oratory, mass gatherings and appreciation of the importance of propaganda, Augustus,the first Roman emperor, and Hitler were not far apart. It appeared natural that Germany should look to Rome as the most successful and longest-lasting of the western empires. Not all Roman provinces were 'conquered'; some were annexed by more diplomatic means. Models of invasion and conquest varied from one part of the Roman empire to another, as did the experience of relationships with Rome, involving for example: the imposition of enforced work and the payment of tribute to the conquering state; compliance with the conqueror's laws and civil organisation; outright opposition and violent resistance; subtle pacifist protest; preservation of traditional customs; and the adoption of the conqueror's traditions, language and values. 'Argoed' takes Welsh readers to the brink of invasion and conquest, as it were, and encourages them to look over the edge. The poem concludes with the inhabitants of Argoed burning their country rather than accepting the yoke of oppression. But there is a moment to reflect before that decision is taken – when all the options mentioned above are available:

> A ched o Argoed a archwyd, deirgwaith,
> A hithau, deirgwaith, a wrthyd Argoed,

Canys Argoed erioed ni roddes anrhydedd
I rymus dieithr na gormes daeog;
Ffyddlon ydoedd ei chalon; ni chiliai
O gof fyth yno gyfoeth ei hanes;[126]

And tribute from Argoed was decreed three times,
And then, three times, Argoed refused it,
For never had Argoed at all given honour
To a foreign might or brutal oppression;
The heart of her people kept faith; richness
Of her history had not lapsed to oblivion;[127]

The fact that the tribute from Argoed is demanded and refused three times brings to mind Julius Caesar refusing the Roman crown three times and Peter thrice denying Christ after his arrest in Gethsemane. 'Deirgwaith' (three times) is not simply how many times something is demanded or offered but involves a suspension of time in which, for example, Caesar might accept the crown and Peter might acknowledge Christ. The poem turns, as do these Roman and biblical narratives, on this moment of suspense which is what all nations and individuals face when confronted with invasion and conquest. It is a space in which the various possibilities that open include violent opposition and non-violent, pacifist resistance as well as compliance.

THE WELSH LANGUAGE

The development of pacifism among writers in Wales cannot be separated from the promotion of the Welsh language as a literary medium and the development of a nationalist, Welsh-language, literary intelligentsia. As soon as we start to probe this we come up against some of Wales's most formidable and radical writers such as T. Gwynn Jones himself, Waldo Williams, Gwenallt Jones, W. J. Gruffydd and the outspoken minister and author Tegla Davies (1880–1967) (whose essays were published as a series of weekly articles in *Yr Herald Cymraeg* between 1946 and 1953). There is also the equally prolific E. Morgan Humphreys, who served as editor of *Y Genedl Gymreig*, where he became a colleague of T. Gwynn Jones, *Cymru* and *Y Goleuad*, while regularly contributing articles also to the *Liverpool Daily Post* under the pen name Celt, and as a special correspondent, to the *Manchester Guardian* in 1927.[128]

Ned Thomas wryly comments: 'sometimes it seems as if the whole of Wales is consumed in endless protest'.[129] He argues that the reasons for the opposition, for example, to the artillery range in Carmarthenshire, the drowning of a mid-Wales valley and the second-class treatment of the Welsh language are different, but 'what distinguishes the protests in Wales from those in some parts of England to preserve the environment, [is] that they converge on a special kind of consciousness which is a national consciousness'.[130]

The importance which Ned Thomas attaches to 'much serious thinking about Wales' being conducted in Welsh suggests another characteristic of Welsh pacifism that must not be overlooked: the extent to which it is underpinned by a national consciousness and by nationalist themes as well as by its support of the Welsh language. In 1925, *The Welsh Outlook*, observing how 'the question of the preservation of the Welsh language is very much to the front just now', maintained: 'In Wales everything centres in the language, and if Welsh ceases to be a living tongue, not even the fullest measure of Home Rule can ever prevent the nation from extinction.'[131] Its assertiveness continued in subsequent issues until it threw down the gauntlet: 'Oes y byd i'r iaith Gymraeg' (Eternal Life for the Welsh language). It argued that this 'has too often been shouted by men who neither speak the language in their homes, nor make certain that their children are taught to use it as their mother tongue'.

Thomas is right, of course, and it is the Welsh language that most distinguishes Welsh and English pacifism. Pacifist thinking in Wales was developed by writers who either worked solely in Welsh, such as Waldo Williams and Gwenallt Jones, or in Welsh and English, such as George Davies and Emyr Humphreys. Ned Thomas points out: 'The most serious thinking about Wales, the most passionate feeling for it, has been expressed in Welsh, and through Welsh literature Welsh-speakers have access to minds that have identified with them and their problems.'[132] The link between the Welsh language and pacifism became stronger between the First and Second World Wars. In *Peace News* in October 1941, John Barclay condemned the excessive attachment of Welsh pacifists at Bangor to the Welsh language and was attacked by Dewi Llwyd Jones of Plaid Cymru for 'arrogantly assuming that all British pacifism must be English in origin and speech'.[133]

Catrin Stevens emphasises the influence of the Welsh language and nationalism on another important Welsh pacifist who has already entered our narrative more than once, Iorwerth Peate. A noted Welsh ethnographer and founder of St Fagans National Museum of 'folk' culture, his background is as traditionally Welsh as one might expect. He had a traditional chapel-going upbringing and his father's literary and religious interests brought him into contact with the charismatic leaders of the Welsh Independent movement, notably Tom Nefyn and the Revd Tegla Davies.[134] During his college years, he remained loyal to this tradition under the guidance of Dr Peter Price, minister of Baker Street Chapel, Aberystwyth.[135] The Revd Tegla Davies himself moved within a circle within the Welsh-language intelligentsia which also included Ifor Williams, T. Gwynn Jones and David Thomas.

A further indication of the close-knit nature of the pacifist Welsh intelligentsia but also of the way in which pacifism in Wales was transformed into a movement interested not simply in anti-war-ism but wider social, cultural and political concerns, is the symposium of tributes to T. Gwynn Jones, published by the Welsh Committee of the Communist Party.[136] Contributors include many of the leading Welsh scholars, writers and pacifists of the first half of the twentieth century: Idris Bell, Ellis Williams, T. E. Nicholas, Keidrych Rhys, W. J. Rees, D. Gwenallt Jones, Dilys Cadwaladr, D. Tecwyn Lloyd and Idris Cox. Central to the symposium is a short essay from Gwenallt himself summarising very effectively his life and work as a pacifist: 'Clwyfwyd delfrydiaeth gan y Rhyfel, ond fe'i claddwyd hi gan Heddwch' (Idealism was wounded by the war but buried by the peace).[137] But the other essays place this achievement in the context of his wider contribution to Welsh-language literature and culture.

Most histories of the interconnection of Welsh nationalism, the Welsh language in twentieth-century Wales and protest make reference to the attack on the RAF bombing school on the Llŷn peninsula, but hardly any mention the link with pacifism, and even fewer mention the attack on the Pencarreg television transmitter near Lampeter in 1979 as part of the campaign for an improved Welsh-language service, which led to the establishment, three years later, of S4C, the fourth channel which now broadcasts programmes in Welsh. In a nutshell, this incident is relevant to this book for the way in which those involved highlight the interconnection of Welsh nationalism, the campaign for the Welsh language, non-violent protest and pacifism. In addition to the academic and Welsh-language campaigner and nationalist Ned Thomas, the others were the theologian, poet and pacifist Pennar Davies and Meredydd Evans

(1919–2015), a senior figure in Cymdeithas yr Iaith Gymraeg (The Welsh Language Society) and historian of Welsh-language folk music, who had won unconditional exemption from military service on religious grounds during the Second World War and was a lifelong advocate of non-violence.

THE TWO INTELLIGENTSIAS

Many members of the English-language intelligentsia looked increasingly away from Welsh-language Wales and the interest of its intelligentsia in pacifism. How rigid the polarisation became in the minds of some monoglot English-language speakers prior to the First World War is evident in many publications from the Victorian period onward. Few expressed the division or set an agenda for debates about Welshness and the Welsh language from an Anglophone perspective more vehemently than the Revd J. Vyrnwy Morgan. He maintained: 'The Welsh language was the mother of the old patriotism – the retrospective patriotism; it was the source of the old idealism, and the reservoir of the old spiritual force.'[138]

The Welsh-language intelligentsia would have seen promoting the 'old idealism' and the 'old spiritual force' as a significant part of their role. What was worrying for them at the time was not so much the accuracy of Vyrnwy Morgan's claims about the value of the English language as the extent to which they found favour in anglicised Wales, where it became increasingly easy to find Welsh people who would agree that Welsh had 'obstructed rather than facilitated the way of Wales in the world' and that 'the sons of Wales who have reached eminence have reached it through the medium of the English language'.[139] Although, as mentioned earlier, pockets of the Welsh language, Nonconformity and pacifism remained in south Wales, sustained by migrants from the north and west, the demand for jobs in the heavy industries, and in the services which developed alongside them, meant that there was always an influx of non-Welsh-speakers from outside Wales, including the continent. Due to the events in Europe in the 1930s, including the Spanish Civil War, and the way the English language facilitated the spread of international socialism across Wales, if the workers of south Wales were pacifists at all, they were conditional rather than absolute pacifists. The influence of the Welsh-language intelligentsia declined with the Welsh language itself in the south Wales English belt. This was not helped by the lack of support by the South Wales Miners' Federation for the characteristics and culture of Welsh-language Wales.

However, despite the softening of the boundaries between Welsh-language and English-language Wales in some geographical areas, the strength of the desire among leading Welsh-language intellectuals to develop a 'pacifism' which was philosophically distinct and structurally different from English pacifism remained, evident in the enthusiasm which greeted the Welsh wing of the Peace Pledge Union. This is not to suggest that Welsh and English pacifists were in opposition to each other, but that Welsh pacifists were driven by convictions which were not relevant to England. This difference was summarised by George Davies when, thinking of Wales, he described how 'Democracy' was 'built from the foundation of small Nonconformist groups which refused to conform to the fashion of the world' (PP, p. 86). This is a line of thought which was developed by the wider Welsh-language community whether pacifist or not. As Ned Thomas says, 'because of its small size, the Welsh-language community feels in extreme form the mindless destruction that is carried out everywhere in the name of economic logic'.[140]

Thomas suggests that the presence of an English-language intelligentsia in the second half of the twentieth century has been stressed at the expense of the influence of the Welsh-language intelligentsia. Discussing the pacifist writer Glyn Jones, Wynn Thomas, who has probably done more than any scholar to promote Welsh writing in English, describes what he calls 'this "genius belt", or at least "talent belt"' of south Wales as 'the Welsh equivalent of the wealthy, well-educated, culturally creative English middle class'.[141] This 'critical mass of intellectuals' emerged as the result of generations educated largely in anglicised schools from the late nineteenth century onwards. John Davies makes a similar point, thinking specifically of Dylan Thomas, Gwyn Thomas, Jack Jones and Idris Jones.[142] However, Wynn Thomas goes on to observe that, in *The Dragon Has Two Tongues* (2001), Glyn Jones argues that the division between the English-language and the Welsh-language intelligentsia was not as clear-cut as some English-language critics have suggested: 'More Anglo-Welsh writers of the first half of the twentieth century come from a background of Welsh-speaking radical Nonconformity than from any other.'[143] John Davies has suggested, also, that 'to judge by the statements of some Welsh authors writing in English . . . it might be considered that despite their hundreds of millions of potential readers they were envious of those of their compatriots who wrote in Welsh'.[144] The three authors he mentions are R. S. Thomas, Emyr Humphreys and Harri Webb, overlooking the fact that each of them learned Welsh as adults and two of them lived in strong Welsh-language speaking communities.

The significance of the Welsh-language intelligentsia to the distinctive way in which the peace movement developed in Wales is evident, of course, in the influence of Plaid Cymru. Plaid and pacifism shared roots in rural, west Wales as Meic Stephens points out in his perceptive obituary of Gwynfor Evans, where he refers to 'his characteristic emphasis on tradition, communal values, the culture of ordinary people and the value of the individual, particularly in the small, rural, Welsh-speaking areas, which were at the heart of his nationalism . . .'[145] Welsh pacifists who objected to the Second World War as the 'English' war were often Plaid members.[146] But while the English Appellate Tribunal formally recorded that Welsh nationalism was a basis for conscientious objection within the meaning of the 1939 National Service Act, few Welsh tribunals were inclined to agree.[147] This proved indicative of the controversy over pacifism which Plaid generated both outside and within the party itself, and in no case more than its alleged 'totalitarianism', which anti-war critics such as Thomas Jones and the Revd Gwilym Davies targeted, while Saunders Lewis's inflexibility on religious matters alienated leading Welsh pacifists such as W. J. Gruffydd and Iorwerth Peate.[148] However, the impact of Plaid Cymru, like that of the peace movement itself, changed with the wider public attitude to war. Following the conclusion of the Second World War in the west and the atomic bombing of Japan, Plaid, the Peace Pledge Union, the Fellowship of Reconciliation and Heddychwyr Cymru, to which we will return in the next section, came together under the leadership of the lifelong pacifist and long-time Plaid president, Gwynfor Evans.[149]

THE WELSH-LANGUAGE PEACE PAMPHLETS AND AFTER

Thanks to contributions from David Lloyd George, Cynan and W. J. Gruffydd, 1937 saw the first modern, Welsh-speaking Eisteddfod at Machynlleth and the beginnings of the Welsh Home Service on radio.[150] In June 1937, a call for a pacifist organisation with more of a Welsh standpoint led to the decision to establish Heddychwyr

Cymru (Welsh Peacemakers) as a Welsh and Welsh-speaking wing of the PPU. George Davies became its first president in April 1938, and Gwynfor Evans, who was given an unconditional discharge as a conscientious objector, served as its secretary from 1939 to 1945. As Llywelyn says, it grew rapidly in the first two years following its founding.[151]

The new pamphlet series implemented by the Christian pacifists of Heddychwyr in 1941 proved important in bringing Welsh intellectuals together in the Second World War as well as promoting the pacifist cause. The list of distinguished contributors is truly staggering including George M. Ll. Davies himself, Eirug Davies, Pennar Davies, Rhys J. Davies, Kate Bosse-Griffiths, Dafydd Jenkins, T. Gwynn Jones, Rhys Davies, the Revd Herbert Morgan, Professor J. Morgan Jones, Ben Bowen Thomas, the first warden of Coleg Harlech, Iorwerth Peate, and Hywel D. Lewis. As Gwynfor Evans points out, it was in a pamphlet in this series that Waldo Williams set out his worldview based on the concept of 'brawdoliaeth' (brotherhood) which is discussed in Chapter 4.[152] George Davies prevailed upon Iorwerth Peate to write the first pamphlet for this Welsh pacifist series, and in 1941 he published *Y Traddodiad Heddwch yng Nghymru*, followed in 1942 by a translation of J. Middleton Murry's *God or the Nation?*[153] In 'Heddychwr Cynnar' (1942), based on notes he made while preparing *Y Traddodiad Heddwch yng Nghymru*, Peate traces Welsh pacifism to Wmffre Dafydd ab Ifan, a Welsh poet during the English Civil War who, refusing to side with the Royalists or the Parliamentarians, chose the way of peace and reconciliation. The essay highlights how Wmffre Dafydd developed a different language in his pacifist poetry from his previous work, which stressed 'llawenydd' (gladness/joy), 'trugaredd' (compassion/mercy) and 'i weithredoedd dynion' (to do the works of men).[154]

As one would expect, the debates in the peace pamphlets, and the debates around them, changed in emphasis in the 1940s. In *Cwymp Cristnogaeth* (Fall of Christianity) (1942), Peate responds to a book from a Dutch academic criticising the church for not opposing the war. The church is seen, as in the writings of George Davies, as too closely bound up with a society and culture that cultivates war and regards it as a necessity. The argument is delivered in the kind of measured way we might expect of one of Davies's sermons: 'yn rhwym wrth y math o gymdeithas sy'n coleddu rhyfel fel angenraid'.[155] In particular, Peate seizes on the book's argument that in the Netherlands, the church will lose the moral right to exist if it continues to support preparations for war: 'Pa hawl foesol, gofyn Heering, sydd gan yr Eglwys tros barhau o gwbl os caniata i baratoadau at ryfel fynd ymlaen yn ei gwlad ei hun.'[156] The argument here, in one of Peate's most startling propositions, is that even in Wales the church is in danger of losing the moral right to exist because it has rejected the pacifist teachings of Christ. Peate's declaration to the churches and chapels of Wales could not be more uncompromising nor his Welsh prose more emphatic: '"Fe'th gydnabyddaf yn unig tra arhosi yn wladwriaeth gyfiawn ac ymwrthod â phob rhyfel." Hon yw neges y gyfrol bwysig hon, ac fe ddylai pob Cristion ei darllen, beth bynnag ei ddaliadau'.[157] He insists that the message of the church must be that righteous nations (wladwriaeth gyfiawn) must abstain from every war (ymwrthod â phob rhyfel) and that this is the duty of every Christian, and in a clause clearly intended to rally pacifists in the face of persecution and prosecution, 'whatever his belief' (beth bynnag ei ddaliadau).

Towards the end of the war, in an essay 'Gorseddu Dyn' (Enthroning man) (1944), Iorwerth Peate focuses on an aspect of the kind of world which he believes will exist after the war. He takes issue with what he sees as a contemporary cultural curse developing in Europe, the sweeping condemnation of knowledge, science and reason. Science was important to Peate, as it was for Raven, whom he quotes in his essay 'Anghydffurfiaeth A'r Trefi' (1944): 'The worst enemies of Christian theology – if not indeed of the Christian religion – at the present time are those who identify the faith with ideas belonging inescapably to the pre-scientific world.'[158] He argues that the problem does not lie with reason or science, but with the faults in the way they are employed. The essay takes issue, too, with the way in which countries and peoples are latching on to ostensibly convincing big ideas. One of the more important for Peate is the obsession with the highways that are connecting different human societies with each other. He fears that totalitarian regimes are putting more emphasis on the highways than the societies which they are connecting, and the former are being developed at the expense of villages and their sense of connectiveness – 'y pentrefi a gysyllta' – which he alleges the anarchists want to dispel completely, 'yn ei dileu'n llwyr'.[159] As a Welsh pacifist, like Waldo Williams and Gwenallt Jones, he was brought up to value the small communities in which people established a society where individuals mattered and were valued. As we mentioned earlier, in his essay 'Anghydffurfiaeth A'r Trefi' he argued for the importance of communities 'small enough for everyone to know everyone else personally . . . little democracies of neighbours'.[160]

These are arguments that were to play a significant part in post-Second World War Welsh pacifism. Gwynfor Evans was as outspoken as George Davies and Iorwerth Peate:

> The great powers were created in response to the demands of military might. What they produce is nuclear bombs and world wars. In such a situation the building of strong peace movements is not enough; we must also try to break and decentralize the great powers and the large centralized system.[161]

Employing the language of post-1945 pacifism in talking not only of anti-war-ism but the future of humankind – and swayed by his own deep-rooted nationalist as well as pacifist convictions – Evans urges:

> The large, centralist, anachronistic power that we in Wales can help to dismantle is Britain . . . We have to strengthen the peace movement in every possible way, but the greatest contribution this small nation can make in the cause of world peace and the survival of humankind is to win full self-government for Wales.[162]

After the Second World War, some of the factors, most notably Nonconformity and the Welsh language, which gave Welsh pacifism its distinctive character contributed to what some might see as its distinctive demise. The 1951 population census showed a decline of over 100,000 Welsh-speakers in two decades, with Welsh virtually ceasing to be the first language in urban Wales. This was accompanied by a sharp decline in chapel affiliation throughout Wales.[163] This, of course, could be traced to the First World War, which disrupted traditional beliefs (the sheer scale of seemingly senseless slaughter raised questions about the benevolence of God) and also the routine of regular chapel attendance. Although chapel attendance recovered for a time, it never regained the levels of pre-war years. In part, the drift from Christian practice in the inter-war period was a product of the influence of the new generation of atheists and agnostics who emerged in the first third of the twentieth century, many themselves influenced by those formidable nineteenth-century atheists Karl Marx and Friedrich Nietzsche, not to mention the establishment, under Lenin and the communists, of the world's first avowedly atheist state.

But, of course, there were economic factors including the redevelopment of town centres. Although rationing did not end until 1954, when it did, the new abundance changed the psyche of the nation, providing a distraction for many ordinary people from the wider gloom and doom of a nuclear world. And it had an impact on the small towns and villages in which pacifism once had its roots. A character in Humphreys's *The Shop*, one of the most interesting Welsh novels in English in the first decade of the twenty-first century, describes the change: 'As soon as rationing relaxed, customers drifted away. Petrol came off ration and people began the habit of shopping in town. Sometimes I used to think the only genuine commodity we have to sell in the shop was sadness.'[164]

However, this is not to say that Wales became a nation of shoppers rather than pacifists. Rather than seeing the 1950s as a watershed, it is possible to talk of the post-war decades as part of the ongoing combination of continuity and change which has always characterised Welsh pacifism. While some of the key exponents of Welsh pacifism met their deaths in the mid-twentieth century (T. Gwynn Jones, d. 1949; George M. Ll. Davies, d. 1949; W. J. Gruffydd, d. 1954; and R. Gwilym Davies, d. 1955), the individual religiosity associated with Welsh pacifism continued to be promoted well into the second half of the century by those who survived, in works such as George Davies's *Pilgrimage of Peace* and Pennar Davies's spiritual journal *Cudd Fy Meiau* (Hide My Sins) (1958); and in Welsh pacifist poetry, particularly the work of D. Gwenallt Jones and Waldo Williams. By the 1960s, the value placed on the individual consciousness, as well as conscience, by Welsh pacifism and Nonconformity, through for example the *seiat*, a meeting in which the faithful shared their spiritual experiences, created a legacy which chimed with a wider 'subjective turn' in everyday spiritual life in which sensitivity to inner life and well-being displaced externally-organised religion.

THE BEGINNING OF THE END OF HUMANITY

There is no escaping the fact that the Second World War made it particularly difficult to be a pacifist for a time, but the later years strengthened the case for pacifism. To return to Aunt Sudwell, the character from Humphreys's *The Shop*; at one point in the book she recalls how 'The power of war grew worse. I remember [my father] muttering to himself at the time the Americans dropped those atom bombs on Japan, "Not once but twice". He thought it could be the beginning of the end of humanity.'[165] It hardly needs pointing out that during the war, aerial bombardment dramatically transformed the traditional understanding of war as fought on distant battlefields to protect homelands, while loved ones and non-combatants sheltered at home. Death, injury and the horror of battle were always brought home from the 'front' in news reporting, art work, photographs and stories, but the distinction between 'home' and 'front', and between 'combatant' and 'non-combatant', became blurred in the Second World War. As White points out, the victims of war 'decisively changed from soldiers to civilian'; unlike in the First World War when only 5 per cent of about 13 million casualties were civilian, more than 50 per cent of the 50–60 million who died during the Second World War were technically non-combatants.[166] The 'Home Front' in the Second World War had a particular impact on Welsh writers, such as Dylan Thomas, Waldo Williams and Emyr Humphreys, who lived through the blitz on London and Swansea, as did the impact of the dropping of the atomic bombs on Japan.

It hardly needs stressing also that as a consequence of Hiroshima and Nagasaki, the nature of pacifism shifted from opposition to war as a threat to particular nations to opposition to war as a threat to the whole human race. Gwynfor Evans summarises the position in which late twentieth-century, and indeed twenty-first-century, pacifists found themselves:

> I find it easier to understand how people can quietly accept that we are likely to be destroyed than to comprehend that they will not react with furious energy against the preparations made in their name for the slaughter of millions of innocent men, women, and children in another country.[167]

Professor Kathleen Lonsdale's Swarthmore lecture, *Removing the Causes of War*, to the Society of Friends in 1953, offers evidence of how the mood of the peace movements in Britain changed after the Second World War. Her principal theme is how the atomic bombing of Hiroshima and Nagasaki was leading to widespread anxiety about what today have been called 'weapons of mass destruction', and to renewed arguments for international reconciliation which she traced to the late 1930s and a quotation from Sir Winston Churchill: 'Either there will be a melting of hearts and a joining of hearts between nations . . . or there will be an explosion and a catastrophe the course of which no imagination can measure.'[168] Grayling offers a useful summary of the 'new' pacifism which emerged in the Cold War: 'As the technologies of war grow ever more sophisticated and destructive so the truth enunciated by John F. Kennedy comes ominously closer, that if we do not end war, it will end us.'[169]

In the 1950s, observations such as these haunted many pacifists for whom the 'piling up of frighteningly destructive armaments . . . [was] a gamble with fear and hatred'.[170] As Lonsdale's lecture demonstrates, rather than celebrating the end of war, the 1950s feared a world where the balance of power depended upon weapons of mass destruction and where 'generations of young people [were] trained for war and conditioned to regard war as a permanent possibility in world affairs'.[171] In the final reflective essay in *Pilgrimage of Peace*, dated 1947, George Davies writes:

> Emerson's words drive one to ask again, 'Is it, in fact, only in the living and leavening of the goodwill of God and the spirit of peace that the conversion of men is possible when their coercion has proved impossible without mutual destruction?' – for that is the position to which modern armaments have brought this generation. (PP, p. 86)

This is a view which the rector in Emyr Humphreys's *Unconditional Surrender* expresses even more memorably: 'The genie is out of the bottle . . . Mankind has found the means to destroy itself. Mankind won't be able to resist the temptation.'[172]

Moreover, there was further concern, as Lonsdale argues, that 'while armaments exist foreign policies are bound to be based on power and opportunism and not on reason'.[173] This is a point of view to be found in much Welsh, as well as English, writing after the Second World War, which Dannie Abse effectively summarises in discussing the title poem of his collection *Funland and Other Poems* (1973): 'In "Funland" power considerations and powerlessness are everywhere put before us. A scapegoat is needed so the blue-haired, red-eyed Thracians become the enemy.'[174] Lonsdale's lecture suggests that, in the 1950s, pacifism became increasingly based on anxieties about fear and hatred between nations, and particularly on how 'fear of espionage and subversion results in oppression, in panic, in secrecy, in barriers between nations'.[175]

Gwynfor Evans was right in suggesting that the war in Korea and especially the hydrogen bomb had more of an impact in turning people to pacifism than even the bombing of London and Swansea.[176] Looking to a future world with nuclear weapons in more than one country's armoury, Evans campaigned: 'We of all people ought not to allow ourselves to be overcome by a feeling of impotence in the face of the nuclear threat, for Wales as a nation has the ability to give an important lead to the rest of the world.'[177] Although support for pacifism in Wales, as in other parts of the UK, has waxed and waned, and pacifism itself has undergone several transformations in response to global circumstances, Gwynfor Evans has ensured that Welsh pacifists think of themselves as 'leaders' and agents of change in public and political opinion. His reflections carefully balance disappointment, even failure, with what has been achieved:

> By its anti-nuclear declaration each of the eight counties made it clear that Wales wishes to be a nuclear-free country . . . We may take pride in the fact that this initiative has raised the hearts of the peace movement from Iceland to Italy, from the United States to Japan.[178]

There is no better example of how Welsh pacifists continued to act as leaders and agents of change than the radical Women for Life on Earth group which led the march to the Greenham Common air base behind a banner made by Welsh women in 1981 and was instrumental in establishing the Greenham Women's Peace Camp, Berkshire, which was active as a protest against cruise missiles. For Welsh pacifists, the march itself invoked the five-day procession of peacemakers through north Wales in June 1926, led by Gwladys Thoday and Silyn Roberts, some of whom joined 10,000 women in Hyde Park, London. But the way in which Welsh pacifists used their identities as mothers to legitimise their protest against nuclear weapons not only recalls the way women used their identities as mothers in the north Wales procession but how, in opening the Cardiff Temple of Peace and Health, in 1938, Minnie Annie Elizabeth James represented all mothers who had lost their children to war. Aaron and Thomas observe that 'there is barely a Welsh woman poet of this era who does not have a Greenham poem in her oeuvre'.[179] But not just women writers. The attempt to establish a Greenham Common-style peace camp at Brawdy, a military base in rural Pembrokeshire, is the subject of an English-language poem by Nigel Jenkins which, through a Welsh-language quotation from the eisteddfod prayer in which the archdruid pleads for peace, invokes the way in which nature, spirituality and peace are interwoven in the poetry of Waldo Williams and D. Gwenallt Jones (discussed in Chapter 4).

The Campaign for Nuclear Disarmament in the 1950s and 1960s promoted Wales and Scotland as sovereign nations of peace. CND Cymru itself embraced some of the key themes of Welsh pacifism in a new context, particularly the connection between pacifism and socialism in south Wales, the interweaving of pacifism and Christianity, its support of the Welsh language and its internationalism. But it also demonstrates how Welsh pacifism particularly has always risen to the moment but never allowed the moment to freeze it, expanding its agenda to include opposition to the new nuclear power stations, as in the march organised in 2012 against the new power station at Wylfa, in which Greenpeace and Cymdeithas yr Iaith Gymraeg also took part.

CND Cymru and Women for Life on Earth exemplify an important distinction between early twentieth-century and post-Second World War concepts of pacifism in their concern not only with the continuation of human life but in sanctifying the quality of human existence, deepening the understanding of peace and synthesising cross-cultural concepts of peace. In this regard, pacifism offered a continuance of how it had extended its reach beyond anti-warism earlier in the century under a new guise. As we shall discuss in Chapter 4, this is very much reflected in Gwenallt's retrospective poetry about the struggle of ordinary people to maintain the spiritual and physical quality of their lives in a harsh industrial environment.

Without employing the term 'post-pacifism', Richmond summarises the development of the concept of 'peace' in a way which points in the direction we are arguing that Welsh pacifism developed:

> A wide range of sources indicate that the emergence of peace is closely associated with a variety of political, social, economic, and cultural struggles against the horrors of war and oppression. Peace and activism has normally been based on campaigns for individual and group rights and needs, for material and legal equality between groups, genders, races, and religions, disarmament, and to build international institutions.[180]

Richmond's point here is highly relevant to Welsh writing in the last third of the twentieth century.

Aaron and Thomas's examples of Welsh writers who 'gave their primary political allegiance to peace and ecological movements in

1980s Wales' include Tony Curtis, who explores 'the dehumanizing consequences of purposeless destructions of natural life and the defilements of war', and Robert Minhinnick, founder of Friends of the Earth Cymru, whose *Life Sentences* (1983) interweaves ecological concerns with the wider issues of peaceful coexistence (cyd-fyw heddychlon).[181] But while this is outside the remit of their book, it is important to note that Welsh-language writers are also addressing Welsh pacifist themes, such as peaceful coexistence and how the innocent are caught up in war, in new contexts, as in Menna Elfyn's well-known poem 'Er Cof Am Kelly' (In memory of Kelly), about a girl shot by British soldiers in the Troubles in Northern Ireland.

White points out that while the etymology of pacifism can be traced to French *pacifisme*, the ancient, Latin derivation points to 'peaceism'.[182] This term is closer than pacifism to the Welsh word 'heddwch' and better reflects the way in which a distinctive preoccupation with peace developed in Welsh culture. 'Heddwch' reflects the way society, as Richmond says, 'requires an everyday peace to prosper and, lacking direct forms of power, experiences the vicissitudes of war and conflict most acutely'.[183] This understanding of 'peace' involves a different focus from the traditional approach to history; one that Richmond describes as 'the private transcript of everyday history that offers a more nuanced understanding of human history and society'.[184] In contemporary Wales, this is exemplified in projects such as 'Poppies: Weeping Window', Caernarfon Castle, 2016; Llwybr Heddwch Caernarfon (Caernarfon Peace Trail), 2016; 'Remembering for Peace' exhibitions and lectures; and locally based books such as Philip Adams's *Daring to Defy: Port Talbot's War Resistance 1914–1918* and *Not in OUR Name: War Dissent in a Welsh Town*.

WELSH EXTREMISM

In its association with the promotion of the Welsh language and nationalism, Welsh pacifism experienced pressures to which English pacifism was never subjected, revolving around the issue of violent and non-violent protest. Ned Thomas highlights the case of the two young Welshmen who killed themselves while laying explosive charges at the government office in Abergele on the night before the investiture of the Prince of Wales on 1 July 1969.[185] Talk of bombing campaigns is more difficult today than in the 1960s. But from a Welsh perspective, it may remain essential to recall them. Thomas reminds us: 'What we have in Wales, and particularly in the Welsh-speaking community, is a situation of extreme stress plus the extreme frustration of attempts to remedy the situation.'[186] Pacifism in Wales in the second half of the twentieth century was forced to confront issues on its doorstep which were distinctively Welsh. The Welsh-language academic, poet and pacifist Bobi Jones highlighted the dilemma in which Welsh-language pacifists who supported the Welsh language found themselves in the 1960s and 1970s. In a letter to *Y Faner* he wrote: 'I am a nationalist of the pen, an armchair pacifist, I do not believe that violence is right.'[187] But there is no real full stop here, for he went on to admit: 'In the midst of our constitutional comforts let us not lose the humanity to see the immeasurable and terrible difference between ourselves and those who risk – and lose – their lives.'[188] In a similar vein, Thomas argues provocatively but pertinently that Welsh people cannot contribute to the 'wider world-community' or 'take part in the world's moral struggles and accept on [their] own doorstep a situation which denies [their] identity as a Welsh-speaker and the value of the centuries which lie behind [them]'.[189]

The arguments in Ned Thomas's iconic book *The Welsh Extremist* have to be addressed in any study of Welsh pacifism because they capture the spirit and the letter of the debates around nationalism and the Welsh language in the 1960s and 1970s. Although not written necessarily from a pacifist perspective, *The Welsh Extremist* engages with pacifism, not only quoting from Bobi Jones but including a chapter on the Welsh-language poet and pacifist Gwenallt.

Thomas is adamant that he is on the side of civil disobedience, taking up a position which identifies him with Welsh pacifists: 'Civil disobedience is not the slippery slope to violence but an alternative to it, provided enough people join the movement to make it effective.'[190] The talk of civil disobedience as a movement here clearly brings the civil rights protests in America to mind. But Thomas is arguing as a Welshman: 'The most hopeful course for an honest Welsh person, it seems to me, is to back the non-violent civil disobedience campaigns of the Welsh-language society.'[191] However, despite his contentious conviction that 'the Welsh-speaker, even when a political nationalist, has hitherto been a natural pacifist',[192] Thomas's book does not distance itself from violent protest. Believing that no one can 'pretend that violence sets back the cause of constitutional nationalism', Thomas argues 'constitutional and linguistic concessions to Wales have been most numerous in the period of multiplying bomb incidents'.[193] As we mentioned above, he cites Bobi Jones's defence of his poem about the two young Welshmen mentioned earlier, who accidentally killed themselves at Abergele, in which Jones argues, 'let us not lose the humanity to see the immeasurable and terrible difference between ourselves and those who risk – and lose – their lives'.[194] Published in the year following Bloody Friday in Northern Ireland and the same year as the Old Bailey bombing, *The Welsh Extremist* favours non-violent protest, while arguing that violent civil rights protests sometimes bring results. Charting this difficult territory, it confronts awkward questions at the heart of Welsh-language pacifism.

SUMMARY

In the light of what we have said in this opening chapter, the words 'pacifism', 'pacifist' and 'peace' are not fixed in time and their evolution in meaning is closely linked to global circumstances and the development of different kinds of war, from aerial bombardment to nuclear rockets, cluster bombs, terrorism and chemical warfare. But an understanding of how the meanings of the words 'pacifism' and 'pacifist' have acquired new associations and meanings over time is no mere academic exercise but an appreciation of the different contexts in which pacifists have had, and continue to have, to live. Welsh pacifists in the First World War had to endure experiences which those in the Second World War did not, and pacifists across the first half of the twentieth century suffered in ways which would be unthinkable to us today.

In the course of the twentieth century, the emphasis in Welsh pacifism shifted from anti-war to a kind of 'social gospel' which in the 1930s promoted alternative ways of life based on pacifist values and became involved, through local initiatives and projects, in the social and economic problems of south Wales in particular. And an equally profound change in Welsh pacifist thinking in the mid-twentieth century was the increased emphasis on the nature of language and discourse and their bearing on how pacifism and war were perceived, together with a more developed interest in how even children are encouraged to absorb a militaristic culture and regard it as the norm.

However, all this is as nothing compared with what has happened in the latter half of the twentieth century, as wars in other countries, including the tracking of missiles, were televised as 'spectacles' in ways that many of the leading Welsh pacifists discussed in this book could not have imagined. This, together with the development of weapons of mass destruction and new technological, chemical and cyber forms of warfare, brought people into the pacifist fold who, if they had been alive earlier in the century, might not have dreamed of crossing this threshold.

In its beginnings, Welsh pacifism was associated with a close-knit, and largely Welsh-speaking, intelligentsia and through them it contributed to Welsh, and substantially Welsh-language, national and literary culture. There is no doubt that the Welsh language has been one of the key factors differentiating Welsh and English pacifism, not least because the most important themes and issues affecting Wales have been raised and discussed most fully in the Welsh language. These issues, such as the future of the Welsh language and the prospects for Wales as a nation, created an agenda for the Welsh pacifist intelligentsia which exerted pressures on it, such as the relative effectiveness of non-violent and violent protest and the wider philosophical discussion of civil disobedience, which were not faced by English pacifists. While there is some evidence to suggest that an English-language intelligentsia has been able to assume an important role in Wales through, for example, its English-language literature, the boundary between the two languages has never been as impermeable as some have supposed. English-language pacifist writing in Wales is often the product of authors who are Welsh-language speakers, some of whom have a preference for writing in English, some of whom write equally well in both languages and others who have learned Welsh as adults or have reclaimed a Welsh they had temporarily lost. Moreover, many of the prominent pacifist members of the Welsh-language intelligentsia wrote in both English and Welsh, while prioritising the latter.

The impact of Welsh pacifism on Welsh culture is most meaningfully and insightfully approached through the prominence and cultural influence of key pacifist writers, thinkers, politicians and theologians rather than the fluctuating numbers of those involved in Welsh pacifism at any one time or through a more limited focus on the wax and wane of various peace organisations. As a result of the close-knit nature of Wales and the radicalism associated with the assertion of Welsh rights and political convictions, Welsh pacifism, especially Welsh-language pacifism, has had a distinctive profile.

2

Disruptive Bibles

> But then might not such a Bible, read through from A to Z, yes, tramped through from Dan to Beersheba, be whisked away by some supernatural agency lest it should fall into the hands of mere ordinary readers . . .
>
> (D. Parry-Jones, 'From an upland road', *Welsh Country Characters*)

Given the Nonconformist roots of Welsh pacifism and the number of conscientious objectors who were imprisoned or lost their jobs, it is unsurprising that the creed of Welsh pacifism was developed in the Bible and tested in the prison. This chapter explores disruptive pacifist readings of the Bible and the next chapter reflections on imprisonment with reference to some of the key Welsh pacifist writers and pioneers of the twentieth century, including George M. Ll. Davies, William Thomas 'Pennar' Davies, T. E. Nicholas, D. Gwenallt Jones, Glyn Jones and Lily Tobias. In doing so, this chapter and the next revisit some of the principal twentieth-century pacifist texts, including the semi-autobiographical prison novel, *Plasau'r Brenin* (The King's Palaces), the relatively neglected novel of the suffering of conscientious objectors *Eunice Fleet*, and the short stories of Glyn Jones.

GEORGE M. LL. DAVIES: PIONEERING PACIFIST

Few would argue that George M. Ll. Davies was one of the twentieth century's most influential and charismatic Welsh pacifists, except, perhaps, Emyr Humphreys who jotted in one of his notebooks: 'Geo M LL D – an idiot busy body . . . or a saint?'[1] However, this comment must be treated with caution; many of Humphreys's notebook jottings are humorous, mischievous and intended to set hares running in his own mind. Davies contributed to Welsh pacifism as an organiser, preacher and author. His essays and pamphlets explore and extend the principles, ideas and convictions associated with pacifism; provide original insight into what being a pacifist involves; and exemplify a reflective literature which conflates personal experience, spirituality, history, philosophy, literature and scholarship. The range of his work, including speeches, letters, sermons, essays, pamphlets and articles, suggests the breadth of the platform available to, and sustaining, the Welsh-language intelligentsia of his day.

The contribution of Nonconformist ministers and theologians to Welsh pacifism led Davies to coin the term 'disruptive theology', by which he meant a theology with an emphasis on Christ's teaching which many would find too uncompromising. Historians have tended to assign this perspective only short-lived significance.[2] For example, Kenneth Morgan draws attention to William Rees's letter in *Y Tyst* (The Witness) (30 September 1914), in which he attacked the war on Christian pacifist grounds, arguing for the absolutist pacifist truths of the Christian message.[3] But Morgan ignores the way in which pacifism in Wales developed in a cyclical fashion, returning to particular perspectives with different degrees of emphasis and rooted in an endless chain of arguments and debates.[4] Rees's letter is not so much evidence of a specific Christian interpretation of pacifism as of how 'disruptive theologies' of different kinds characterise Welsh pacifism.

Davies traces his concept of 'disruptive theology' to the image of Christ on the cross, arguing that it involves 'unmasking', 'insurrection', 'disruptive outbursts' and the 'downfall of a repressive civilisation' (PP, p. 29). It is an idea which he can only fully express in the Welsh language: 'Yr Arglwydd sydd yn teyrnasu, gorfoledded y ddaear; llawenyched ynysoedd lawer' (PP, p. 35). This leads to one of his most powerful images, from his essay 'In Forma Pauperis': 'God is made partial, and the whole of humanity, which is His body, is dismembered, wounded and crucified.'[5] The uncompromising, almost aggressive, nature of Davies's writing comes partly from the extent to which he sees Christ himself as a controversial figure: 'It was because He antagonised so many that He agonised so much' (ETP, p. 65).

For Davies, the church was at the centre of a schism between anti-war pacifists and war supporters (ETP, pp. 62–3). In his 1942 pamphlet, he criticises the relationship between the Church and the State, arguing with the forcefulness that characterises many Welsh pacifist publications that 'it is almost unknown for the national

Church to oppose any war'.[6] In this regard, Davies anticipates arguments over the role of the church in contemporary military spectacles where the church, as David Gee observes, is 'mobilised to provide divine sanction'.[7] Davies's argument is that the church's support of war is contrary to how the 'prophetic Scriptures themselves describe the way of peace' (RQP, p. 7). To his mind, the church had a foot in two camps and thus, to employ Gee's words, was 'unavoidably compromised by their service to two masters'.[8] On the one hand, 'they serve the state and are enrolled into the worldview of the armed forces' and, on the other, they serve a religion 'whose prophets foretell an end to war'.[9]

The Foreword to *Pilgrimage of Peace* begins with a quotation from the American philosopher Ralph Waldo Emerson: 'There is a word of Emerson "we are always hoping to get settled down. There is only hope for us so long as we are unsettled"' (PP, p. 13). It captures Davies the intellectual socialist pacifist exactly, so it is unsurprising that he returns to Emerson in the last reflective piece, with a quotation from 'The Abolition of War', encapsulating how his own life and work as a pacifist, like Emerson's, was rooted in radicalism and protest on the one hand, and reflection, prayer and meditation on the other. This quotation is appropriate also in that it appears to speak to both political necessity and Davies's inner troubled self:

> For the only hope of this cause is in the increased insight, and it is to be accomplished by the spontaneous teaching of the cultivated soul, in its secret experience and meditation – that it is now time that it should pass out of the state of the beast into the state of man; it is to hear the voice of God which bids the devils that have rended and torn him come out of him and let him now be clothed and walk forth in his right mind. (PP, p. 86)

Although Davies did not have first-hand experience of trench warfare, he was well aware of its horrors through his brother's letters. Writing from Gallipoli in 1915, Stanley described the dead 'swollen up into hideous things with faces that have blackened' and the not-quite dead with 'half their faces and their feet blown off'.[10] He warned his brother but was really warning his fellow Welshmen: 'If anyone talks to you about the field of battle as an ennobling place, refining and strengthening character and exalting human sacrifice – take it from me . . . it is a horrible and damnable deception.'[11] But Welsh history also provided domestic examples of ruthless militarism. Davies's parents belonged to a generation which still talked about farmers in the Vale of Clwyd who refused to pay their church tithes being confronted by hussars with drawn swords, and he himself saw real unemployment and poverty in the Rhondda Valleys, where pacifism developed beyond an anti-war movement (ETP, pp. 65, 115, 126).

Although he was only one of a number of ministers who published arguments against war, Davies's essays and pamphlets are among the more sophisticated, arguing against the wider militaristic culture embedded in civic, political and educational institutions. *Religion and the Quest for Peace*, for example, discusses subjects such as reprisals and the aftermath of war; the mobilisation of public opinion; the nature of ecclesiastical and peace politics; and Christian democracy.[12] Of course, Davies was very familiar, from the chapels in Liverpool where he was brought up, with the sermon as a reflective, philosophical and imaginative text, and the different ways in which its narratives might be structured. His mother encouraged him to hear the visiting preachers at the Toxteth Tabernacle during the religious revival of 1904–5, including the Welsh charismatic preacher Evan Roberts.[13] Davies was ordained himself in November 1926 at a time when prospective Calvinist Methodist ministers did their training through undertaking preaching engagements, after which he was appointed pastor at Tywyn.[14]

That Welsh reflective writing should exemplify as many literary qualities (multiple story lines, images, refrains, biblical allusions and anecdotal and proverbial material[15]) as they did may seem surprising. T. Gwynn Jones pointed out that the Nonconformist movement 'held aloof from Eisteddfodau' and even put an end to dramatic activities which had their roots in the eighteenth century.[16] But this simply forced Welsh literary efforts into a reflective or scriptural mould. Almost any of Davies's reflective pieces might be selected to demonstrate the literary strengths of his writings, but none more so than 'Est nihil vobis, O viatores omnes'. Although it is undated, the content clearly betrays that it was written in 1915. It opens and closes with 'voices' from outside Davies's usual world – the conversation and anecdotes of the soldiers at the beginning and the cries of the wild geese at the end. Meanwhile, it takes the reader from the thunderous motion of a troop-carrying train to moments of stillness, recollection and reflection. The excited movement of the present is contrasted with the quietness of the past. In the soldiers' description of the charge from a trench, Davies hears what he had not expected: 'Everyone appeared to have been swearing or shouting, some even laughing . . .' (ETP, p. 9). The behaviour of the soldiers is comparable to the boys chasing the wild geese which Davies remembers: 'It was great fun for us boys to chase the foolish birds and to laugh at their ungainly run, their shrill cries and their vain, ineffectual attempts to fly' (ETP, p. 12). The soldiers and the boys appear to give expression to a natural energy which is different from the mechanical energy released by the train. But the soldiers have been 'regimented' and the wings of the geese have been clipped, so that both seem to 'recapture the lost freedom and joy of flight' (ETP, p. 12).

At a literary level, too, the essay has several levels of organisation, not only through the different ways in which movement and stasis are used, but the way in which it employs different places to signify different meanings: the train carriage, the rectory, the tin chapel and the wind-swept common. It is also structured around anecdote: the soldiers' story about their lieutenant who was shot; the villagers' anecdotes about the geese; and the tale of the preacher who had one text about the Christ-figure. Images, too, are important to its textual structure: the walled garden, reflecting the English Georgian poets, 'heavy with the fragrance of flowers and busy with the mellow murmuring of bees' (ETP, p. 10); the 'tiny trigger that 'explode[s] the slowly accumulated joys of twenty years' (ETP, p. 11); and the 'miserable-looking donkey standing still and disconsolate under the lea of the hedge through which the wind wailed' (ETP, p. 12). Contrast between sound and silence is equally important. The silence and tranquillity of the rural night sky, the stars and the fields are described as 'intolerable', as nothing in nature or the cosmos seems to have been affected by the 'world tragedy' of the war (ETP, p. 13). However, the cry of the wild geese is exhilarating because they appear to have been lifted and strengthened by the winter winds.

The wartime mood is conveyed also by the emphasis upon chance, evident in the coincidence that the rectory, which was the home of the lieutenant about whom the soldiers talk, is known to the author/narrator, and unexpected juxtapositions and contrasts, such as that between the soldiers' laughter over the way in which the lieutenant is shot and the gloom and silence that descends on his home. The essay's refrain is provided by the repetition of a key question, 'What does it all mean?' The wartime mood which Davies tries to capture through the essay's emphasis on chance, coincidence and surprise stands in contrast to, but at times is also blurred with, a narrative voice that seems to look beyond the war. This voice is capable of disentangling itself from complex ideologies and patriotic symbols as is encapsulated in the image of the 'plain tin tabernacle', without crucifix, chalice, high altar or rich window (ETP, p. 13). Without suggesting that Davies was in any way influenced by Virginia Woolf, her essay on the Second World War, to which we referred in the discussion of Humphreys's *A Toy Epic* in Chapter 1, effectively summarises what this essay achieves: 'it is our business to puncture gas bags and discover seeds of truth'.[17]

Davies's ongoing reflections on biblical quotations and moral imperatives constitute a meditation on what is perceived as an *absolute* rather than *conditional* interpretation of Christ's teaching. From evidence in the essay, this is a Welsh Nonconformist contribution to pacifist thinking. His cousin Dolly summarised their developing pacifism in a letter from Gallipoli in July 1915: 'Is there not only a striking but an overwhelming need for a return to the first principles of our Faith without modifications to suit the clamourings of an infidel Press.'[18] At the end of 'Second Bests' the reader is memorably urged to shun 'that graceful compromise which accepts [Christian teaching] with the lip and denies it in the life, which marries it at the altar and divorces it at the church door' (ETP, p. 21).

In a later essay, 'In Forma Pauperis' (1922), Davies's criticism of the call to action develops into an indictment of 'the sufferings of the imprisoned life' and how individuals are not free to pursue their own moral and spiritual potential (ETP, p. 64). Again, this brings Woolf's essay, referred to earlier, to mind: 'If we could free ourselves from slavery we should free men from tyranny. Hitlers are bred by slaves.'[19] But Davies has a different perspective. The social, as well as theological, 'disruption' of his essay is rooted in the way in which it envisages how the educational system, which he labels 'our educational machine', prepares students 'not for service, but for servitude' (ETP, p. 64). Here, he is developing ideas that were later to have prominence in the Peace Pledge Union. Charles Raven, who wrote the Memoir at the beginning of *Pilgrimage of Peace*, maintains in a pamphlet published in 1940: 'we have for so long ignored the human way and been content to organize our education and citizenship and business in neglect of it' while people are looking to free themselves from 'enslavement to economic and political exploitation'.[20]

Davies and Raven pursue comparable arguments and employ similar terms. Raven argues, like Davies, that people exist 'not for economic activity' but 'a place in a fellowship whose service is or should be his [*sic*] freedom and fulfilment'.[21] The difference between the two is that Davies's writing is more impassioned, drawing more overtly on the pulpit and the sermon. It is most obviously disruptive when at its most rhetorical. In this essay, it is evident in Davies's repetitive insistence that people are controlled through social imperatives: 'has to marry', 'has to preach', 'had to oppress', 'has to bully' and 'has to maintain order' (ETP, p. 64). The repetitive use of the same verb recreates the social 'cage' where individuals lose control over their own lives, confuse vocation with necessity, and transfer their moral responsibility to the wider social and political system.

The structure of the sermon helped Davies develop even his more political essays such as 'Work among the unemployed' (1936). In 1933, he began work at Maes-yr-Haf, a Quaker settlement in Trealaw in the Rhondda, and became the warden at the Malthouse, which was intended as a summer camp for single unemployed miners. But the settlement became what it had never intended to be, a centre of relief, because of the donations that came flooding in, while it also offered Sunday groups and adult classes to workers who were particularly well read and culturally aware: 'One has only to pass through the streets to notice how frequent are the announcements of choral and orchestral concerts and dramatic performances.' (ETP, p. 115) This gave the Welsh pacifist movement a distinctive philosophy for which Davies was largely responsible. It had one pragmatic eye on world poverty and the need for material relief, and another on cultural and spiritual development: 'Urgent as the money need so often is, it is a great misconception and an affront to the unemployed man to think of his need as being on a lower level in things spiritual and cultural than that of the professional man' (ETP, p. 115). T. Gwynn Jones made the same point in the 1920s when he argued that there was a 'hidden life' in Welsh communities where people were 'interested in things of the mind, in religion, in poetry and music', believing that 'among those brought up in a Welsh atmosphere, intellectual interest is general'.[22]

Davies's engagements with contemporary social issues of the 1930s are rooted in critical, analytic thinking but driven by pacifist convictions such as the importance of individual freedom, self-worth, fellowship and an inner and external peace. These themes bind together the reflective pieces in Davies's *Pilgrimage of Peace* (1951). Collated retrospectively, the book seems to have been designed to confirm faith 'not only in the worth of personality; but in its work and influence and persistence in the long view of life' (PP, p. 88). At one level, its inspiration appears to have come from the bells of King's College, Cambridge, recalled in the opening reflection: 'Fragments of harmony would peal out and cease abruptly, leaving one hanging in expectation of some grand chorale' (PP, pp. 17–18). This is analogous to the experience with which *Pilgrimage of Peace* provides the reader; individual essays/reflections offer 'fragments of harmony', but they are part of a wider pursuit of 'some grand chorale'. In the last essay, this is attained by juxtaposing William Wordsworth's long, autobiographical poem *The Prelude* and Christ's Beatitudes. *The Prelude* is conceived as 'the story of pilgrimage from republicanism and revolution to the evolution of personalism in its ways and values' (PP, p. 89), which is linked to the Beatitudes through the conviction that 'it is the meek who seem to us to have most truly inherited the earth, and not those who talked and acted "lebensraum"' (PP, pp. 88–9).

Pilgrimage of Peace moves through cycles of moods beginning with a reflection on the beginning of the First World War, written in Cambridge, and concludes with a piece, dated 1947, on 'the pessimism and optimism of post-war idealism' (PP, p. 82). Each of these moods is linked with specific locations and, as the 'pilgrimage' progresses, the sequence of locations expands, as does the circle of human contacts. Individual relationships send out suggestions of harmony and peace, like the chapel bells at the beginning of the book. The first of these is with a member of the Fellowship of Reconciliation who has spent two years as a prisoner on Dartmoor and has an important message for all: 'The idealism of Christ or Tolstoy must be lived not "imitated"' (PP, p. 24). This belief leads to the pacifist conviction that individuals must 'be prepared here and now to stand for peace' (PP, p. 24). However, as in all of Davies's writings, the possibilities of peace are regularly countered by more pessimistic observations. For example, everyone in the 1920s is said to be 'living in a world of men, unconsciously dominated by . . . herd instincts' (PP, p. 25). But most pessimistic of all is the replacement of the physical imprisonment about which he writes in his essays and letters with a broader, more permanent, psychic imprisonment, causing him to exhort his fellow pacifists: 'The sufferings of the imprisoned life and the agonies of breaking free are all around us' (PP, p. 25).

Davies was an intensely religious person and, as is the case with many intensely religious individuals, what scares him most is failing 'to see spiritual things at the time in their true perspective' (PP, p. 35). Thus, envisaging the spiritual in the material world is one of the key motifs in *Pilgrimage of Peace.* This means that while the book is Emersonian in the twists and turns of its arguments, at its best, like Emerson's work, it is also imagistic. Some of its most powerful images are suggestive of the triumph of darkness over light, as in the Cambridge University chapel. But more than Emerson, Davies hears as intently as he sees, so the *vox humana* rises high, 'yearning like a god in pain', while the base is said to have 'boomed and throbbed in disconsolate harmony', only to be followed by silence (PP, p. 18). The prospect of the failure of spiritual insight is never far from any point in the book which keeps returning to the conditions necessary for its successful achievement. The antithesis that humankind has lost God is countered by the thesis that 'when the Grace and Peace of God are in the heart then is man strong so that he can neither be cast down by adversity or puffed up by prosperity' (PP, p. 55). *Pilgrimage of Peace* addresses the church and educationalists as well as fellow or would-be pacifists, urging them to 'develop human beings of full stature' (PP, p. 57).

What makes *Pilgrimage of Peace* such an important work is that it argues for the relevance of pacifism to a post-Second World War world. For Davies, this entailed 'turning away from crowd-patriotism' (PP, p. 54) – upon which be blamed the rise of fascism and the war itself – to a beatitude of his own that says, 'Be fair, show mercy and companionship every man to his brother' (PP, p. 55). This, in 1930s pacifist parlance, opened the way for true human affection and interaction to be rekindled through 'personalism' and 'individual contact' (PP, p. 46).

Although Davies suffered from bouts of doubt, he was a committed pacifist who, like Merfyn Turner in his support of ex-prisoners, became an important social pacifist through his pioneering work with the unemployed in south Wales. His essays consistently sought to define pacifism and its relevance to the post-war world. But they were also highly literary and, at times, breathtakingly learned, reflecting the influence of essayists such as Emerson and fellow Welsh-language pacifist Iorwerth Peate. Pacifist writing of the time betrays the influence of his thinking about pacifism, through concepts such as 'personalism', which Welsh pacifism, as we shall see, made its own; debates within and around pacifism in which he participated; and even his interest in the contradictory nature of the Bible in which pacifists sought to take solace.

THE REFLECTIVE DIARY: WILLIAM THOMAS 'PENNAR' DAVIES

The reflective diary has a long tradition in Welsh Christian, confessional writings and, as in the case of Pennar Davies's *Diary of a Soul*,[23] often follows the principal convictions of the post-Calvinist Nonconformist pacifist creed which we find in the work of George Davies, including the importance of recognising the spiritual potential of individuals and returning to a Christ-centred reading of scripture. But like many of the works discussed in this chapter, it is compelling reading because of its darker and contradictory elements.

Diary of a Soul was originally published as a weekly diary in *Y Tyst* (The Witness), the Independent Congregationalists' journal, between 20 January 1955 and 16 February 1956. Published as a book in Welsh, *Cudd Fy Meiau*, in 1957 and 1998, the first English translation was published in 2011. Generally recognised as an insightful, independent-minded and challenging account of Pennar's own spiritual journey, in which he wrestles (like George Davies) with doubts and deep-rooted personal anxieties, it is a more enigmatic text than has often been acknowledged. Welsh Nonconformist reflective writing often makes use of what is called, in Welsh *saeth weddïau*, 'unpremeditated, direct, immediate prayers'.[24] The diary could be seen as written around such moments of prayer because it is in them that Davies is revealed as a troubled Christian, in awe of Christ and challenged by him.

But throughout there are hints that it is not only Christ who is challenging him but something much deeper which, as the diary unfolds, is unveiled as being linked to the 1950s. Even from the first paragraph, it is not completely clear why Davies, who felt that diaries were a waste of time, chose to keep one for a limited period. Through the diary's entries, the theological doubts that plague him come to the fore, particularly around his need to find convincing evidence of Christ's presence in the world and his intellectual, as much as spiritual, search for what will bring everything together. These provide the diary with a compelling sense of purpose but in entry after entry further depths are plummeted. As the diary unfolds, new anxieties and insights reveal themselves while leaving much unrevealed.

At the beginning of the diary, Pennar admits that 'none of us live far from Bedlam'. This somewhat alarming confession is not entirely offset by his expressed faith that 'Bethlehem is near also.'[25] It is not necessary to read very far into the diary to realise that the text is haunted by this kind of binarism – a little later he contrasts the 'stinking and flea-ridden body' and 'a clean body as the habitat for a pure soul'.[26] Again, he tries to make sense of this binary in terms of a more comprehensive image of wholeness. But the one that he chooses is an almost gothic-inspired image of the body of a saint who chose not to wash, erupting in sores where worms are crawling. Here, as in many parts of the diary, Davies seems pulled by the dark forces within life and which life has to withstand, signified by Bedlam and putrefaction, as much as – if not more than – Bethlehem and cleanliness.

The references to Davies's reading in science in the diary leads him to wonder at the sense of emptiness in the spaces of the universe and around atoms and molecules.[27] The language here is intriguing, Davies talks of the 'wonderful emptiness' and 'the strange world of the molecule'. In a reflection on the Bible, he seems surprised to discover that 'darkness' is as crucial as light and in an attempt to bring the two poles together, he becomes 'conscious of powers in the bright darkness'. [28] These various strands – around putrefaction, emptiness and darkness – eventually reveal what has been half-hidden all the way along and what it is that is really pulling Davies towards Bedlam. A key entry in the diary concerns his attendance as a Christian pacifist at a discussion of the challenges posed by nuclear warfare and the threat hanging over all nations in the 1950s. Again, Davies is drawn to the towering, defamiliarising images spawned by the twentieth century, aligned with the emptiness in space and around atoms and molecules such as the hydrogen bomb, the 'loathsome', and in the eyes of extreme Christian pacifists (thinking of the revengeful God of the Old Testament), the 'godly' weapon.[29]

The diary gradually unveils why, in Davies's mind, Bedlam is so near and why he is pulled in that direction. The central question in the diary is whether atomic science, and the emptiness which it unveils, is a creation of a new Bedlam or the creator of it. In this regard, the diary reveals a mind tormented, and at the same time fascinated, by the sense of 'emptiness' brought about by nuclear science and by the prospect of a peace, such as it will be, created by a balance of nuclear powers and overshadowed by the threat of a nuclear apocalypse. This peace is not that which comes from within and would be a dark and depressing conclusion, except that the diary is brought to a close at the end of a year where positive strands of the pacifist creed, which have been running through all the entries, come to the fore. Here there are suggestions that Davies will discover the inner peace for which he has been searching. A phantasm of the risen Christ, appearing as an irruption into the world which nuclear science has created, wishes him peace, and he finds peace in sharing the festivities among old friends, returning the reader to those diary entries in which Davies talks of the pleasure and everyday peace which he finds working among ordinary people.

GLYN JONES AND THE DISRUPTIVE BIBLE

No Welsh pacifist writer was as preoccupied with the contradictory nature of the Bible, or as plagued with doubts about the peace and support pacifists were supposed to find there, as Glyn Jones (1905–95). Generally associated with the English-language Welsh literature that flourished in south Wales between the wars, Glyn Jones is an interesting example of an author whose discovery of himself as a pacifist was linked to the reclamation of his Welsh, Nonconformist roots and of the Welsh language itself which he almost completely lost as a result of the anglicised schooling in Wales at that time. His great-grandfather had left the family farm and had come to Merthyr to find work. Jones's own upbringing there, two generations later, brought him into contact with the political pacifism of Merthyr but, through his mother's family roots in Carmarthenshire where he spent many summer holidays, he was also familiar with Welsh-language, rural Nonconformity.

How Carmarthenshire fuelled a particular type of Nonconformist pacifism is evident from D. J. Williams's *Hen Wynebau* (Old Faces) (1934), written in the same decade as Jones's first collection of stories, *The Blue Bed*. Williams was a participant in the 1936 arson attack on the bombing school on the Llŷn peninsula and although he worked as a miner in the Rhondda, his *Hen Wynebau*, a collection of character sketches and anecdotes, and subsequent volumes of stories,[30] bring to life the type of rural society in which he spent many summer holidays as a boy, and how these parts of Wales, despite their ostensible tranquillity, fuelled a combination of pacifism and radical nationalism.[31] Williams's stories feature pacifist opposition to war as in 'Ceinwen', as well as more ethically dubious episodes in which patriotism is assumed as a means of self-advancement, as in 'Meca'r Genedl' (Mecca of the Nation).

Although critics have noted the influence of the industrial Valleys on Jones's boyhood, the importance of Merthyr to Welsh pacifism has often been overlooked. Described by George Davies as the 'old hearth-stone for the fire of Peace' (PP, p. 62), Merthyr attracted prominent pacifist speakers including Bertrand Russell. By the 1930s, Jones had come to recognise the town's strong and distinctive pacifist tradition, which he described as 'a combination of the pacifism of Welsh nonconformity and of left-wing politics', and to appreciate how its Nonconformist ministers had demonstrated great courage in preaching pacifism when the First World War was in progress.[32] However, it was Jones's move to Cardiff that enabled him to redefine himself as a Welsh pacifist. Membership of the Minny Street Congregationalist chapel, 'an island of Welshness' (GJCS, p. xxviii), enabled him to rediscover his Welsh-language and Nonconformist roots, while involvement with the Peace Pledge Union educated him in political pacifism. Summarising the mood of many pacifists in the 1930s, he wrote in his journal after the fall of Barcelona in 1939 that 'I feel as if my fate is pressing in on me' (GJCS, p. xli). But it is a quotation in his journal from Milton's *Areopagitica* that provides most insight into his pacifist state of mind: 'When I kill a man I kill a reasonable human being, the image of God' (GJCS, p. xli). Unlike Gwenallt and George Davies, Glyn Jones was not imprisoned for his pacifist beliefs. But he did suffer a fate similar to that of Iorwerth Peate and Waldo Williams. As soon as he registered as a conscientious objector, he was suspended from his teaching post in Cardiff and cold-shouldered by colleagues in his next appointment at Oldcastle Boys' School in Bridgend (GJCS, pp. xli–xlv).

Given the way in which Glyn Jones's pacifism had roots in Welsh-speaking Nonconformist Wales and in industrial south Wales, one might have expected his writings to involve a sustained negotiation between these two perspectives. But his stories turn to pacifism in unexpected ways, almost at times appearing to turn on pacifism. The first story in *The Blue Bed*, 'I Was Born in the Ystrad Valley', is usually approached through the narrator's alienation from the working class in which he grew up; its tactile, physical sensations; the sense of wonderment in the descriptions of the collieries' machinery; and the way in which the organic world of nature and industry are interwoven. But it may be read as a narrative in which the narrator, Wynn, looks back on his earlier life before he discovered the key principles of Welsh pacifism, articulated by George Davies, and what being a pacifist and a radical socialist really means. In this regard, the title may be read as referring to his physical birth in the Ystrad Valley or to his later spiritual birth there.

Wynn's spiritual rebirth is brought about by the discovery of a mode of pacifism which is closer to the Marxist-inspired, revolutionary socialism of the industrial south than the more overtly religious pacifism of west Wales. The first part of the story is focused on Wynn's enrolment in university; his contact with the middle class in the evening classes he teaches; his association with working-class people through a club for unemployed boys; and his visit to the home of one of the young people he meets there. He looks back on this period through a lens which seems to have been provided by Jones's work for the Peace Pledge Union and Welsh Christian pacifism: 'I knew nothing of love for people then, I had no experience of their suffering' (GJCS, p. 8). The key word here is 'then', for the self through which the story is narrated is not Wynn's former, alienated and somewhat patronising self on which he is constantly looking back. As he says: 'I should have known that the sufferings of the working class are more real than any I had read about' (GJCS, p. 5). The narrative points towards the true awareness of others which the pacifist ministers preached, stressing how Wynn's awareness of others is frequently distorted by class consciousness, judgement and labelling. The latter is evident in the case of Gwilym Morgan, the unemployed boy in whom he shows an interest: 'But I could tell by his clothes and his broken boots that he was very poor' (GJCS, p. 7). When he visits Gwilym on his sickbed at home, he admits: 'But I could see all the same signs of poverty, and defeat and hopelessness' (GJCS, p. 9). Even when he thinks he remembers experiencing true love of another as a human being, for example for Gwilym's father, the way in which it is described betrays its inadequacy in comparison with the pacifist emphasis upon love. Looking back, he knows this: 'What this man felt towards me was of no importance now, it was airborne and nullified by the gush of love I felt for him, my pity for his suffering and his despair' (GJCS. p. 11).

This judgemental, and at times dismissive, view of others is a major motif in the story, evident in the way in which Wynn describes his evening-class students: 'and a fine lot they were when I lectured in bourgeois Cardiff, arty, conceited, gutless, merely anxious to be impressive and to show off their knowledge' (GJCS, p. 6). He comes to believe that art and culture separate working-class people, including himself, from their true roots, which contradicts the views held by Welsh pacifists such as George Davies. While some critics have taken Wynn at face value, it is important to recognise that he is always looking back on an earlier self, implying that he no longer believes what he thought then. The more mature Wynn's views are more closely aligned with those of George Davies (even though Davies tended to idealise the working class).

Written from a post-Christian pacifist perspective, 'I Was Born in the Ystrad Valley' explores the difficulties of practising what Christian pacifists preached: recognition of the value of another's life and loving others despite their flaws and weaknesses. For Wynn, these difficulties include his tendency to make hasty judgements; his preoccupation with the unpleasant personalities and physical aspects of others; and also the way in which his view of others was shaped by what he calls his 'naturally sensuous and impressionable nature' (GJCS, p. 4).

Although Jones is interested in the way in which pacifist ideals can be frustrated by the so-called 'realities' of human behaviour, he is fascinated by darker subconscious motives and desires. Usually Wynn's detailed observations of others are linked to his negative impressions of them, but sometimes they betray his desire for them, usually for young men whom he feminises, as in the case of Gwilym: 'He was a pretty, rather small and delicately made boy with a Welsh name. His eyes were blue and although he must have been about sixteen he had a mop of yellow curls' (GJCS, p. 7). This is similar to how he describes a young socialist, 'a nice-looking, fresh complexioned boy not long out of Oxford' (GJCS, p. 14). While Wynn as the participant-narrator looks back critically on aspects of his former self, there seems to be no awareness, at the time or retrospectively, that he feminises and desires young men. On joining the revolutionary socialist movement, he, again, feminises his cell leader:

> As he sat opposite in the clear electric light, reserved and watchful, a bit touchy, I noticed his brilliant pupil-black eyes, and the smallness of the bones of his thin yellow face . . . and the hard nails of his tiny delicate hands tapping the scarlet glass top of the table like the elegant hands of a girl. (GJCS, p. 21)

In this story, the reader feels that the author as much as Wynn himself is struggling with the ideals of pacifism. George Davies's faith in the spiritual potential within every individual enters into every corner of the story and every aspect of Wynn's life where it is sorely tested, including love for others which becomes thwarted by Wynn's judgementalism and by a desire for young men which never rises above a kind of menacing eroticism. The pacifist 'social gospel' is transformed into a revolutionary, socialist threat to the wider social and economic order with no prospect of anything much better in its place when it is overthrown. The story ends in a mirage of fragmented images of horror and dissolution. This is the psychic disintegration which some pacifists such as George Davies himself – who (as we noted earlier) was subject to bouts of depression – experienced and many others feared. But in this story, Jones seems to hang on to the coat tails of violence in nature itself. The natural environment which, viewed from a different perspective, nurtured the pacifism of Waldo and Gwenallt, becomes worse than the worst kind of human horror – violent, destructive and consuming. But throughout the last few pages of the story, bleak and confusing as they are, there are hints of the love and optimism of Christian pacifism and the possibilities of discovering an inner peacefulness. Although far less convincing than the pacifist publications which Jones sold on the Cardiff streets, the promise of pacifism never entirely deserts this story. Buried deep within even the apocalypse with which it ends is the pacifist voice which reminds even the most disillusioned of pacifists that it does not have to be this way. A product of the reflective, retrospective narrative voice, this 'no, things could be different' may not be 'No' in thunder, but it may just be enough.

Nowhere does Jones appear to turn on, rather than to, pacifism more than in his engagement with the Bible. He seems fascinated by the way in which the New Testament, as a Bible of love and peace, disrupts the more overtly violent Old Testament while at the same time being a continuity of it. For William Jones, the leading character in the Welsh-language novel bearing his name by Glyn Jones's contemporary T. Rowland Hughes, whom we introduced in Chapter 1, the Bible 'contains fundamental, lasting mighty truths' but was a 'dry book devoid of interest'.[33] The Bible was no dry book for Glyn Jones but not so much for its truths as its violence, especially in connection with Christ's bouts of unreined 'human' behaviour. William Jones's next-door neighbour was always in his shed, reading his Bible and chewing extra-strong peppermints. Most readers would need extra strong mints to read Glyn Jones's version of the Bible.

Given the close link between Glyn Jones's rediscovery of his pacifism and his Nonconformity, which demanded a close reading of scripture, it is unsurprising that Jones's first collection of stories should use passages and images from the Bible to explore and test some of the core principles and beliefs of Welsh pacifism. This is evident in the story 'Price-Parry' based on a prophecy of peace from Isaiah: 'The wolf also shall dwell with the lamb, and the lion shall lie down with the kid . . . and a little child shall lead them' (11:6). Price-Parry is a spiritual Scrooge, divorced from his congregation by his pride in being a descendant of a Welsh prince even though the girl who leads his horse and cart has a better claim as Geta Glandwr. The story is about transformation, in this case Price-Parry's conversion brought about, as in Charles Dickens's *Christmas Carol*, by the ghost of someone he knew. She is the most excluded of his parishioners, Mati Rees, known after her cottage as 'Mati Tŷ-unnos' (Mati of one-night house) because of her one-night stands (GJCS, p. 377n). The irony is that while Mati is perceived by Price-Parry as a pariah figure, he is the more abject, displaying decay and putrefaction in his house and in himself: 'the hat had a round disc of grease on the top as though all the fat of the vicar's body was slowly oozing out through the top of his head' (GJCS, p. 162). The odious nature of his spiritual being is conveyed also in the warts of his neck that in keeping with a folk remedy are tied with ribbon. Such is the Reverend Mr Price-Parry's pride that he does not see the ridiculous nature of the name with which he has burdened himself, 'The Reverend Roderick Pari Pryce Price-Parry'.

Allusions to biblical prophecies of peace and to biblical teachings of mercy, love and forgiveness are to be expected of Nonconformist pacifist writing. But Glyn Jones's work often betrays the other side of Welsh pacifism, fascination with the violence and abjection in the Old Testament. This is evident, for example, in the story 'It's not by his Beak you can Judge a Woodcock', the title of which is a translation of the Welsh idiom 'nid wrth ei big y mae prynu [barnu] cyffylog', the equivalent of 'do not judge a book by its cover' (GJCS, p. 387n). It is based on the curious figure of the Revd Gwilym Nantwig, a simple man capable of mixing up points in his sermons, who goes to great lengths to help his parishioners. However, the narrative revolves around a moral dilemma created by the abject figure of Ahab, a drunken, violent and carnal man who lives with a young mother, Phoebe Harris, but has a mistress, Mrs Watkins, known to everyone as 'Ahab Nantwig's fancy' (GJCS, p. 227). Ahab is an allusion to the Old Testament ruler who was accused of permitting Jezebel to patronise the cult of Baal of Tyre (1 Kings 18:17) and to the false prophet of that name accused of adultery and impropriety (Jeremiah

29:21ff.). Alongside this fascination with Old Testament immorality, the narrator takes refuge in a pacifist God evident in the biblical allusions with which the story concludes. Thus Gwilym 'thanked God that He had made some as cunning as serpents and as harmless as doves, that out of the mouths of babes and sucklings should come forth wisdom' (GJCS, pp. 230, 388n). Alluding to the Psalms, this passage invokes the merciful God of the New Testament: 'Out of the mouths of babes and sucklings hast thou ordained strength because of thine enemies, that thou mightest still the enemy and the avenger' (Psalm 8:2). The second, equally telling, allusion, however, is to the Old Testament God of deliverance through war (as in 1 Kings 9:16; Judges 2:16, 8:22, 12:3).

PACIFISM AND ABJECTION

In the 1930s, with the possibility of another world war just around the corner, one can see how people were encouraged from church pulpits to take refuge in a militaristic God intent on victory over the enemy and on revenge. But one can also appreciate that pacifists were encouraged to take solace in the New Testament. As Zipes observes, 'no matter how dark and sinister are those forces that violate our lives, we can discover our own human powers to resist such violence without imitating the gods and the devils and playing with other people's lives'.[34] But Jones's handling of biblical themes that might be expected to provide believers with solace sometimes offers anything but an inner peacefulness. 'The Kiss' concerns a collier buried alive in a pit accident who manages to dig himself free. There are several ostensibly reassuring biblical narratives behind this story: the raising of Lazarus from the dead by Jesus (John 1:11–46) and, of course, the resurrection of Christ himself. As Jones's workman digs himself out and gradually regains consciousness, the violence of the crucifixion and resurrection become increasingly pronounced. He is said to have sickness filling his mouth 'like bitter water', reminding us of the vinegar which the Roman soldiers lifted to the crucified Christ; 'sinking his legs out straight again with agony' recalls Christ's bent legs on the cross; 'his pulses tapping softly like piano-hammers among the bones of his wrists' suggest the nails holding Christ's body to the cross which would have been driven through his wrists; and the worm deep in his feet and his 'putrid' hands focuses on where in the biblical account the nails were driven (GJCS, p. 41). On seeing him when he arrives home, his mother's reaction is redolent of Mary's on discovering Christ in the Garden of Gethsemane: 'Are my eyes open or my lids glass?' (GJCS, p. 42).

Through its multiple biblical allusions to the crucifixion and the resurrection, Jones's story seems to turn against the love and peacefulness preached in the Christian faith in which pacifists sought solace. But the last part of the story juxtaposes the collier's brother unwrapping his bandages (comparable to unwrapping the cloth in which Christ's body was laid) with him kissing the damaged hand. The collier's injuries are of the kind with which people in the 1930s would have been familiar, directly or indirectly, from the First World War: 'It was terrible to see, pitiful beyond anything the workman had imagined, and at the horror of it he felt numb, he could only bow his head and remain silent' (GJCS, p. 48).

The emphasis upon putrefaction, typical of war injuries, is significant; his hand is 'a great heavy mass of black flesh, soft and thick, swollen up with black spongy decay and larger than twice its normal size . . .' (GJCS, p. 48). The psychoanalytical critic Julia Kristeva maintains: 'A wound with blood and pus, or the sickly, acrid smell of sweat, of decay, does not signify death.'[35] More than this, as she says, 'these body fluids, this defilement, this shit are what life withstands, hardly and with difficulty, on the part of death' which places us at the border of our human condition.[36] Thus, wounds, decay and putrefaction become, in Kristeva's language, 'abject'; 'that of being opposed to I'.[37] In placing a character, and the reader, at the border between life and the defilement that life withstands, Jones's story conceives of a border which is both physical and religious. It provides, as Kristeva says, a possible basis for reconciliation: 'A source of evil and mingled with sin, abjection becomes the requisite for reconciliation, in the mind, between the flesh and the law.'[38]

The conclusion of the story in which the 'resurrected' man's hand is kissed by his brother is symbolic on a number of levels: 'very tenderly, with tears running down his face, he bent forward and kissed the putrid flesh of his brother's hand' (GJCS, p. 48). Jones's use of the term 'putrid', in tandem with the reference to the brother's tears, conflates the two aspects of abjection to which Kristeva draws attention, 'the poisoned cup in which man drinks death and putrefaction, and at the same time the fact of reconciliation'.[39] In the Bible, a kiss is symbolic: divine images are kissed (for example, Job 31:27; Hosea 13:2) and a kiss is a greeting (Luke 17:45). In kissing the injured hand, the brother's act signifies a 'brotherhood' to which Welsh pacifism, as we saw in the discussion of George Davies's writings, aspired through an appreciation of the value of others.

While the brother's act reminds us that Christ was betrayed by a kiss, the kiss at the end of this story signifies an acceptance of the value of another life in the face of death and decay. The impending 'brotherhood' is based, like the Christian Church itself, on a resurrected body and on wounds which bleed and discharge pus. The emphasis on the smell and sight of putrefaction and decay is important to the personal courage which the brother shows which is also the bravery displayed by pacifist non-combatants working as medical orderlies at the front (another aspect of the pacifists' war which has been overlooked). Here, with the brother so close to the realities of putrefaction and decay, the ideal love of another to which pacifism aspired can only be seen in spiritual and religious terms: he unwraps the bandages 'as though his ministration were sacred, laying them gently aside with slow priestlike tenderness and deliberation' and 'his calm absorption in this eucharistic task seemed child-like and complete' (GJCS, p. 47).

MRS JEFFREYS'S DILEMMA

None of Jones's stories are based as much on core Nonconformist religious and pacifist principles as the later story, 'Mrs Jeffreys', an example of Welsh pacifist-dilemma writing. Ostensibly, Lowri Jeffreys would appear to be one of the Welsh Nonconformists who thought of themselves as the 'Elect': 'a kindly motherly woman zealous for her family and her chapel' with 'a deep piety and an unexpected tenderness of conscience and a brooding awareness of a divine guidance in her life' (GJCS, pp. 255, 256). But at its core, the story is a compelling study of what happens when the pacifist creed of forgiveness comes up against what it is difficult to forgive, an issue especially pertinent for pacifists in the 1930s faced with fascism and Nazi-led Germany. It revolves around Lowri's secret about her father, that he is a violent, abusive drunk, even worse than Ahab in the earlier story. Neither of them has an inner peacefulness and it is for this that both are searching deep within their beings. Lowri lives with a hidden bitterness and resentment towards him. As she admits: 'Every memory I have of him was evil' (GJCS, p. 256). One of these memories is of him kicking a felled opponent almost to death in a bareknuckle boxing match which, to employ Kristeva's words, threatens her sense of 'I', her innermost sense of self, which she tries to expel: 'I ran away horrified and before I reached home I was sick. The only memories I had of my father was of his violence and cruelty and ever since childhood I had hated and feared him' (GJCS, p. 12). In the story, she becomes associated with two types of language, one connected with her public, chapel self (recognising the values embodied by words such as 'motherly', 'piety', 'tenderness'), and the other linked to her secret self, dominated by words such as 'fear', 'hate', 'violence' and 'cruelty'. In effect, one is a pacifist language, expressing its creed of love and forgiveness, and the other the language of 1930s Nazism. The story develops this tension between her 'private' and 'public' self, a familiar pacifist dilemma in the 1930s, encouraging the reader to question her zealous fidelity to her family and chapel and her confidence in 'divine guidance'. The sight of her father's crouching victim becomes so fixed in her mind that it freezes her emotional self. Of her dying father, she says: 'I felt no pity for him and I found forgiveness hard' (GJCS, p. 257). This became the central dilemma for pacifists in the Second World War, who were confronted by overwhelming hatred and evil on all sides and found themselves struggling even to pity the perpetrators.

The tension between these opposites is dramatically encapsulated in the contrast between the peace and love of Lowri's new family home and her father's residence in the 'workingman's lodging house' in the 'old rough part of the town' (GJCS, p. 257). The emphasis on the light and warmth of her home, even to the point of repeating the word 'brightly', suggests that it is a protection against the darkness and defilement, associated with violence and death, which for her is signified by her father: 'and I felt a strong wish to hurry with my baby out of the bareness and the dark and the feeling of defilement around me' (GJCS, p. 258). The journey which she takes to his lodgings mirrors the one Wynn takes to visit Gwilym. Not only are the physical details similar – damp, peeling plaster and little light – but the journey involves crossing safe boundaries (physically, socially and psychically) which the impending Second World War demanded of pacifists.

In Lowri's case, the border crossings ('the iron work's railway line' and the threshold of the workingmen's lodging house) take her to the outer limits of her spiritual beliefs, as were pacifists by the war itself in which they had to confront mass destruction, genocide and evil technologies. Her father's room is lit by 'a candle end stuck in the wrinkles of its own grease' (GSCS, p. 258). The candle grease, along with the decay and damp in the room, signifies the boundary that Kristeva envisages between life and the death and putrefaction which life withstands.[40] The nearly extinguished candle signifies the ebbing of life, light and love. But just as the story brings us to the outer limits of the pacifist creed, it turns the tables, offering evidence that no one (not even Hitler?) is totally evil. As Lowri has carried her hatred of her father, her father has borne guilt over the man he beat to death. He wants his daughter to reassure him that there will be forgiveness for him.

In Glyn Jones's stories what happens almost out of sight, as it were, proves to be highly significant. In this text, as Lowri is talking with her father, a blind man near the struggling fire reads from a braille bible. Here Jones turns from his fascination in other stories with the Old Testament to a New Testament story of forgiveness. The blind man reads the account of the angel Gabriel's annunciation to Mary of Christ's coming (Luke 1:26–7; GJCS, p. 392n); the Magnificat (Luke 1:50–1) and an Old Testament passage exhorting people to cease their evil ways (Isaiah 1:16–20), concluding with the story, from one of the gospels, of Simeon, an old man who did not want to die before setting eyes on Christ the boy child (Luke 2:25–32; GJCS, p. 392n). The two narratives, of Simeon and Lowri's father, are interwoven around the possibility of peace and forgiveness. Simeon finds salvation when he sees the baby Jesus (Luke 2:13), as does Lowri's father when he sees his daughter and grandchild. The blind man reads a significant line from the biblical story of Simeon which relates to both Simeon and Lowri's father: 'Lord now lettest thou thy servant depart in peace' (GJCS, p. 264; Luke 2:29). In its conclusion, the story turns to, not away from, Christian-inspired pacifism, not only in suggesting that there is no deed so evil that it cannot be forgiven (a large assumption in the Second World War), but that forgiveness brings absolution to those who forgive as well as those who are forgiven. This is what Lowri now hopes for herself through her reconciliation with her father, and the story finishes with a quotation from the New Testament in which pacifists, even in the war, might find solace: 'In the world ye shall have tribulation: but be of good cheer; I have overcome the world' (John 16:33).

In the early part of 'Mrs Jeffreys', Jones confronts the dark 'reality' of human nature on which the pacifist and New Testament creed of forgiveness teeters and almost collapses. While at the end of the story, the value and beauty of forgiveness are powerfully retrieved, the reader cannot help wondering whether this might always be the case. Jones's stories give us no cause to doubt his pacifism but a strong sense of how he struggled at times to keep the Christian pacifist faith. This is evident in 'The Blue Bed', a story which almost drowns beneath a torrent of scriptural allusion through conflicting, half-stated and worrying references to biblical stories, anecdotes and images.

AN IMPETUOUS CHRIST

The characters in 'The Blue Bed' – the gardener and the lady with the lamp – are unnamed and the story has no identified location in time and space. In a brief synopsis, the gardener's garden has flooded and the woman who shared his bed seems to have fled. He makes his way to the house in which she appears to be living and while she is at the riverside, he finds the cold, newly born child laid on a table, whom he holds close to his chest until warmth and the flow of blood return.

The most important of the biblical allusions suggest how in the 1930s images of the end of nations and an impending apocalypse loomed large; for example, the flood, the drowned dove-leaves, 'the meaningless cold perfection of the roses unfolding into death', and even lamp light whose many biblical connotations include, with its extinction, the destruction of Judah (Jeremiah 25:10). The gardener's hatred of the 'peaceful' garden and the meaninglessness which the rose and the other flowers now have for him are linked to his displays of violence and impetuosity. In beating the empty bed with a laurel branch, the gardener appears to be inflicting imaginary violence on the woman who has left him, 'slashing deep weals across the blue silk like crossing whip-marks, with the frenzied weight of his blows' (GJCS, p. 81). The dove, rose, blackbird and laurel bush all have sacred significance. But to capture the mood of the 1930s the story inverts their traditional meanings. For example, the biblical image of the dove returning with a leaf in his beak (as many pacifists and anti-war politicians returned from Europe) is undermined by the more ominous image (especially given the impending prospect of war) of the blackbird with 'a red worm writhing in his beak' (GJCS, p. 83). The story exploits the contradictory nature of its symbolism, sometimes opposing two antithetical images as here, employing ambiguous images like the lamp which in different contexts can signify different things, or turning sacred images (like the blackbird) into ones of violence. Of all the images, the one with the profoundest link to the

1930s, is the laurel leaf. In ancient times, this symbol of peace when worn as a wreath denoted the Roman emperor or the victor in Roman games, but it became a symbol also of the Roman imperialist culture which Nazi Germany deliberately invoked and whose propaganda and mass rallies the regime imitated.

As in most of the stories in which Jones appears intent on taking the darkness of scripture as far as he can, just when the reader is close to the abyss the story pulls back from it. Often, it is through an event that brings the story to a close (such as the collier's brother kissing his wounded hand and Lowri Jeffreys finally forgiving her father). Here, it is the gardener hugging the baby to bring it back to life with his body warmth, an inversion of the mother giving her child life through her body milk: 'He was giving up the great heat of fiery body to him, pouring out his animal blood-warmth through the contacts of his flesh into the heat-parched inner body of the child' (GJCS, p. 84). But it is also a two-way process, in which the cold and death are drawn out of the baby's body in a way similar to Christ drawing death and the devil from human bodies: 'His heated body began to suck out the outer cold like a poison from the child, receiving the chill of his limbs and his heavy shell-cold head into the burning warmth of his body' (GJCS, p. 84). But another reason for this image's powerful impact is that it underlines the gardener as an enigmatic combination of love and violence, as was Christ himself, especially as he is represented in St Mark's gospel.

The biblical scholar Aichele points out that Christ's life is surrounded by violence in some of his actions, such as driving the moneylenders out of the temple; in the events described in some of his parables; and in his exorcising of demons.[41] His impetuosity can be seen in some of the Bible stories, too, such as the story of the fig tree, where a hungry Christ, failing to find fruit to eat because it is outside the fig season, declares the tree will never bear fruit, despite others later being dependent on it (Mark 11:12–14). There is evidence that Jones as a pacifist was worried by the Jesus of St Mark's gospel. In the later story, 'Robert Jeffreys', a seriously injured miner is visited by a minister, who is described as 'a grim old man', arrogant and authoritative, and as one who 'worshipped the Saviour who blasted the fig-tree, and foretold for his followers the sword, who declared that the fruitless branch should be cast out into the fire, who drove out the money-changers from the Temple with the twisted cords' (GJCS, p. 239). Here Jones recalls not only the Christ who destroyed the fig tree and drove the money-changers out of the temple, but the one who said to his disciples: 'Think not that I am come to send peace on earth; I came not to send peace, but a sword' (Mark 10:34).

The violent and impetuous actions of Christ stand in contrast to his acts of mercy and love. This antithesis is central to 'The Blue Bed', where the gardener's initial hatred, violence and impetuosity contrast with his recovery of the baby; to when 'he watched the blackbird for a moment with pleasure'; and when he falls exhausted 'ready for tears' (GJCS, p. 82). The 'miracle' in which he brings the baby to life is anticipated by the flame which an imaginary woman hands him saying: 'To kindle under-flame for the cold point of a heart' (GJCS, p. 82). The flame, which warms his cold heart and changes his hatred to love is compared with a flower which brings to mind the sunflower in 'The Kiss'. But while in that image the emphasis was upon strength, here, as in the pacifist creed, it is upon tenderness and malleability, signifying the capacity of individuals to transform themselves, be transformed, and discover their true spiritual potential and an inner peacefulness:

> a flame with a long slender stem like the green stalk of a flower, opening out above her fingers into the cup of a golden crocus bloom, but not stiff like any flower, quivering, transparent, gold-green, changing its shape and its clear golden colour, a real flame with shivering fire-petals growing on a thin stalk of threaded flame. (p. 82)

Thus, the work of Glyn Jones and George Davies share a concern with peace not as something that comes from outside but from within, and an interest in a shared human aspiration for a peaceful mode of being. At their core, each seeks to supplant separation and violence by a much deeper sense of union and a positive inner peace but these aspirations are tested, if not undermined at times, by doubt, fears and negative experiences to which each bears witness. Each returns to the Welsh post-Calvinist reliance on the Bible. But while for Davies scripture is a source of meditation and reflection, Jones seizes the fantasy and ambivalence of biblical texts in stories that ultimately grapple with threats to the pacifist creed.

3

Prison(s)

> Pe câi'r carcharor ysgrifennu llythyr at ei rieni neu at ei gyfeillion byddai hynny iddo'n ddihangfa.
>
> Were the prisoner to write a letter to his parents or to his friends then that would be an escape.
>
> (D. Gwenallt Jones, *Plasau'r Brenin*)

T. E. NICHOLAS'S PRISON SONNETS

Any discussion of prison writing in Welsh must acknowledge the staggering achievement of T. E. Nicholas's sonnets written while he was imprisoned as a conscientious objector. They were undoubtedly inspired by the *Ballad of Reading Gaol* (1898) by Oscar Wilde (1854–1900) which was published after his release from prison in 1897 after serving a two-year sentence for homosexual offences. A narrative about a Royal Horse Guards trooper executed for killing his wife, it exposes the brutalisation of the prison system to which all convicts, including Wilde himself, were subjected. But Nicholas may also have been inspired by Wilde's pamphlet *Children in Prison and Other Cruelties of Prison Life* (1897) and *De Profundis*, published posthumously in 1905, which traces Wilde's spiritual journey.

A selection of Nicholas's prison sonnets was originally published in Welsh as *Llygad y Drws: Sonedau'r Carchar* (1940) (Eye of the Door: Prison Sonnets), introduced by D. Gwenallt Jones, *Canu'r Carchar* (Ysgrifennwyd yng Ngharcharau Abertawe a Brixton) ([1942]; rpt 1943), and *Ail Gyfres* (Prison Poems: Written in Swansea and Brixton Prisons) (second series), with a preface by the Welsh-language poet Dewi Emrys and a concluding translation, 'To a sparrow', by H. Idris Bell. In 1948, an English translation of some of these poems – by the pacifist and poet Daniel Hughes, who provided most of the translations, Dewi Emrys, Eric Davies and Wil Ifan – was published with a preface by Iorwerth Peate and a translator's foreword by Daniel Hughes.[1] 'To a sparrow' clearly had profound significance for Nicholas, to which we will return shortly, as the only translated poem included in *Llygad y Drws* and, by another translator, in *Canu'r Carchar* and selected again for inclusion in the English-language version of the poems.

The English translations of the prison sonnets are not slavish imitations of the Welsh but creatively develop Nicholas's poetics, and especially the way in which visual, pacifist and spiritual insights are interwoven, as in the final couplet of 'The black sheep': 'All men have faults; go thou, black sheep in peace; / The morning frost shows white on thy black fleece' (PS, p. 26). However, there are important differences between the reading experiences which the respective texts offer the reader, beyond the obvious point that one version is a translation of the other. The poems selected for the English version are grouped according to who translated them, which means that some of the resonances between the poems in the Welsh version, and the effect of some of the juxtapositions there, have been lost. The prefaces are written by different authors – Dewi Emrys and Iorwerth Peate – each of whom has a different perspective on the importance of the sonnets. While both texts close with a translation of 'To a sparrow', as we said, the translation in each version is by a different translator – H. Idris Bell and Wil Ifan (whose translation was originally published in *Llygad y Drws*) – and therefore are slightly different.

NICHOLAS'S PACIFISM

The poems certainly were, to quote the historian Kenneth Morgan, 'a powerful riposte by "No 2740" to the injustices and coercions of prison life'.[2] In his introduction to *Llygad y Drws*, Gwenallt distinguishes between Nicholas's Marxist poems, which he acknowledges are based on sincere political ideals, and his rural poetry, which in his view has more depth and 'poetry'. However, this says as much about Gwenallt as Nicholas and how in the 1940s rural west Wales had come to mean more to Gwenallt than the politics of the south Wales coalfield. Bell, writing in the 1950s, takes a similar approach, pointing out that 'only a minority [of Nicholas's poems] can fairly be described as propagandist; in the best he expresses his longing for the open air and the life of nature, his sympathy with living things, and, forgetting for a while his internationalism, his love of Wales'.[3] Nicholas's first collection of peace poems – *Dros Eich Gwlad: Cerddi Heddwch* (For Your Country: Songs of Peace) – was published in 1930 and embraces, albeit in embryonic form, some of these motifs.

However, while Gwenallt and Bell provide good insights into the selections of Nicholas's prison poems, they gloss over how protest, sympathy with nature and other living things, Welsh nationalism and socialism were closely interconnected in Welsh pacifism and are closely linked as a cluster of motifs in Nicholas's sonnets. The Welsh versions of the sonnets should be read as a book in which Nicholas set out to reveal the interlinking of aspects of his psyche. For this reason, it is a pity that there is no English-language translation of the Welsh versions in their entirety which respects the ways in which the poems pick up on resonances from each other in subject matter, imagery and, above all, language. If Nicholas is reclaiming any 'tradition' of Welsh writing, it is poetry with deep roots in the Nonconformist (and non-conformist) politicised communities of rural west Wales, where pacifism, protest and the Welsh language were closely interconnected.

The preface to the English version by Iorwerth Peate, to whom *Llygad y Drws* is dedicated, is a sharply focused introduction to the sonnets as Welsh pacifist texts, mentioning Nicholas's emphasis on the 'common man'; on the value, dignity and 'abiding worth of the individual man'; on what he calls the 'complete life'; and on peace, justice and 'brotherhood' (PS, pp. 9–10). In '1940', Nicholas spells out the Welsh pacifist creed to which he adheres: 'My faith was in a brotherhood unarmoured, / In love as limitless as human need' (PS, p. 40). Peate as a pacifist himself also finds in the sonnets a legacy of pacifist thinking which he dates to Nicholas's work and activism and to Thomas Rees's influence in the earlier decades of the twentieth century. However, he not only helps the reader to see Nicholas as a pacifist poet but to be conscious that the English version of the poems, despite the translators' best efforts, have lost some of the core of their Welshness in translation. While in their publication during the Second World War the sonnets were meant to bolster conscientious objectors and opponents of war, Peate, three years after the conclusion of the war, recommends them to post-war pacifists and, in doing so, redefines the relevance of pacifism for the post-war world, arguing that Nicholas's principles 'commend themselves to all men of goodwill who, amidst the ashes of a war-shattered civilisation, wish to build a new and better community on the bedrock of the Brotherhood of Man' (PS, p. 13).

The sonnets are haunted throughout by an image of the poet incarcerated in a bare cell ('Y bydd garcharor rhwng y muriau llwm') (CC, p. 31). This image is important because it is a constant reminder to pacifists, especially imprisoned conscientious objectors, that the discourse of military heroism cannot violate the view that pacifists have of themselves as brave, silent sufferers. The sonnets draw upon the same heritage as Gwenallt and Waldo in seeing pacifism as the fulfilment of a destiny that has scriptural origins. They develop the final couplet of 'Y Llais' (The voice) at the outset of both Welsh- and English-language versions of the sonnets: 'Minnau, freuddwydiwr tragwyddoldeb pell, / Yn disgwyl am ei neges yn fy nghell' (CC, p. 25) (And I, a dreamer of eternity's far spell, / Await his message in my lonely cell) (PS, p. 23). 'His' here refers to Christ, and at the core of the poem is the rejection of the false gods of war in favour of the 'one voice [who] alone in all the crowd announces / Humanity's deep curse on blood and guilt' (PS, p. 23) (un llais yng nghanol miliwn yn cyhoeddi / Melltith dynoliaeth ar y gwaed a'r farn) (CC, p. 25). This line of thought mirrors George Davies's writings in returning to the Nonconformist pacifist reliance on scripture – here the emphasis on peace in Christ's gospel – and compares the courage which pacifists need to come out as pacifists with that required by the early Christians.

But the poem also introduces another theme which the sonnets share with George Davies's work, the indictment not just of war *per se*, but of the church for blessing weapons of destruction and encouraging its congregations to participate in war. An important sonnet in this regard is 'Dafad Ddu' (The black sheep) – obviously written to bolster the courage of pacifists in wartime – which challenges the scapegoating of conscientious objectors by the church and society generally as 'black sheep'. In countering discourse that constructs pacifists as 'aliens' (a word Nicholas employs as a title to a poem in *Llygad y Drws*) and transfers notions of 'strangeness' to conscientious objectors, the poem readdresses the binary. In a world of 'the gross festivities of flesh and crimes' (A chellwair â phechodau trychinebus) (CC, p. 30), Nicholas makes the point that it is nonsensical to treat conscientious objectors as if they were 'some monstrous evil power' (PS, p. 26) (A'th drin fel anferth o droseddwr mawr) (CC, p. 30).

ACTIVISM AND MYSTICISM

The redefinition of conventional views of war in the sonnets is rooted in Nicholas's political pacifism. Poems, such as '1941', invoking the Home Front, often render locations and bombers anonymously so that the poem can be seen as talking about Home Fronts anywhere and as blurring distinctions between enemy and defender. Seeing ordinary people involved in war everywhere as victims of social inequality, the sonnet contrasts the 'common man' who faces death and terrible injury at home and on the front with the rich in their mansions who continue to laugh and drink wine. It goes beyond depicting the immediate physical horrors of aerial bombing – 'Homes burst to flame' (PS, p. 44) – in identifying an even greater outrage, that ordinary people are but 'the playthings of the mad things' (PS, p. 44). The sonnets are uncompromising as pacifist poems, drilling down to where there is neither 'heroism' nor 'service to a higher cause', but only the insanity of war.

This highly charged political pacifism is woven throughout the sonnets. Although the arrangement of the English-language sonnets displaces the resonances and telling juxtapositions in the organisation of the original Welsh-language text, it sets up new but equally significant juxtapositions. Of these, some of the more important relate to the interweaving of political argument, biblical allusions and moments of insight and transcendence. While Bell correctly refers to Nicholas's sympathy with nature that relationship is redefined in the sonnets so that the beauty of the Welsh landscape retained in the prisoner's memories provides a glimpse into something that is within and beyond nature. In this regard, Nicholas reminds us that he has two sides, as we said there were to T. Gwynn Jones in the previous chapter, although they cannot be easily separated. He is both a socialist-driven thinker, speaking up for ordinary people, and a solitary, meditative mystic searching to discover, and sustain, an inner peacefulness.

Among his most important poems are those concerned not simply with sympathy with nature but the sheer pleasure in it which brings its own insights into a 'reality' that transcends war, violence, suffering and turmoil. Such a moment occurs in the sonnet 'To a sparrow': 'Your constant pecking its own comfort bringing' (PS, p. 91); 'Your pecking strikes my ear, a comfort bringing' (CC, p. 53). A bird visiting and providing prisoners with an inner peacefulness is a recurring motif in prison literature. For readers familiar with the *Mabinogi*, it may bring another bird to mind, with different connotations from Nicholas's sparrow – the starling that carries a message from Branwen across the Irish Sea to her brother, the king of Britain, after her husband, the king of Ireland, has banished her to work in the kitchens. In the Bible, the sparrow (like the imprisoned conscientious objector) is a symbol of loneliness and isolation, but, despite its apparent insignificance, it is used by Christ to illustrate the importance of all things in God's eyes (Luke 12:4–7). In classical mythology, sparrows escorted the chariot of the goddess of love, although once again 'love' here has different suggestions from the New Testament and the Christian pacifist creed. Feeding the bird pieces of bread, Nicholas imagines that he is conducting a kind of communion, but one that is very different from the communion and religious services which are offered in the prison by those who bless weapons of war. In the concluding couplets of this sonnet the 'communion' with the sparrow becomes the meeting of two open hearts which is at the core of the spiritual side of Welsh pacifism and which, tellingly, closes both collections: 'Gift of a heart that ever open lies' (CC, p. 53); 'The offering of a heart that knows no bars' (p. 91). In some of Nicholas's poems there is a binary between the crowd and the solitary mystic which, as in 'The crowd', favours the latter; 'The passion of the crowd is not of those / Lone pangs that give to truth and beauty birth' (PS, p. 80). But what is distinctly Welsh about Nicholas's sonnets is the way in which they seek to bring the different dimensions of his work together within the Welsh Nonconformist concept of intellectual and spiritual independence: 'I neither lead nor follow, I just yield / To that Great Urge which moves in every field' (PS, p. 80).

One of the most significant sonnets in this regard is 'Midnight', which has an original and independent take on war. An intriguing poem, it brings to mind the visitation of divine judgements in the Old Testament, the apocalypse in the Book of Revelation and inter-war American science fiction films. The core of the poem is a contrast between the mechanical powers of destruction and ordinary people who want nothing more than to live together in peace, fleeing like rats, and a mother, personifying love and family, who desperately wants to get her child to shelter. But the real subject of the poem appears to be not the 'midnight' of Western society in the event itself but the voyeuristic interest which readers and viewers have in destruction and carnage, suggesting that it is this which is the real 'midnight' of Western societies. Again, Nicholas is extending the conceptual reach of social or political pacifism as an ideology which exposes and challenges the fetishisation of violence.

'Affinity', too, is an important sonnet in that it revisions how pacifists are perceived by 'others' and see each other. It is concerned with how the way in which the people who pay to visit an imprisoned ape – although the species is not fully identified – are viewed by the ape itself. Nicholas's own imprisonment clearly informs the text which also invokes the interest in zoos among early modernist writers. The ape recalls the jungle in which he was once free, as Nicholas thinks of the Welsh mountains in other poems; and the ape, again like Nicholas in other poems, thinks of itself as one of many who might have been caught and imprisoned. Instead of thinking in terms of the imprisoned and those who imprison, the poem links the imprisoned 'brother' to those brothers – 'His kindred, [who] happily, live near, free men' (PS, p. 75) – who visit him, keeping alive, through a network that is not fully acknowledged, a hope that 'bites deeper than the captive's chain' (PS, p. 75). At one level, Nicholas presents pacifists as a close-knit family in order to encourage others who might be imprisoned or be facing incarceration. But more importantly, this is another of the sonnets which challenge the way in which imprisoned conscientious objectors are defined by discourses which render them 'alien' and 'other'.

Nicholas's tremendously high level of creative output; his impressive poetic and political erudition; and the vehemence, and at the same time impatient zeal, of his polemics made him a strong presence in twentieth-century left-wing politics and in Welsh pacifism. Alongside such varied personalities as T. Gwynn Jones, Waldo and Gwenallt, he demonstrated a high sensibility to poetry, to nature and to the pacifist mode of being. His poetry, articles, letters and speeches convey the complexity of the world in which he was living and which he was trying to transform.

However, he never achieved the iconic status in Welsh letters of Gwenallt and Waldo. This is partly due to their development of key pacifist principles in ways which, as we shall see in the next chapter, have given their poetry philosophical depth and a vivid sense of the kind of society for which Nicholas argues. Their work still has relevance, even (perhaps especially) for a post-nuclear age which has developed new forms of technological, chemical and cyber warfare. While Nicholas's Welsh veers at times towards the polemic and political exegesis, which is one of the reasons he is able to make such effective use of the final couplet in his prison sonnets, their work has a richer sense of poetry and, it must be said, a considerable care for the Welsh language, rooted in their understanding of its linguistic traditions and of its figurative and imagistic potential. Their work has always been admired for the way in which it brings the past and the living 'present' of the Welsh language together in nuanced ways which point towards the future of the language itself.

Nicholas's work, as we have noted, draws on the same pacifist heritage as the poetry of Waldo and Gwenallt. But his prison sonnets are inspiring because of the way they develop an ideological pacifism and create original discourses around ethical and social issues. They are impressive for the way they integrate the spiritual or inner sphere with the external sphere of social and political life. They convey, too, the speed with which Nicholas, within individual sonnets and across the Welsh-language sections as a whole captures insight after insight; the skill with which he adapts what was once for him a traditional, rural Welsh into a more urban, political Welsh; and the adroitness with which he adapts a difficult poetic form, in Welsh, to the social and political concerns of ordinary people. While aspects of his work mirror Gwenallt and Waldo, his voice can also be quite different, as if all the time he is writing back to ordinary pacifists, intent on encouraging different ways of perceiving war, violence, nature, human relationships and peace, and constantly challenging discourses which construct pacifists and conscientious objectors as 'other'.

GEORGE M. LL. DAVIES'S PRISON WRITINGS

Writing from prison, as the biblical scholar Gilpin reminds us, has 'a long and variegated Christian literary tradition that reaches from the Apostle Paul to such twentieth-century figures as Dietrich Bonhoeffer, Dorothy Day and Martin Luther King, Jr'.[4] As a public declaration of protest and belief intended to encourage others, it features strongly in Welsh pacifist literature not only through the writings of T. E. Nicholas but also George Davies. In the course of his imprisonment, before he was moved to the camp for conscientious objectors at Caeo in Carmarthenshire, Davies smuggled out essays and letters with the assistance of visiting Quakers. They exemplify the importance of religious conviction and acts of conscience to Welsh pacifism. Their influence undermined the state's argument that conscientious objectors must be imprisoned as an example to others and provided documentary evidence of conditions in the prisons, of the demeaning prison work and of the social isolation. It was as if society wanted to punish the pacifist's mind for conceiving alternatives to militarism and war, and the pacifist's body for being unavailable to the war machine. Davies's reactions to his incarceration are much the same as those of other pacifists who found themselves imprisoned. Merfyn Turner, for example, describes how

> Prison did many things to me as it did to my fellow-prisoners. It caused physical discomfort by depriving me at first of my mattress, and sufficient bed-covering to combat the chill of a poorly-heated cell, and by keeping me in a state of perpetual hunger. It caused humiliation and degradation.[5]

They both emphasise the shock of being catapulted from a life over which they had control, that was structured around respect from and respect for others, to one where they are shouted at, bullied and physically intimidated on a daily basis. This is a point which Turner could not have made more strongly: 'But the greatest injury it inflicted on us all was psychological, for by exerting complete external control over our life, and thus making us totally dependent on the prison for all our needs, it forced us to regress into our childhood.'[6]

Llywelyn stresses how Davies's 'own humanity and compassion enabled him to see humanity in others'.[7] His prison writings interweave accounts of his shame and suffering with anecdotes of support, for example, from fellow prisoners in the guard room; the prisoners who encouragingly wink at him on the parade ground where he is publicly sentenced to hard labour; and the subaltern who talks to him quietly about the importance of love. But they also depict a system that, as Llywelyn says, Davies found 'dehumanised both inmates and warders'.[8] From, albeit brief, exchanges with warders and the prison governor, he discovered that warders behaved as they did because they could be fined if they were overheard talking sympathetically with a prisoner, and even the governor would have introduced a more liberal regime if the Home Office had allowed him. Thus, there is a strong suggestion in the prison letters that, left to their own devices, people in authority would be more inclined to follow pacifist convictions than might be supposed.

Inevitably, the Bible features strongly in Davies's prison writings, reminding us that it may be read from different perspectives in different circumstances. Thus, it is possible to talk of a feminist or Black Bible, for example, and, as in Davies's letters, a prisoner's Bible which can sustain those who suffer incarceration, torture and abuse for their faith. As Llywelyn points out, in the course of his life Davies's own reading of the Bible changed from 'a conventionally Christian gospel to the "gospel of personalisation" – his principle and practice of seeing the individual as "more important than belief, or rule, or dogma"'.[9] 'Personalisation', or 'personalism' as Ralph Waldo Emerson preferred to call it, was at the core of Welsh pacifism. Welsh pacifist intellectuals were introduced to it not only through Davies's reading of Emerson but through the work of David Gwenallt Jones and Waldo Williams. Waldo, as we shall see in Chapter 4, developed the concept differently from Davies. While Waldo stressed individuals realising their full potential through community with others, Davies emphasised spiritual insight arising from reflection on Christ's teachings.

As is evident from the works of Davies, Glyn Jones and Gwenallt, irony also features strongly in Welsh and English pacifist writings. Hardly any of the ironies around the way in which the Bible was used in the prison system escaped Davies's attention, including how it could promote freedom of thought among those imprisoned for their freedom of thought; that the only book with which pacifist prisoners were provided in their cells was the very work on which their pacifism was often based; and that the officials who sentenced them usually kissed the New Testament.

However, Davies's irony did not protect him from bouts of severe depression brought on by the brutality of the regime and the hard labour although perhaps his realist writing did. 'Bottom Dogs – II and III' captures the slow laborious nature of the road gang in a single sentence: 'So the road is made, yard by yard, and, as the weeks pass, mile by mile'[10] while the torture of the labour is encapsulated through the change in the primary sense from sight to sound: 'the rattle of pick and shovel, the sharp crack of the 16-lb sledge hammer, the clank and roar of the steam tractors dumping heaps of iron slag, to be smashed and laid on the roads' (ETP, p. 52). Ironically, the road building mirrors the manual work undertaken by troops, and prisoners of war, in other parts of the world, all of whom may be seen as mere extensions of their tools. The conscientious objectors are 'treated as "criminals" by those aware of their prisoner status and viewed as "navvies" by the local people':[11]

> So much pretence is laid aside, for a group of dusty navvies, who may chance to lean on their shovels and look up, are – well, just navvies to the

> rich, and just men to the poor. The other navvies pass by with a jest, the little farm servant maid with a smile, the children look up wonderingly and unafraid, the little farmers or their wives passing by in their carts have generally a friendly word, the better-off farmers in their gigs have their status to preserve and just nod condescendingly, the Priest and the Levite pass by on the other side, the Council official (a heavy portentous man whom the other navvies have christened 'The Hun') comes by once or twice a day to find fault, and to look it. (ETP, p. 52)

Throughout, it is easy to equate 'soldiers' with 'navvies'. Both are recognisable by their uniforms – the navvies by their 'corduroys' and 'red kerchief' – and both are confined as a body of men under orders. But at the heart of this essay is the story of the Good Samaritan in which the Priest and the Levite 'pass by on the other side'.

The warmth of the good Samaritans whom Davies found among the lower classes and fellow prisoners lightens even his darkest prison prose. In 'Bottom Dogs – II', drawing inspiration from the Beatitudes of Christ, Davies declares: 'At any rate, I am sure one sees life – the spontaneous expression of men's hearts – more truly and easily on the open, dusty road than from any other vantage ground I have known' (ETP, p. 52). One of the most uplifting passages describes Davies's encounter with gypsies which begins when he calls out to them 'Good-night brothers' (ETP, p. 57). As Davies would no doubt have noted himself, it is an appropriate greeting for a Christian pacifist to use, exemplifying the concept of 'brawdoliaeth' (brotherhood) which became important to Davies's life and writings and, also, to the poetry of Waldo Williams. In inviting Davies to share their fire, the gypsies exemplify the generosity of the poor, which is a key refrain in the New Testament, as well as recognition of a shared humanity. A key image is 'the strange ring of bright-eyed boys and swarthy-faced girls, with the dogs nosing in between us' (ETP, p. 57), which reflects both an external sense of peace and an inner peacefulness. Pointedly recalling Psalm 23, Davies declares how his 'cup runneth over' (Psalm 23:5): 'my empty cup was refilled and piece after piece of thickly buttered bread was handed to me' (ETP, p. 57).

Davies's twentieth century and Christ's ancient Palestine are merged when Davies admits to the gypsies that he is a prisoner working on the road and describes himself, as Christ might have done, as 'going about speaking for peace' (ETP, p.57). On hearing that he was imprisoned for this, the gypsy wife exclaims, ironically, 'Jesus Christ have mercy!' and is herself described by Davies in a way that brings the Madonna and child to mind, as 'the woman with the brown baby in her arms' (ETP, p. 57). Indeed, the location, 'a caravan, a rough shelter, three horses browsing by, some dogs' (ETP, p. 57), conjures up the stable in Bethlehem. Never one to overlook an irony, as we said earlier, Davies contrasts the symbol of the fire, as hearth, with gypsies as examples of 'precariousness, homelessness and transitoriness' (ETP, p. 57).

R. GWENALLT JONES, *PLASAU'R BRENIN* (1934)

No novel in the Welsh language was more important to Welsh pacifism in the inter-war years than the largely autobiographical *Plasau'r Brenin* (The King's Palaces), which deals with the experiences of a conscientious objector imprisoned in the First World War. I call it 'semi-autobiographical' because it is a novel, and while it undoubtedly draws upon Gwenallt's own experiences it utilises those of others, including stories that Gwenallt would have heard from, and about, other conscientious objectors. Thus, whether, for example, Gwenallt actually suffered the violence reported by Myrddin Tomos – being left naked in a cell for long periods at a time, being stabbed by bayonets and made the subject of mock executions – is immaterial. The experience of pacifists varied considerably, dependent upon how and where they were imprisoned, and, as Gwenallt suggests, the important point is that how prisoners were treated often depended upon the attitudes of warders and other officials towards others as fellow human beings.

The title of the novel most obviously refers to the prisons in which the central character, and Gwenallt himself, were incarcerated, but it also invokes the gospel of St John which, of all the gospels, most obviously tries to summon optimism and hope following Christ's ascension: 'In my Father's house are many mansions: if it were not so, I would have told you. I go to prepare a place for you' (14:2). There is some debate as to why Gwenallt refused military service. Bell suggests that it was because he was unwilling to fight for the British Empire.[12] However, arguments as to whether Gwenallt was imprisoned as a pacifist or as someone opposed to British imperialism unhelpfully separates motivations that were often combined in the minds of Welsh conscientious objectors and, in any event, by the time Gwenallt came to write this novel he was certainly an absolute pacifist.

The novel looks back from the 1930s to the First World War, asking the question posed by *The Welsh Outlook* on the twelfth anniversary of the Armistice, 'Have we moved at all along the path to peace?'[13] In his critical introduction to Gwenallt's work, the pacifist author Dyfnallt Morgan, who was himself imprisoned as a conscientious objector in the Second World War, points out that the time lag between the events which are described and the publication of *Plasau'r Brenin* is common to a number of reflections on the war such as Herbert Read's *In Retreat* (1925), Edmund Blunden's *Undertones Of War* (1928), Robert Graves's *Goodbye to All That* (1929) and David Jones's *In Parenthesis* (1937).[14] However, in Gwenallt's case the time lag is not between the experience of the front and reflection on it but between the experience of being a conscientious objector and its documentation. Through his experience as a student and later a teacher at the University College of Wales, Aberystwyth, and the visits he made to Ireland, Gwenallt in his early years was an intensely political man profoundly influenced by socialism, nationalism and campaigns in support of the Welsh language.

The time lag is important to the exploratory nature of *Plasau'r Brenin*, many of whose debates – although they date back to the formation of the Independent Labour Party – belong more to the 1930s than the First World War. Why Gwenallt in the mid-1930s chose to write this book about an experience upon which he had remained extraordinarily silent has often been the subject of discussion. The prospect of a further war which would put pacifists through the mill again may have been a factor, but also the extent to which Gwenallt in the 1930s, like Myrddin Tomos in the novel during the First World War, was being pulled by political and cultural forces in many different directions. Perhaps, it was the experience of finding parts but not the whole of his self-identity which had prevented him from writing about his incarceration and smuggling out writings as did George Davies and T. E. Nicholas.

RADICALISM AND RADICALISATION

A central theme in *Plasau'r Brenin* is not simply the sufferings of incarceration but the radicalisation of the prison experience for many Welsh pacifists. However, Gwenallt's approach is not to focus on the radicalisation as a straightforward linear experience but as a series of internalised debates and disruptions. In this regard, the novel mirrors the experience of pacifists in the 1930s as much as in the First World War. Thus, the psychological journey which the novel's central character, Myrddin, undertakes is interwoven with political, religious and pacifist debates that would have been familiar to Welsh readers of the 1930s when the book was published.

Not unusually for a novel concerned with imprisonment, the text moves between different timescales and takes the reader into Carmarthenshire's rural past. Myrddin's memories recreate 'the image of a really human society' which Ned Thomas finds in Gwenallt's poetry.[15] Nowhere is this clearer than in the recollections which torment him when he is left 'wandering' in his mind back to the Welsh rural Sabbath: 'Ar y Sul, yn y carchar, eisteddai ar ei ystôl drithroed gan adael i'w feddwl grwydro yn ôl yn Sir Gaerfyrddin'[16] (PB, p. 62). 'Crwydro' is a verb generally used to suggest 'roaming' and 'rambling', emphasising the freedom of the countryside he once knew, but, like many pacifists who were born and raised in the Welsh countryside, he did not fully appreciate at the time.

Myrddin remembers how it had been possible during the week for him not to see a single friend or neighbour on the roads. By contrast, the Sabbath brought friends and neighbours together in the spirit of peace and created, importantly to a Welsh pacifist from the area, a holism centred on God, nature and community. This was encapsulated in the way in which the chapel congregation expressed their gratitude to God for the sun, rain, seasons and the harvest. The striking rhythm and alliteration in the Welsh here – 'am haul neu law, am sychin a hinon' (PB, p. 64) – capture the sense of completion in the harvests (cynaeafau) and in rural life generally. Recollections of travelling in his family's trap and engaging in conversations with farmers about mundane matters recreate the romantic idyll of his parents' life, and these memories prove important as one of the means by which he survives his confinement.

However, this is only part of the story. Prison provides Myrddin with a deeper understanding of the subversive politics of rural Wales. Interestingly, because Gwenallt is describing Myrddin here from his own post-imprisonment experiences, this knowledge comes to Myrddin through his 're-memory' of the politics of rural Ireland – inspired by being moved to a cell in which Irish republicans had been detained – and memories of the Nonconformist hymnists and poets from pre-industrial Wales when it was a centre of popular uprisings. Densil Morgan says of Glamorganshire:

> Despite the early influence of Marxism and the continuing presence of religious apathy within its borders, industrialization there did not conform to the English or continental stereotype by indicating secularity. Well into the twentieth century, religion, especially in its Nonconformist guise, remained an important social phenomenon in South Wales.[17]

But another means of support was provided by the socialist-cum-communist politics of south Wales and his fellow prisoners from that area, especially Jac Niclas (whose name is a fusion of those of two well-known conscientious objectors of the time, T. E. Nicholas and Jack Rees), a south Wales coalminer and communist committed to the Welsh labour movement. The industrial community of south Wales had had as strong an impact upon Gwenallt, as did the bitterness of the 1910 strike, after which he joined the Independent Labour movement. Morgan highlights how after the introduction of conscription in 1916, the nature of relationships within Gwenallt's home valley changed.[18] Bridge House, where Gwenallt met other well-known conscientious objectors, became a centre of strong socialist debates, and the valley was visited by prominent socialists like Philip Snowden, George Lansbury and Keir Hardie.[19]

One of the subjects which Gwenallt's novel examines is the difference between pacifism in west Wales, which was largely based on Nonconformity, and south Wales, which, having its roots in the unrest and unemployment in the coalfields, was more political than religious and, in the 1930s, increasingly relied upon Marxism. When the prisoners in *Plasau'r Brenin* hear the news of the Russian Revolution, the whole prison seems to erupt in renditions of 'The Red Flag' and the 'Internationale'. But there is need for caution when discussing this aspect of Gwenallt's work. A native of Pontardawe, and the son of Nonconformist parents, Gwenallt grew up in a mining and industrial area, and in his early adult years became all too familiar with deprivation, unemployment and social unrest. As Bell recorded, 'he was in those years a Socialist of the extreme left, hostile to organized religion, and showing little specifically Welsh patriotism'.[20] Unsurprisingly, therefore, Jac's documentation of industrial south Wales seems more 'real' to Myrddin at times than his memories of Carmarthenshire. Gwenallt's own parents belonged to a hill-farming community until they were eventually drawn away by better prospects for work in the industrial south.[21] Not surprisingly, therefore, *Plasau'r Brenin* captures, like Gwenallt's poetry, what Ned Thomas calls 'the pull between the rural and industrial communities'.

The former is a pull towards a way of life, as Angharad Price demonstrates so effectively in a novel discussed in Chapter 6, that was intellectually limited, and limiting, but emotionally expansive. This was especially the case for women, as D. J. Williams remembers of his mother. He recalls her as 'possessed [of] depth and intensity of character and true spiritual humility', but also pointedly notes that she 'had many of the components of a great character if she had the opportunity to develop them fully'.[22] The pull towards the industrial communities, on the other hand, is informed by social critiques and ideologies that are intellectually more expansive and globally more transformative but emotionally and spiritually more limited. In the period to which the novel looks back, rural life was safeguarded and contained within clear regional, linguistic and cultural boundaries. But at the time when the novel was written these boundaries had broken down under the weight of transformative but destructive economic and social forces that caused many to leave rural Wales for more industrial parts. The gravitation towards rural life and towards socialist ideologies at different points in Gwenallt's novel mirrors the debates within Myrddin's own mind and his conversations with his fellow prisoners. Myrddin carries his experience of community and neighbourliness in rural Wales into the prison with him but it was in the prison that he discovered the communist commitment to a different kind of society. The negotiation between these forces gives the novel a to-and-fro structure and creates a narrative that revolves around conflicting perspectives, different social aspirations, and debates that are only partly resolved even at the end of the novel when Myrddin and Jac decide to go their separate ways on their release. Jac intends to return to his work as a miner for a while, but his ambition now is to devote himself to the labour movement, while Myrddin looks forward to returning to the farm where he hopes to reclaim the shared sense of belonging rooted in neighbourly relationships with others.

However, the novel leaves the reader with a sense that these are not necessarily the best decisions for the individuals, which is in keeping with the troubled nature of the book as a whole. This is partly because of Myrddin's conviction that the Welsh nation should be repelled by Europe's social and moral disorder and that pacifism in this novel is not a woolly idealism but a head-on encounter with very real, pressing historical forces. As a prison novel, *Plasau'r Brenin* enables Gwenallt to grapple with a courage of conscience imported from the shadows of European prison literature, that made possible the risky embrace of quite specific Welsh fears of being outcast and powerless within their own nation.

Thus, pacifism in this text is not an escape from war and military discourse but an engagement with it as part of a search for an inner spiritual peacefulness. The novel has an external focus on the discourse and structures that create war, existing in tension with the aspiration of human society to live in peace, and an inward focus on the search for a peaceful mode of being in contact with nature and rural community. Ironically, it is in the military camp that Myrddin finds the 'conversation' and social intercourse of Welsh rural society. But it goes beyond the farmers' talk of their daily lives. The soldiers, like the prisoners, appear to be prepared to enter into debate with each other. But a key word which brings the conscientious objectors, the farmers and the soldiers together is 'cyfeillgarwch' (neighbourly friendship).

THE 'WELSH NOT' AND THE YELLOW DISK

One of the striking contrasts in the novel is that between the 'conversation' (ymddiddan) which Myrddin recalls with the local Carmarthenshire farmers and enjoys in a more spirited fashion with the soldiers, and the enforced silence of the exercise periods in which the prisoners are prohibited to speak to each other. Tellingly, the images of enforced silence follow Myrddin's induction into the prison system, and they are analogous to the attempts by an anglicised education system in Wales to eradicate the Welsh language. However, although watched by warders, the prisoners manage to snatch a few words with each other, quickly and craftily (yn gyflym ac yn gyfrwys), as did Victorian Welsh children making secret use of their native language in school under the threat of the 'Welsh Not'. The alliteration here underscores the subversive conspiracy of the prisoners, and the close-knit nature of their inner society within the prison which is comparable to that of the rural Welsh communities which enabled periods of dissent such as those associated with the Rebecca Riots. The 'King's Palaces' present Myrddin, as they did Gwenallt himself, with bastions of impenetrable Englishness. Like George Davies, Gwenallt sees the prisoners as part of a large oppressive machine. Approaching the imposing gates of the prison, Myrddin recalls Dante: 'Rhoddwch heibio bob gobaith, chwi sydd yn myned i mewn' (PB, p. 46). Warned, as it were, to put aside all hope, Myrddin struggles in prison to retain his faith but the experience enables him to discover a deeper hope.

The interrogation of the conscientious objectors in the courtroom suggests that everywhere human beings are classified within a system, as they are asked for details of their nationality, their residence, their religion and their occupation. Inside the prison, the only prisoners' details that really matter to the prison authorities are their background, the nature of their offence and the term of their punishment. No scene in *Plasau'r Brenin* is more shocking and telling than that in which Myrddin is inducted into the prison system. Stripped naked and humiliated, his body is scrutinised for every identifying mark. There is an allusion here to Christ being stripped naked before being flogged. In fact, the novel as a whole makes a number of references to events surrounding the crucifixion. For example, the court martial of one of Myrddin's fellow conscientious objectors is compared to Christ's trial before Pilate, and the final page of the novel alludes to the image of the wounds on Christ's feet and hands. As part of his prison induction, he is forced to surrender his belongings, including his money and pocket knife, but above all his books. Deprived of them, like his fellow conscientious objectors in the courtroom, he is stripped intellectually. However, although he no longer has access to them, he remembers and uses what he has read to make sense of experiences at once horrifying but also, as in the case of being sent to chokey for looking at a young woman, bizarre.

In addition to having to wear prison clothes, Myrddin's name is taken away from him and he is given a number A3.43. A short, emphatic sentence summarises everything perfectly: 'Collodd ei hunaniaeth a'i bersonoliaeth' (He lost his identity and personality) (PB, p. 48). At the end of the novel, he reclaims his possessions, but most importantly his name, described in a clause which is as emphatic as the sentence which originally described them being taken from him: 'chafodd yn ôl ei frws dannedd, ei arian a'i enw' (PB, p. 129). Once again, his toothbrush is stressed because its removal seems to emphasise that the prison left him without a 'mouth', in the sense that it robbed him of his everyday use of the Welsh language. In the course of the novel, Myrddin tries to write out a letter in Welsh, but prisoners are banned from using the Welsh language. The coat which Myrddin has to wear in prison has his number on a yellow disk which is redolent of the way in which Jews in Nazi Germany, at the very time the novel was being written, were being forced to wear a yellow signifier. This link suggests that the British and German establishments may not be so dissimilar in what they are capable of when it comes to stereotyping and stigmatising those they perceive as outsiders and a threat to hegemony. A Welsh reader would not be able to avoid comparing the yellow disk which Jews were forced to wear with the 'Welsh Not' which Welsh-speaking children were made to wear when they were overheard speaking Welsh. The yellow disk becomes an important image in the novel and, placed on the door of the punishment cell, it becomes a signifier of a psychic prison within the physical prison.

CHRISTIAN PACIFISM

The way in which the prison strips away the identity of conscientious objectors in layers, as it were, is not unlike the treatment of Christians in ancient Palestine or Rome before its conversion to Christianity. This, again, is unsurprising, for Christianity, alongside socialism and the politics of rural west Wales, is one of the forces pulling at Myrddin. The novel concludes with the discovery of an enlightenment that is very much based on the Christian pacifist creed of the 1930s in its emphasis on 'personalism', a 'joyful heart', 'calon . . . yn llawn o lawenydd', a 'generous spirit', 'ysbryd hael', and forgiveness or absolution, 'maddeugar' (PB, p. 134).

Rediscovering Christianity was as important to Gwenallt in the 1930s as the reclamation of Nonconformity for Glyn Jones about the same time (it is part of Myrddin's prison experiences, too, through his friendship with the devout Christian prisoner, Bill Mainwaring), and Ned Thomas points out that 'all Gwenallt's published poems date from after his return to Christianity'.[23] Unsurprisingly, then, the novel reflects some of the salient features of Gwenallt's Christian poetry identified by Dyfnallt Morgan: the direct manner, the vivid imagery and memorable phrases.[24] Gwenallt never fully lost his faith, even when he was at his most agnostic, and Myrddin uses the Bible, as did George Davies, to make sense of his prison experiences. Like the ironic George Davies, too, he often turns to wry humour, for example when he says that he was sent to 'chokey' for the offence committed by Lot's wife, in this case looking back in the prison chapel to the Master's daughter.

The condition of being a pacifist aligns with one of the grand narratives of the Bible and metanarratives of centuries of hymns, that to be a stranger in the world is the normative condition for a Christian. In Emyr Humphreys's novel *Outside the House of Baal*, the pacifist minister J.T., quoting a hymn, describes himself as 'a stranger in this world. My home is outside time'.[25] Perhaps the connection between these pacifist texts is not too surprising, as Gwenallt came from the same area as many Welsh hymn writers such as Thomas Lewis and Williams of Pantycelyn, to whom he wrote one of his best-known poems. However, in both novels, the central protagonist exchanges a fixed identity for one that transcends his former self and is more fluid. In Myrddin's case, he discovers a more complex sense of identity than he had in west Wales, based on an assimilation of different discourses, not only pacifism but socialism and Marxism. But as a budding Christian socialist, he finds a 'religion' in which the whole course of history, albeit threatened by militarism and war, still has a future. *Plasau'r Brenin* can be seen as a portrait of Gwenallt as a young man grappling, like Myrddin, with different contemporary discourses which the concept of a coherent 'religion of progress' promises to bring together.

CONNECTEDNESS AND DISCONNECTEDNESS

A strength of this novel is that it not only recognises the importance of being able to believe in desirable futures but tries to define what this means. Thus the text, which is pulled by the tensions between rural and industrial forces, and between religious pacifism and secular socialism, is also pulled by the friction between the pre-modern and the modern. Speeding towards London in the train, Myrddin is 'refreshed' (although the Welsh word 'amheuthun' has a stronger meaning than its English translation) by the speed, greenery (gwyrddlesni) and the sense of openness (ehangder). The words which Gwenallt uses to describe what Myrddin sees from the train windows, especially the lusciousness of the green fields implied by the word 'gwyrddlesni' and the freedom of 'ehangder', reflect not only the 'joy' experienced by a prisoner glimpsing what he has missed for so long but the spiritual importance of being close to nature.

But Myrddin also finds the train's speed invigorating. The irony here is that the speeding train that brings Myrddin into contact with the countryside also keeps him distant from it. In his rural life,

Myrddin would have moved at a walking pace which would have kept him close to nature, while the landscape would have influenced how fast or slow he moved and provided him with opportunities to wonder at the order of nature all around him. Yet in that former life, the pony and trap or the horse and cart would have been introducing opportunities to experience speed in his everyday life, at the level of mental and physical sensation. But the horse and cart not only made local journeys faster, they accelerated the way in which individuals were being pushed, without their knowing, into functioning faster. In doing so, they became more like machines, anticipating the replacement of horses with horsepower.

At the end of the novel, the description of the bus journey which he and Jac share to Paddington station stresses Myrddin's wonder in, and excitement at, cities, especially London, emphasising the height of the buildings, the brightness of the large shops and the general expansiveness. Deprived of ordinary life for so long, the two men now find everyday things exciting. As they walked from the prison, they passed different types of shops, the categories of which became almost a kind of inspirational chant: 'y siopau dillad, y siopau cig, y siopau ffrwythau a'r siopau tegannau' (PB, p. 130). If this sounds like a list from a child's Welsh-language primer, the association may not be coincidental, for on their release from prison, Myrddin and Jac rediscover the sense of wonder they possessed as children.

The desirable future which is worked out in this novel is one which has as much emphasis upon human relationships as solipsistic reveries with nature. This is evident in the writings of another pacifist to which we referred earlier, D. J. Williams. His memories of his parents' lives in rural west Wales reveal the origins of the pacifist creed which he clearly cherished. His mother exhibits the inner spiritual side of pacifist relationships – 'the peacefulness and natural respect for one another' – while his father exemplifies the more public face of the rural community in its neighbourliness: 'I know he was on the best terms possible with his neighbours every hour of the day and every day of the year. That was a part of the secret of the life of the Old Neighbourhood.'[26]

In this regard, *Plasau'r Brenin* is again pulled by conflicting forces – connectedness and disconnectedness. This is exemplified in the opening discussion between Myrddin and the army sergeant who is escorting Myrddin to a military base where he is to face a military tribunal. The two men appear to connect with each other in as much as Sergeant Evans confides in Myrddin about his health and how he has been affected by his war experiences in France. Suggesting a newly discovered allegiance with pacifism, he admits he is worn out by it all: 'Rwy' wedi blino ar y blydi busnes' (PB, p. 7). Another finely crafted sentence describes the sergeant spitting into the sawdust on the floor: '[p]oeri'n syth i'r blawd-llif a oedd ar y llawr' (PB, p. 7). Its alliteration and brevity encapsulate not only the action itself but links the suffering of soldiers with how the working conditions in the coalmines and heavy industries in south Wales affected the health of thousands of Welshmen, many of whom might have been seen spitting to clear their lungs. But while the two men are drawn together through their shared despair, they remain distant from each other. This sense of disconnection is underlined by the nature of the room in which they talk, where the different pieces of furniture, unlike those in Myrddin's own bedroom, do not relate to each other.

Objects are frequently used to convey a sense of coherence or a sense of disjointedness. The hard labour to which Myrddin is sentenced is introduced to the reader, as to Myrddin himself, through a variety of objects: 'cynfas' (canvas), 'edafedd' (yarn), 'cwyr' (wax), 'nodwydd fawr' (a large needle), 'gwniadur' (thimble) and 'siswrn' (scissors). As we see in other parts of the novel, Gwenallt often employs literary techniques, such as alliteration and internal rhyming, to suggest that relationships between objects can reflect a sense of connectedness which is somehow greater than the individual item, analogous to how positive relationships between people mirror a greater community of which they are a part. But this is not the case here. In a farmhouse in west Wales, all these objects would be associated with crafts and skills employed to make something which is necessary and/or a thing of beauty. Contributing to a punishment of hard labour, they are only vaguely connected even to something that is truly necessary, and reflect only a greater sense of disharmony and disconnection.

However, the emphasis on objects in this novel is linked to a further tension between the way in which the text pulls towards individuality and the way in which it steers towards companionship, neighbourliness and friendship. Each brings different degrees of fulfilment and unfulfilment. In isolation, Myrddin can crave the company of others but, in the company of others, he sometimes seeks creative, meditative solitude. Not coincidentally, the novel opens and closes with Myrddin experiencing pain that is associated with the head and the heart. In the opening of the novel, Myrddin suffers 'homesickness', but the English here does not do the Welsh 'hiraeth' (PB, p. 7) justice. At the end of the novel, sharing a railway carriage with his friend Jac Niclas, Myrddin suffers from the kind of headache to which language does not do justice. The pounding rhythms – 'Mae 'mhen i bron â hollti gan boen ac mae 'nghalon i yn curo fel injan' (PB, p. 136) – are enough to convey his head splitting with pain and his heart palpitating like an engine, analogous to the different forces pulling him in different directions.

Anticipating the later socialist novels of writers like Raymond Williams, Gwenallt's text examines, and begins to deconstruct, the different motivations that drive and sustain political, and in Gwenallt's case pacifist, activism. At the time he wrote this novel, Gwenallt was on the way to becoming one of the foremost pacifist poets in Wales. But in this novel, he has found a prose genre where he can engage with, and seek to resolve, the wider tensions between different pacifist perspectives, socialist and communist ideologies, and religious aspirations. The pacifist author Lily Tobias, whose novel is discussed in the next section is admittedly more adept at creating characters who are more fully alive in the writing and easily seduce us into believing that it is their motivations and desires that are driving the plot. But the strength of Gwenallt's novel is the convincing way it depicts what imprisonment involved for conscientious objectors and relates this to issues around Welsh identity and Welsh language. The difference between the two authors is that Gwenallt's novel is one of perspectives and conflicting arguments while Tobias is a writer of conflicting relationships, behaviours and contexts.

LILY TOBIAS, *EUNICE FLEET* (1903)

Lily Tobias (1887–1984), like Gwenallt and Glyn Jones, was familiar with industrial south Wales. She was born in Swansea and grew up in the mining village of Ystalyfera. But she did not share the Welsh-language, Nonconformist backgrounds of the writers discussed previously. Her parents were Jewish immigrants from Poland, and her father opened a decorator's shop in Ystalyfera. As a child, she spoke Yiddish at home and English in school, although she had some knowledge of Welsh from living in the village. She was a committed pacifist and two of her brothers were conscientious objectors to whom *Eunice Fleet*,[27] her second novel, is dedicated.

Eunice Fleet, like *Plasau'r Brenin*, is an important pacifist text because of its concern with the sufferings of pacifists rather than soldiers. As such, it is a response to the challenge facing writers at the time: how to present a 'realist' account of pacifist suffering when 'realism', as Virginia Woolf was demonstrating in her post-war fiction, was losing its credibility as a viable mode of writing. It is not news that in the 1920s and 1930s, innovative modes of writing and art were addressing the demise of the 'grand narratives' such as patriotism, empire and nationalism which took the country into war; responding to new theories of consciousness and unconsciousness; and deconstructing notions of objectivity and empiricism.

Reflecting post-First World War modernist writers' interest in non-linear time, *Eunice Fleet* consists of three parts, the first and the third set in 1930s London and the second set in pre-war and wartime Britain. The way these parts are arranged means that the novel presents the reader with a different, at times more challenging and in some respects more interesting, reading experience than Gwenallt's *Plasau'r Brenin*. However, in each of these novels, the narrative is interrupted by memories which enable the text to explore the pacifist experience. In Gwenallt's novel, as we have seen, they take the reader back to the rural roots of the central character. In *Eunice Fleet* the first and third parts constitute a continuous London-based narrative which is interrupted by an extended flashback to the First World War and the experience of a conscientious objector, with whom Eunice has a relationship, who appears before a tribunal and is then imprisoned.

The first part introduces the reader to Eunice Fleet, who is managing a lingerie business owned by her friend Hava Casson; her relationship with her sister Dorry; the men with whom Eunice and her sister become involved in the 1930s; and the involvement of Eunice's acquaintances in pacifism and political groups. As Donahaye says, it describes London very evocatively, 'it is all smog and clubs and theatres'.[28] But more than this, it presents 1930s London, from a middle-class, womanist perspective, as a racy and exciting decade. In this respect, it is different from Part 3, the mood of which is determined by the suicide of Eunice's housekeeper and Eunice's own decline, socially and mentally, leading eventually to the suggestion that she, too, has committed suicide. From a global perspective, the raciness of the decade becomes almost parochial, as the decade is overtaken by the prospect of another war and the political and social turbulence in Europe. But, for a while, it becomes one of the ways in which Eunice preserves her character and resists pacifist arguments which eventually come to make more sense to her and overturn everything she has hitherto believed.

PREJUDICE AND STEREOTYPING

In the 1930s, Eunice is in her thirties, so that her life charts the first three decades of the twentieth century: the optimism of the opening decade; the impact of the First World War and its aftermath; and the initial, spirited years of the 1930s before economic depression, political turmoil in Europe and the Second World War. The Eunice whom the reader meets in the 1930s is like the decade itself, overcoming the First World War but haunted by it. At a personal level, she has suffered long years of depression after the death of her partner, Vincent, imprisoned as a conscientious objector, and, like the nation itself, wrestles at times with a sense of hopelessness.

Pacifist themes run throughout the book: the experience of being a conscientious objector, the resistance among the English-speaking middle class to pacifism and pacifists, and the impact of becoming a conscientious objector on non-pacifist friends and family. The structure of the novel is determined as much by its exploration of how conscientious objection affected non-pacifists such as Eunice as the sufferings of conscientious objectors because of the way the two are interwoven. In doing so, Tobias's novel captures the different strains constituting the public mood of disillusionment which followed the war and haunted the 1920s. Those who served were led to believe that they would be returning to a land fit for heroes, only to find unemployment and poverty. The wounded who thought of themselves as heroes found themselves as pariah figures to the middle class. Eunice's associate Hannah Jay describes, with a sense of wishing to distance herself, how 'it's awful to see the wounded soldiers limping about . . . it gives one the horrors to pass the hospital. But the unemployed round the docks are an ugly sight too' (EF, p. 169). Through characters like Hannah's mother, there are strong suggestions of a growing anti-Semitism in Britain. She declares outspokenly 'a Christian C.O. was an unnatural coward and traitor, but a Jewish one a *natural* kind' (EF, p. 171).

A key theme which is developed through the sufferings of the conscientious objector is the complicity of wider society in sanctioning prejudice and stereotyping. One of the achievements of the text is the way in which Tobias creates a plausible character in Eunice Fleet, who has difficulty in coming to terms with pacifism and whose thinking is determined by the wider middle class to which she aspires. Part 2 begins with Eunice as a child and introduces her privileged, and somewhat 'careless', life. This enables us to understand how the 1930s in London and conscientious objectors during the war years are perceived from her perspective. In most respects, Eunice is a shallow character who is made to look as such by a narrative voice which treats her more seriously as a character than she probably deserves, and by the intellectual superiority of her pacifist partner. When Eunice accepts an invitation to attend a meeting of conscientious objectors, she sees them as 'cranks' and watches them 'silently under her sullen lids' (EF, p. 79). In Glyn Jones's 'I Was Born in the Ystrad Valley', the older Wynn feels that his failure as a young man to love others as fellow human beings rested in the 'reality' of what he saw. But in Tobias's novel, Eunice, having formed a negative, stereotypical opinion of others, assigns them physical features that confirm her prejudicial view of them:

> The chairman's face was sanctimonious; his high voice vexed her drums. The boys wore their eager air falsely, since it aped that of youths who ran to the trenches . . . Women offended in the opposite style. Some were too dowdy to matter in their shabby coats and appalling hats: the younger had clothes in character – misfits, wrong jumpers and skirts, absurd necklaces; a mixture of the jaunty, the frumpish, and the crazed. (EF, pp. 80–1)

Her thoughts here stand in contrast to the message from the chair: 'We hold that human life is sacred' (EF, p. 80). More than that, the pacifist speech suggests that their position is the result of a logical argument which would have to be met by logical argument: 'Some of us think this particular war unjust and unnecessary. Most of us believe all war to be wrong' (EF, p. 80). But Eunice's mode of thought is not even impressionistic, it is the projection of an image upon others which to her mind they then become. The novel juxtaposes her fragmentary observations and projections with the coherence of the speech which the chair makes.

However, there is a need for caution here, too. The chair's address makes an argument, offers evidence and anecdotal detail, but it does not invoke or seek to address counter-arguments. Its rhetorical devices, mode of language and structural organisation are intended to impassion as much as to persuade logically. Like a sermon, a lawyer's jury address or a political speech, it has a structure which addresses but also shapes and determines the thoughts and perspectives of the audience. There is a suggestion here of the cautionary note which Kristeva sounded in relation to political commitment: 'any political commitment . . . settles the subject within a socially justified illusion'.[29]

Eunice's attitude to the lower classes is similar to that of Glyn Jones's Wynn, not only in its negativity but the way in which they both fail to recognise their own judgementalism. To borrow a concept from Kristeva's psychoanalytic discussion of identity, Eunice's judgementalism serves as a barrier against the disintegration of her identity. In other words, her definition of others creates boundaries which keep her own sense of self intact. Eunice tells herself, and Vincent, that she hates the lower classes because they are 'low common things'. Her hatred is projected on to others, as the Nazi stereotyping of Jews in the 1930s, until seeing only 'ugly habits, coarse talk, sordidness', she no longer sees individual people but loathsome 'types'. In the final analysis there is little distinction between her day-to-day contact with the lower classes and Nazi contact with Jews: 'she shrank from the vulgar boys, the sluttish girls, and rough adults' (EF, p. 73). However, as in Nazi Germany, what she does as an individual is what society does collectively, as is evident in the way in which Vincent is shunned as a conscientious objector: 'Her family's disapproval spread to friends, and finally to strangers. The hints became taunts and the silences vocal with threats' (p. 75). Here the prejudice against conscientious objectors, like all forms of prejudice, develops and spreads because it is based in a community. But once it has spread, it determines the nature of a community so that hatred of pacifists and conscientious objectors becomes one of the things that define the community and the community becomes more confident in the legitimacy of its prejudice.

However, as Donahaye points out, an important event in the novel is the transformation of Eunice's life when she meets George Furnall, a former member of the No-Conscription Fellowship who had known Vincent. Through him, and his work for peace, she hopes to 'begin to make up for her failure to support Vincent, whose ideals belatedly, she has come to understand and to share'.[30] Her relationship with George Furnall initially reinvigorates her and enables her to enjoy what London in the 1930s had to offer, and what had provided a barrier to her past with Vincent which she was refusing to face up to. But she also comes to see middle-class London for what it is. As Donahaye says, Tobias's depiction of London stands out for the amount of 'accurate detail and closely observed dialogue, which is peppered with the new expressions and idioms of the day'.[31] However, what the reader experiences here is not simply Tobias's London but Eunice's city. While Eunice engages with 1930s London, she comes to understand the attitudes behind the new expressions and idioms.

Eunice finds herself a witness not only to how modernity is bound to technology but how sensibility itself is changed by technology. An important moment of transformation for Eunice occurs at a theatre when she comes to realise that sensibility has become so changed by technology that our own technological destruction becomes an aesthetic experience. There, she is shocked by the response of the audience to *Journey's End*, a play by R. C. Sherriff, first performed in the Apollo Theatre, London, and made into a film, directed by James Whale, in 1930. It is set in an officers' dug-out over four days from 18 to 21 March, 1918 during the run-up to Operation Michael, a major German military offensive. Eunice finds that 'the scenes of trench warfare, its filth and degradation, its pity and terror, drawn with quiet art and conveyed with realism in a single dug-out, beat on her sense with a retributive force'. She observes how she sat 'as if in a spell, unable to smile, while the "comic relief" drew vociferous acclaim in the crowded theatre. "How can they laugh?" she murmured to Furnall' (EF, p. 46).

STRUCTURES OF DISCOURSE

But for all the attention paid to Eunice's sensibility, the novel revolves around how Vincent thinks differently from Eunice in ways which reflect Welsh pacifists such as George Davies. Vincent, like George Davies, sees others such as soldiers and prison guards, as being caught up in a system of which they are not fully aware. He tells Eunice that she is 'absolutely right to hate filth and poverty but don't you see – it isn't human beings you can't bear – it's the dirt they're cased in' (EF, p. 74). This is important to an understanding of Welsh pacifism at the time the novel was written because it suggests how Welsh pacifism, as is evident from George Davies's work, developed into a social gospel based on the deconstruction of social systems. In the 1930s, pacifism shifted its emphasis from anti-war-ism to arguing against systems which create, and are in turn determined by, militarism. In this respect, Vincent sets out a case for seeing the enemy as ordinary people who are caught up in a system; this is similar to Humphreys's arguments underpinning *A Toy Epic*. He argues that most of the Germans 'are not doing what they like – wretched conscripts! – only what they are forced or deceived into doing' (EF, p. 76).

The white feather which Vincent is handed signifies how members of a community can ostracise those of whom they disapprove because they believe they have been given the right to do so by the wider community. But in developing this incident, Tobias shifts the focus, innovatively, from the recipient to the recipient's partner, who, not sharing their pacifist beliefs, is 'shamed'. In doing so, the novel questions what is meant by shame and disgrace. In Eunice's case, it involves the internalisation of the prejudice of others. The irony which she does not appreciate is that how others now see her, or she thinks they see her, is similar to how she sees others, like pacifists, conscientious objectors and the lower classes. She has turned others, as she is now being turned, from a subject in their own life narrative to an object in someone else's. Unlike Vincent, whose sense of self is rooted in his carefully thought-out principles, Eunice's identity is based on the values and opinions of the middle-class society to which she tries to belong.

Vincent brings Eunice into contact with what she had hitherto avoided. When he tries to explain to her what will happen to him once he has been arrested, she can only repeat the single words that grab her attention: 'A policeman?' and 'Prison' (EF, p. 104). When she attempts a more cohesive response, she garbles ideas that are not clear in her mind: 'And I'm not sure that physical cowardice is a "frightful disgrace" – it's a disability, rather: But *moral* cowardice – that's another thing' (EF, p. 76). Confronted with Vincent's impending imprisonment, she regresses into a pre-linguistic state of being: 'she wanted suddenly to beat against him – to clamour, to rend. But her hand lay helpless, her tongue mute . . . The melting oil soaked back in her flesh, blotting her fibres – nauseous, clogging. She couldn't fight: she was devitalised' (EF, p. 105).

The inability to argue, to use words effectively and construct sentences are exposed in the novel as the disadvantage many ordinary pacifists faced at their tribunals. By contrast, the tribunal members who sit in judgement on them appear incisive and eloquent. But Vincent's ability to argue and defend himself exposes the inadequacy of the bench, intellectually and linguistically, as a Chair reveals:

'That's all tommyrot. We have to get on with the war now we're in it, and our brave fellows fighting to keep the Huns out' (EF, p. 95). Vincent argues eloquently that he is not able to participate in the war in any way, but his case does not impress a bench locked into its own prejudices. He is imprisoned, tortured and, at one point, threatened with death by firing squad for refusing to comply with a military order. What happens to Vincent is not summarised in any single phrase or sentence in the novel, but in the image of him in prison which haunts Eunice: 'her mind obsessed by Vincent, by pictures of his prison solitude, the torment of his pale, pleading face, strained in anguish to catch her withheld word, would seize upon her suddenly' (EF, p. 167). In describing the sufferings of conscientious objectors, *Eunice Fleet* and *Plasau'r Brenin* contribute to our understanding of Welsh pacifism. In doing so, they produce innovatively structured narratives in which conventional authoritative arguments are challenged and displaced by a radical, if in some respects pessimistic, pacifist discourse.

PEACE AND PEACEFULNESS

4

The Spirit of Pacifism: Waldo Williams and D. Gwenallt Jones

> The universal does not attract us until housed in an individual.
> (Ralph Waldo Emerson, 'The Method of Nature')

That these two Welsh-language pacifist poets, each of whom served prison terms for their beliefs, are known by their bardic names is a testimony to their contribution to the Welsh language and Welsh culture. They share an ambition to relink their own lives, and twentieth-century Welsh life in general, to a fuller realisation of the spiritual potential of the individual, pacifist values and the importance of 'community'. Their work demonstrates how pacifism is not only an anti-war movement but is concerned with alternative ways of living and of social organisation. In this regard, their work is a development from the writings of George Davies, whose direct, or indirect, influence can be detected in key aspects of their poetry. But, as was suggested in Chapter 1, their work combines a focus on external harmony, respect for others and alternative social systems, with an orientation towards personal virtues and inner qualities.

ORIGINS

The roots of Welsh pacifism in the rural communities of west Wales is important to Waldo's *Dail Pren* (1956), one of the most important twentieth-century collections of Welsh-language poetry and the only one which Waldo published.[1] One of its recurring themes is that of an adult reclaiming the wonder he enjoyed as a child, and a sense of wonder clearly became a cornerstone of what the Welsh-language poet and translator Anthony Conran has described as Waldo's 'confident spiritual message' (WW, p. 22).

A notable poem in this respect is 'Preseli', a response to the War Office's plan to take over Preseli and increase its holdings to 16,000 acres, which involved the total requisition of 105 farms and the loss of the village of Mynachlog-Ddu (WW, pp. 31–2). Its subject is how the working countryside of Preseli provided Waldo with the perspective on life that came to mean so much to him as an adult: 'Hon oedd fy ffenestr, y cynaeafu a'r cneifio' (This was my window, the harvest and the shearing) (DP, p. 20; WW, p. 114). Through the window in 'Preseli' he believed that he experienced true 'wonder' for the first time, inspired not only by nature but also by the rural community and the traditional skills practised by those who lived and worked there.

As one of the most insightful Waldo scholars, Alan Llwyd maintains that Waldo's father did much to develop his son's spiritual insights into a philosophy, noting how it was from him 'that Waldo inherited the principle of brotherhood'.[2] He wrote to his son just before his baptism: 'The Highest Religion I have had glimpses of is that which makes man a brother, Life a Sanctuary and the common deeds of life sacred by purity of motive.'[3] Here we see the origins of what was to become one of the distinctive hallmarks of Welsh pacifism which was further inspired by his reading in the influential English socialist poet and philosopher Edward Carpenter (1844–1929) who 'believed that man should keep in close contact with the earth, live in harmony with the earth, in fact, and man should also live in harmony with his fellow-men'.[4]

While Waldo's poetry would probably never have been written without those original insights at Preseli, it can also be seen as a development of the sense of wonder in nature which pervades early twentieth-century Welsh-language poetry more generally. A notable example of this type of writing is R. Williams Parry's poem 'Yr Haf' (The Summer), which won the Crown at the Colwyn Bay Eisteddfod in 1910. Idris Bell described it in a way which anticipates Waldo's work, 'instinct with imagination and suffused with a kind of shimmering sensuous beauty which contrasts strikingly with the average *awdl* of the nineteenth century'.[5] But Parry's poem, focused on the transitoriness of summer, anticipates Waldo's work also in its allusions to the wider anxiety of the early twentieth century and the sense of impermanence in the order of things which characterised this period. Within its post-world war context, the full collection of poems in which 'Yr Haf' was eventually published, *Yr Haf a Cherddi Eraill* (The Summer and Other Poems) (1924), anticipates not only Waldo's appreciation of nature but a sense of the interconnection of all forms of life. A key achievement of this collection, as Bell says, is that Parry 'portrays the creatures of the wild not with the condescension of a human observer looking at them from outside but as if he had himself shared in their life'.[6]

Seeing themselves as sharing their lives with everything around them, including the non-human, Waldo and Gwenallt develop a kind of Christian animism. That said, it must be noted that there is a strain in Parry's poetry which occurs more overtly in Gwenallt's work than Waldo's. It involves looking beyond the specificity of the countryside to the interplay of what Bell describes as 'natural forces, the wind in the telegraph wires, the sunshine on the hillside, the mountain solitudes'.[7] Much of Gwenallt's poetry puts greater emphasis than Waldo's work on a transcendental reality that is embodied in but beyond individuality, subjectivity and the particular. By contrast, Waldo's poetry is much more rooted in the tripartite themes of nature, community and rural life. Waldo strove to redefine human activities from the perspective of a conscious link between humankind, nature and the divine, positing that the kind of rural communities he knew in west Wales were most capable of realising the ideal of the 'integral life' he sought. His work revolves around the spheres of creativity, spirituality and practical activity.

Trying to recapture the different levels of wonder he experienced through his window, Waldo describes the skills that he witnessed: 'Pedair gwanaf o'r ceirch yn cwympo i'w cais, / Ac un cwrs cyflym' (Four swathes of oats felled at each sweep / On the one swift way) (DP, p. 20; WW, p. 114). The poem integrates movement in the landscape with the moments of stillness which are necessary to grasp the full meaning in the scene. The varying but close pattern of sound in the Welsh – 'cei', 'cwy', 'cai', 'cwrs', 'cyf' – and the clipped effect of the line capture not only the speed of the activity but the child's wonder at the men's adroitness. Recapturing this sense of awe, the poem links these hereditary skills to a sense of fraternity and a way of living which for Waldo is an alternative to a world dominated by commerce, profit and militarism. Llwyd points out that 'a key word in Waldo's poetry is "elw", meaning "profit" as a "destructive force"'. Developing this argument, Llwyd notes that 'elw' is often juxtaposed in Waldo's work with 'awen', which, Llwyd explains, means 'the inspiring force which binds mankind together, as opposed to "elw", which always creates havoc and disorder, and drives men [*sic*] apart'.[8]

The harvesting and shearing in 'Preseli' bring people together as a community which recognises each other's worth individually and collectively. As Rowan Williams says, 'what comes first in the universe is connectedness – recognition'.[9] Llwyd explains that for Waldo, 'agricultural work . . . would draw a whole neighbourhood together and create intimacy between the various members of the community, and this intimacy and pulling together created a natural, practical brotherhood between men'.[10] David Cadman develops this kind of argument in ways which are important to appreciating both Waldo's and Gwenallt's work, stressing the importance of the symbiotic relationship between community and peace: 'If living systems are always precarious and self-contradictory, there is a necessary co-existence between individuals and the community and an essential reciprocity between them.'[11] This is encapsulated in key phrases in 'Preseli' such as 'ar aelwydydd fy mhobl' (on the hearths of my people) and, particularly, 'a bro brawdoliaeth' (brotherhood's country') (DP, p. 20; WW, p. 114). The importance of a 'fully personalized social order' is a key thesis in Charles Raven's pamphlet *The Starting Point of Pacifism* (1940), which describes small communities in ways very similar to Waldo's poetry: 'a community, the members of which have attained an organic solidarity one with another, and are "one heart and soul", finds itself fully possessed of a dynamic capacity literally unlimited in its possibilities'.[12]

This perspective can be placed within a larger framework not only in literature but also in late nineteenth-century English and European art where it is part of a wider, positive revisioning of rural life and the organic relationship between nature and humankind to be found there. The art critic and historian Kenneth McConkey draws attention to paintings such as Henry Herbert La Thange's *The Last Furrow* (1895) that celebrate what is clearly perceived as the healthy vigour of rural work.[13] To an extent, it is this altered attitude to life in the countryside from the mid-1890s onwards which can be seen in the Welsh poets of the first half of the twentieth century. But in Welsh-language poetry, this perspective is more politicised. Ned Thomas points out that poets such as Waldo and Gwenallt might stand accused of idealising small rural communities; they do not mention 'rural poverty, damp cottages, the puritanical repression, the deaths from tuberculosis'.[14] But he argues that such an approach overlooks the value of the 'remarkable collection of small, politically radical, religiously cultured communities' and their 'image of a really human society'.[15] This becomes an important perspective in the context of the social dislocation brought about by agricultural change and industrialisation in, for example, south-west Wales, which resulted in an extraordinarily high rate of suicide among people in their middle years.[16] Reclaiming a sense of a 'really human society' became an important motif in the work of Welsh pacifist writers and Welsh writers interested in privileging peace over war, as in W. J. Gruffydd's *Hen Atgofion* and D. Parry-Jones's *Welsh Country Characters*.[17]

How rural west Wales was depicted in Welsh-language writing as 'small, politically radical, religiously cultured communities' and/or as a 'really human society' was very different from the way in which it was represented in nineteenth- and early twentieth-century English literature from English publishers and intended for an English readership. For example, in S. Baring-Gould's historical romance *In Dewisland* (1904), set at the time of the Rebecca Riots in 1839–43 (protests by local farmers and agricultural workers against, among other things, tolls charged to use the roads), rural Carmarthenshire and Pembrokeshire are depicted in dark, almost Gothic terms as beyond 'civilisation': 'the great promontory of South Wales, that is thrust into the ocean . . . the sky bending sullenly over it with a scowl . . . [into] which the finger of God has not been thrust to divide the light from the darkness'.[18]

In writing that brings together cultural memories from his archival research and his own memories, T. Gwynn Jones, in the 1920s, argued that the cultured and neighbourly nature of Welsh rural communities was one of the distinctive characteristics of Welsh life. While allowance must be made for Jones's tendency to over-idealise Welsh society and the fact that he is writing for the peace movement Urdd y Deyrnas, it is clear that he came to believe that Welsh pacifism had roots in rural Wales where he found that a 'generosity and hospitality were practised to an extraordinary degree amongst all classes'[19] and, like Waldo and Gwenallt, discovered 'an atmosphere . . . artistic and the conversation intellectual'.[20] All three possessed pacifist convictions which had their origins to some extent in this kind of romanticism, even though Waldo and Gwenallt seem closer to rural community as something actually lived on a daily basis. No wonder then that Preseli, as Llwyd says, 'came to be regarded by Waldo as a microcosm of a perfect world, a world-wide community in which all mankind lived as one enmeshed in brotherhood'.[21] As we have seen, this is an idea that is important in Welsh pacifist pamphlets and essays. In some of George M. Ll. Davies's work, such as his essay, 'Est nihil vobis, O viatores omnes?', written shortly after the outbreak of the First World War, this leads occasionally to an over-romanticising of rural life but, as Ned Thomas argued, not one that should distract from the sense of a 'really human society': 'Felt it all – the gladness of the morning, the labourers coming forth into the fields, the sweetness of human life and affection, the beauty of the wide undulating landscape – pulse into my heart a great joyous optimism.'[22]

Given the significance of small, rural Welsh communities for Waldo, it is important to note, as Siwan Richards has pointed out, how the principal spiritual concepts in Waldo's poetry are integrated through recurring key words referring to family, home, brotherhood and community such as 'brawdoliaeth', 'teulu', 'tŷ', 'adnabod' 'goleuni' and 'awen'.[23] Developing Ned Thomas's argument that one of the subtleties of Waldo's poetry is the way in which it employs linguistic strategies in order to pull people together, the Welsh-language writer and academic Jason Walford Davies maintains that these include the use of words with the prefix 'cyd' or variations of it such as 'cymod', 'cymdeithas', 'cyfannu', 'cyfannwr', 'cyfeillach', 'cymdogaeth' and 'cydymdeimlad'.[24] But he goes on to suggest that the subtlety of Waldo's Welsh also lies in the way in which he put his personal stamp on popular idioms through his inventive use of prepositions, as in the idiom 'fel haul haf' in 'Cwmwl Haf', interlinking key ideas with old, small words from the language.[25] But it is Ned Thomas who provides a key link between Waldo's Welsh and his social outlook, arguing that Waldo's small communities bring 'people together for necessary social organisation without turning them into a mass huddled in the shadow of all-powerful institutions'.[26]

The emphasis upon small Welsh communities in Waldo's poetry is politically important given the direction that government thinking about rural Wales took in the late 1920s and early 1930s. Waldo, and also Gwenallt, valued their significance in terms of 'brawdoliaeth', their sense of belonging and their importance in preserving the Welsh language and Welsh cultural roots. *The Welsh Outlook* in 1930 suggested that this was threatened by the emergence of a more commercial and economically motivated approach to farming. The small Welsh farming communities were seen as 'problems' caused by the want of capital; the uneconomic division of the land; the unwillingness on the part of many farmers to eschew traditional methods of agriculture and trading; and a lack of education, including technical knowledge, in the agricultural industry generally.[27] While Waldo saw the small, rural communities as providing an alternative to the capitalism which many pacifists like himself believed generated war, this new mode of thought saw Wales as a 'unit' within the UK contributing 'their due share to the life and prosperity of the nation'.[28] It struck at the heart of pacifist thinking by stressing that 'somehow or another the farmer's own attitude of mind must be changed'.[29]

MORE THAN ONE FIELD

While the spiritual heart of Waldo's poetry is the concept of 'brawdoliaeth', responsible for the subtlety of much of his writing, its drama sometimes lies elsewhere. The assertiveness, and even at times the violence of his poetry, reflect the forcefulness of its engagement with pacifism and anti-war-ism, as in the conclusion of 'Preseli' where the wall around his boyhood home is threatened: 'Cadwn y mur rhag y bwystfil, cadwn y ffynnon rhag y baw' (Keep the wall from the brute, keep the spring clear of filth) (DP, p. 20; WW, p. 114). But much of the drama of his poetry lies in the way in which he often positions himself, to borrow the title from another of his poems, 'Mewn Dau Gae' (In Two Fields).

Thus, 'Preseli' has a foot in the past and in the present, in boyhood and in adulthood, but also in peaceful, industrious communities and in war. Like a number of poems, including 'Mewn Dau Gae' itself, the way in which the countryside is described suggests war. Thus, in 'Preseli', specific words allude to the sights, noise and violence of war, such as 'Lle tasgodd y gwreichion sydd yn hŷn na harn' (Where the sparks flew that are older than iron); 'gelaets' (flag iris); 'ceirch yn cwympo'(oats felled); and 'Mae rhu . . . Mae rhaib' (There's a roar, there's a ravening) (DP, p. 20; WW, p. 114). In 'Mewn Dau Gae', there are references, for example, to 'y saethwr' (the marksman); 'yr eithin aeddfed' (crackle of gorse); 'ffoadur a phererin' (the fugitive pilgrims); 'O, trwy oesoedd y gwaed ar y gwellt' (ages of blood on the grass); 'goleuni y galar' (the light of grief); 'y dihangwr o'r byddinoedd' (escaper from the armies);

and 'cyrch picwerchi' (forayed with pitchforks) (DP, pp. 17–18; WW, pp. 133–4).

Subtle allusions to war in poems that are not specifically about war are a feature of Waldo's work which he developed in the late 1930s in poems such as 'Eirlysiau' (Snowdrops), one of Waldo's least discussed poems, and 'Y Tŵr a'r Graig' (The Tower and The Rock). 'Eirlysiau' is focused on snowdrops emerging ahead of the real warmth of spring. They suggest the young going to war, ahead of their time: 'For all their modesty, like steel / To bear blows . . .' (Er eu gwyleidd-dra fel y dur / I odde' cur). The poem asks, remembering perhaps the famous First World War Welsh-language recruiting poster referred to in Chapter 1, 'Are there braver than they?' (Mae dewrach 'rhain?) (WW, p. 153; DP, p. 41). The horror of war is suggested in the image of the shards of the flowers scattering 'like a myriad fires' (Pan elo'r rhannau ar wahân / Ail llawer tân fydd lliwiau'r tud) (WW, p. 153; DP, p. 41). But there is also a sense of light emerging from the darkness of the 'black earth' (y ddaear ddu) and of warmth reaching into the soil. Analogous to spiritual growth, the poem provides an alternative to the growing disillusionment of the inter-war years.

However, 'Mewn Dau Gae', one of Waldo's most sophisticated poems in the way in which it interweaves allusions to war, was written after the Second World War and is, in part, a response to the Korean War. Like 'Preseli', it looks back to a moment of epiphany in Waldo's life. Llwyd has worked out that the poem is rooted in a moment of revelation which he experienced at the age of fourteen, in the last year of the First World War.[30] Waldo remembers: 'tua deugain mlynedd yn ôl sylweddolais yn sydyn, ac yn fyw iawn, mewn amgylchiad personol tra phendant, fod dynion, yn gyntaf dim, yn frodyr i'w gilydd' (about forty years ago I suddenly and vividly realised, in a very personal manner, that men are, first and foremost, bound by brotherhood).[31] In a note to 'Mewn Dau Gae', he recalls that there was a gap between two fields, 'Weun Parc y Blawd' and 'Parc y Blawd'. The reference to two specific fields is important because it makes the memory all the more convincing.[32] But the poem is written both within two fields and between two fields, in that it attempts to recreate this moment of realisation as a 'new way', in which there is holistic synthesis rather than division. Rowan Williams translates a crucial phrase in 'Mewn Dau Gae' differently from Anthony Conran. Whereas Conran translates 'awen' as 'goodwill', Williams translates it as 'a new voice', implying a 'third way':[33]

A thrwyddynt, rhyngddynt, amdanynt ymdaenai
Awen yn codi o'r cudd, yn cydio'r cwbl,
Fel gyda ni'r ychydig pan fyddai'r cyrch picwerchi
Neu'r tynnu to deir draw ar y weun drom.
Mor agos at ei gilydd y deuem –
Yr oedd yr heliwr distaw yn bwrw ei rwyd amdanom. (DP, p. 17)

And on the two fields his people walked,
And through, and between, and about them, goodwill widened
And rose out of hiding, to make us all one,
As when the few of us forayed with pitchforks
Or from heavy meadows lugged thatching of rush,
How close we came then, one to another . . .
The quiet hunter so cast his net round us. (WW, p. 134)

Damian Walford Davies has discovered as many as eight published translations of this poem,[34] but recommends Rowan Williams's rendering of the poem as 'a creative negotiation or "free translation" rather than "a crib of the Welsh"'.[35] But this particular translation benefits from Rowan Williams's own pacifist inclinations and his profound appreciation of Waldo as a pacifist poet. This is evident in the fact that he alone translates 'saethwr' as 'marksman' while the other translations, as Damian Walford Davies has noted, have opted for 'archer' and 'bowman'.[36] The strength of the latter are that they bring to the fore the reputation which Welsh archers acquired in early medieval warfare. But the term 'marksman' brings the poem up to date, suggesting how the scope of pacifist thought has expanded in the twenty-first century to embrace terrorism and war on the streets. The word 'marksman' is a particularly potent signifier, a sign of how militaristic responses to violence have increasingly displaced other non-violent strategies.

However, it is important not to let this single word take the poem out of the contexts to which it refers. I say 'contexts' because, although the poem is based on an event which occurred at the time of the First World War, Damian Walford Davies stresses that it must also be considered in regard to global events at the time when it was written, over thirty years later. He reads the poem convincingly in relation to events in Cyprus, but especially, as mentioned earlier, in relation to the Korean War (1950–3), arguing that Waldo's 'philosophical anarchism and pacifism' drove 'the campaign he was waging throughout the 1950s against conscription, war, imperial possession and the superstate'.[37] Indeed, he describes 'Mewn Dau Gae' and the prose pieces,

'Brenhiniaeth a Brawdoliaeth' (Sovereignty and Brotherhood), which was initially delivered as an address to the Peace Society of the Welsh Baptist Union Conference, and 'Why I refused to pay the income tax', as a 'remarkable summer [1956] triptych of protest'.[38] However, it is important not to overlook the fact that Williams's concerns over the destruction of the Korean countryside and the division of the country bring to mind the destruction of Japanese cities by atomic bombs and the division of Germany. The effectiveness of 'Brenhiniaeth a Brawdoliaeth' lies in the way it conflates the atomic bombing of Japan with the bombing of Korea:

> People's homes were burnt, others were forced from their homes, and according to one report they were burnt together alive, by being driven into a barn and the barn set alight. In other places correspondents saw people whose skin had been burnt on their faces, and on the greater part of their bodies, as a result of the napalm . . .[39]

But equally important to 'Mewn Dau Gae' are themes and concerns from the essays of Iorwerth Peate and George Davies written in the 1940s which, as we have seen, also regard with suspicion the increasing importance attached to the authority of the state, state hierarchies and the superstate. This is a key theme in Waldo's 'Y Tŵr a'r Graig' (The Tower and the Rock) in which, as Nicholas says, 'the Tower stands for State oppression, the Rock for the refuge of the "gwerin", the ordinary folk who inevitably lose their freedom which leads to suffering under oppression'.[40] In 'Y Tŵr a'r Graig', 'Mewn Dau Gae' and 'Brenhiniaeth a Brawdoliaeth', Waldo looks forward, as did Peate and Davies, to an alternative social system based on smaller units and the significance of the individual.

At the heart of 'Mewn Dau Gae', like 'Preseli', is the adult poet's quest to understand a far-off experience from his childhood in this respect. Waldo comes to believe that a single moment in his childhood caused him to see farm work and the rural community differently, as the heart of an alternative lifestyle based upon peace and upon close, neighbourly relationships between people. Immediately after the acknowledgement of the heaviness of farm labour, the rhythm and syllabic construction of the line changes, to convey one of Waldo's most important spiritual convictions: 'Mor agos at ei gilydd y deuem'. In their respective but different translations, Conran and Williams try to capture the meaning of this conviction for the poet and, ultimately, his pacifism: 'How close we came then, one to another —' (WW, p. 134) and 'So near / we came then to each other.'[41] Rowan Williams tries to capture the emotional effect of the Welsh by repeating 'Mor agos' which he translates as 'So near' while Conran, trying to keep as close as possible to the rhythm of Waldo's line, translates 'Mor agos' slightly differently to suggest an even greater sense of intimacy by using the word 'close' rather than 'near'.

ADNABOD

The spiritual sentiment of 'Mewn Dau Gae' is developed in a number of key poems in *Dail Pren*, particularly 'Adnabod' and 'Brawdoliaeth'. As Llwyd explains:

> the exact meaning of 'adnabod' is difficult to convey. 'Adnabod' means 'to know', 'to recognise', and the closest translation of the word, and of Waldo's usage of it, would be 'to know someone intimately', and it is this kind of knowing that binds men [*sic*] together in brotherhood and love.[42]

The origin of the concept of 'adnabod' in Waldo's poetry is difficult to determine because of his knowledge of authors who influenced each other. His reading in Emerson, and possibly even in Whitman whom Emerson influenced, was undoubtedly significant, but there were contemporaneous pacificist influences too. Waldo's concept of 'adnabod' mirrors the first Peace Pledge Union affirmation, published in all its 'Bond of Peace' pamphlets, 'attaching supreme value to the human person and the integrity of the individual'. In his PPU pamphlet, Charles Raven argues that 'the human way, the way of persons, is to be our way, the human way by which man can recover his integrity as body and spirit'.[43] Whereas George Davies stressed the importance of the individual's personal relationship with God and developed a concept of personalism based on the gospels, Waldo puts more emphasis on individuality within a communal solidarity. Personal reflection was important to both Davies and Waldo but whereas Davies's sermon-inspired essays emphasise exegesis and interpretation, Waldo's poetry explores experience as a means to spiritual insight and an inner peacefulness.

The poem 'Adnabod', as its title suggests, is an exploration of the concept which is the crux of Waldo's 'personalism'. Conran translates the Welsh as 'acknowledge' (WW, p. 109). But, as so often,

Waldo has an eye on more than one perspective, in this case the interconnectedness of all things. Those whose lives are impelled by this concept stand in contradistinction to those who, in Conran's translation, 'dissect and sever' and let the world 'slip through their fingers' (WW, p. 109) (Rhag y rhemp sydd i law'r dadelfennwr / A gyll, rhwng ei fysedd, fyd) (DP, p. 50). The poem opposes the 'dissector' (y dadelfennwr) with the 'hen gyfannwr'. The latter is a difficult phrase to translate; Conran suggests the slightly awkward 'old wholeness-bringer' (WW, p. 25).

The poem seeks to give voice to what it calls the 'imagination of a saint' (dychymyg y sant) that transcends binarism and hierarchy: 'Sydd â'i naws yn cofleidio'r yrfa (the moment of light / That embraces the way we pass) (DP, pp. 50–1; WW, p. 111). The poem's rhythm, metre and repetition have an energy that emerges from, and encapsulates, this sense of wholeness, culminating in the repetition of 'Ti yw'r' (you're) in the penultimate and the last verse, where the alternate rhyme acquires a drum beat: 'ddoedd, ap, lau, rfa'. Through its rising rhythm, beat and repetition, the poem, like the imagination which it celebrates, binds everything together, enabling the reader to become a participant in its energy.

'Brawdoliaeth' (Brotherhood) develops the concept of 'adnabod' in a different way from the poem 'Adnabod', utilising the rhythm and pace of a sermon rather than a song. It has the drama, assertiveness and challenge which we might associate with the Welsh preachers, opening with a theological and philosophical concept which is gradually developed: 'Mae rhwydwaith dirgel Duw / Yn cydio pob dyn byw' (Each man alive is knit / Within God's secret net) (DP, p. 66; WW, p. 89). The Welsh has more impact than this English translation, opening powerfully with the image of God's clandestine net and suggesting, through the language and rhythm of the second line, how all living things are linked by life itself. The poem unfurls the image of the net, 'rhwydwaith', stressing how we are all held together, through a phrase 'Myfi, Tydi, Efe' (Of I, Thou, He) which is repeated in the third verse. The assertiveness of this conviction which underpins Waldo's pacifism drives the poem, unequivocally speaking up for a united world, until the impact of the last line in which violence destroys the unity and sense of 'brotherhood' expounded throughout the poem: 'Pa werth na thry yn wawd / Pan laddo dyn ei frawd' (What value ends up other / Than mockery, when a man kills his brother) (DP, p. 66; WW, p. 90). The poem takes the reader back to its beginning and the opening image of a life that is shared by all, now undone in the allusion to the brothers Cain and Abel at war with each other.

HOPE AND DOUBT

There are two dimensions to Waldo's poetry: on the one hand, there is its positive vision and, on the other, bouts of doubt. While Waldo's vision is one of the most admired features of his poetry, there are times when the level of doubt becomes stronger, evident in the image at the end of 'Preseli' of 'fforest ddiffenestr' (windowless forests). There is a fine line, too, between confidence and doubt at the end of 'Mewn Dau Gae' in the phrase 'Diau y daw'r dirháu' (Surely these things must come) (DP, p. 18; WW, pp. 135). It is a suggestion of doubt which the following question underlines, 'a pha awr yw hi / Y daw'r herwr' (What hour will it be / That the outlaw comes) (DP, p. 18; WW, p. 135).

At one level, the drama within 'Mewn Dau Gae' stems from the tension between the sense of a 'troubled self' (helbul hunan), and a wider sense of calm and stillness (o'r hollfyd weithiau i'r tawelwch). Key poems written after *Dail Pren*, such as 'Llandysilio yn Nyfed' (Landysilio in Dyfed), pursue this dichotomy in a very tight and disciplined way, exemplified in this poem by the choice of the sonnet form. It is a poem which can be read on many levels. It is an anti-war poem but also a 'religious' poem in the sense of 'relinking' with the interconnectedness of things. It begins with the word, 'mynych' (often),[44] and as in 'Preseli' and 'Mewn Dau Gae', the poet tries to reclaim the wonder he felt as a child and now understands more fully. The poet is in two worlds: that of a child in the present of the poem, as part of the community waiting at Tysilio's church for the New Year bells to ring out hope for the future, and that of the adult poet looking back. But the poem occupies more than one world in another sense as well. There is the world of the small village in which the boy is living and experiencing his sense of wonder and the wider world in which the village is situated: 'When life for us was brutal, full of wrong, / Made great by neither purpose nor ideal?' (WW, p. 179) (Pan oedd ein byw yn farus ac yn frwnt / Heb fawr o'i fryd na'i ddelfryd ar ein clai?[45]) The poem is aware of two types of society, the village and the larger commercial world: 'We'd see small companies, / Without exploit of cities, yoke the world one / And among them, salvation clear' (WW, p. 179) (Gwelem y fintai fach / Heb ddinas camp yn ieuo'r byd yn un, / Ac yn eu plith gwelem yn glaerwyn iach [46]). In making reference to

Tysilio, the poem invokes a third level of time and space, taking us back to the Age of the Saints in the sixth century CE when Wales became a Christian country and Tysilio, a Lord of Powys, chose the monastic life and small communities. In addition to the First World War, the poem alludes to the collapse of the Roman empire although there is no suggestion in the poem that it was its demise that brought about cruelty and barbarity. As mentioned in Chapter 1, many pacifist writers and scholars were sceptical of Pax Romana and thought of it as no different in many respects from what followed and preceded it. George Davies, for example, pointed out that the Romans were responsible for the executions of Christ and St. Paul as criminals under Roman law and, more generally, drew attention to their 'ruthless oppression' (RQP, p. 6).

Waldo's evident admiration of Tysilio reflects the attention given to early saints and monks in pacifist religious writing. George Davies reminds readers that 'the early Franciscans . . . consciously and deliberately accepted a minority and subordinate position in society, with poverty and personal disarmament as the condition of their proclamation of peace upon earth through goodwill between men' (RQP, p. 6). A key image in Waldo's poem is 'yoke the world one' (yn ieuo'r byd yn un) for it tries to supplant the linearity of time and the distinction of past, present and future by the sense of timelessness that comes with inner peacefulness. The boy Waldo, who is in the poem's present and past, also signifies the kind of future into which the adult poet hopes the world will develop. Like many of Waldo's poems, it has a binary structure – drawn sword/sheathed sword, Lordship/exile, monastery/community, brutality/ideal, darkness/light – which represents the duality which the poem seeks to transcend.

The binary of war and peace is particularly important in 'Y Tangnefeddwyr' (The Peacemakers). The poem begins with a recollection of the blitz over Swansea, which occurred in February 1941 and left at least 230 people dead and over twice that number injured: 'Uwch yr eira, wybren ros, / Lle mae Abertawe'n fflam' (Rose-red sky above the snow / Where bombed Swansea is alight) (DP, p. 31; WW, p. 91). This is compared with memories of his parents, who are 'the peacemakers', and the home in which he was brought up. There, as Nicholas says, 'he learnt sympathy, consideration and compassion for others from his parents' but also, from his father, 'the cornerstone of his philosophy of life' that 'man's mission is to be a brother' (Cennad dyn yw bod yn frawd).[47] Before a Conscientious Objector Tribunal at

Carmarthen in February 1942, Waldo declared: 'I consider all soldiering to be wrong; for it places other obligations before a man's first duty to his brother, a brother he cannot regard as a cipher to be wiped off the other side.'[48]

ABSOLUTE PACIFISM

Whatever the differences between their work, Waldo's declaration encapsulates the absolute pacifism which unites his poetry with that of D. Gwenallt Jones. Although both Gwenallt and Waldo experienced imprisonment for their beliefs, Waldo was imprisoned late in his life, while Gwenallt, like George Davies, was imprisoned during the First World War as a conscientious objector. Gwenallt's 'Cymru a'r Rhyfel' (Wales and the War), which recalls his forefathers, becomes a rallying cry as much against English responsibility for the war as the war itself:

> Fe awn er dy fwyn yn ferthyron y tu ôl i farrau'r carchardy,
> A disgyn i hanner tywyllwch di-fwyd, diddiod y daeardy;
> Ac fe gawn sgwrs â gwallgofrwydd, yr unig ffrind yn y celloedd,
> Ac ysgwyd llaw â marwolaeth a'i dilyn i un o'i stafelloedd.[49]
>
> We will for thy sake become martyrs behind the bars of the prison,
> Go down to the subterranean foodless and drinkless darkness,
> We will hold discourse with madness, the only friend of the captive,
> And taking death by the hand, will follow to one of his chambers.[50]

'Dartmoor', in the same collection, extends the meaning and significance of being 'tu ôl i farrau'r carchardy'(behind prison bars). Beginning, 'daw eilwaith farrau heyrn ar draws ein trem' (Once again iron bars fall across our sight), it conflates physical and psychic imprisonment as in his novel, *Plasau'r Brenin* (GCC, p. 132; WP, p. 251). References to the actual prison – for example, hearing keys turning in double-locked doors and the murmuring of prisoners at their enforced labour – lead to the use of crime and prison metaphors to describe the weather beyond the bars such as 'hau niwloedd creimllyd' (criminal, warped fogs) (GCC, p. 132; WP, p. 251). In doing so, the poem suggest that it is difficult to separate the external from the internal prison while the weather imprisons the moor and the prison. The second section of the sonnet frees the imagination through its invocation of fiends, hobgoblins, ghosts and sprites while suggesting that they are as much a part of rural life as the more solid working with hay and corn, questioning whether such folklore frees or, in a different way, imprisons the imagination.

The introduction of mythic beings from folklore into a poem which opens with the poet-narrator looking through iron bars makes a profounder point to a readership familiar with Welsh folklore. Iron acquired a special value in both world wars and especially the Second World War when all forms of non-essential ironwork were dismantled and recycled. But iron has a special significance in Welsh folklore concerning the Tylwyth Teg where it is associated with invasion and the imposition of an alien culture on another. W. J. Gruffydd points out that Owen Edwards suggested that the Tylwyth Teg were the 'dreamy and artistic' original inhabitants of Wales before the 'practical hard-headed' and 'iron-using Celtic invaders became the dominant race'.[51] Moreover, one of the characteristics of the Tylwyth Teg was 'their deeprooted objection of the green sward being broken up by the plough' which assumes additional significance in the light of the many objections by Welsh pacifists to the Welsh grasslands of south-west Wales being ploughed up to serve the war effort.

Like Waldo's work, Gwenallt's poetry has its feet under more than one table, for example modern and medieval Wales; contemporary Welsh issues, such as the status of the Welsh language; Welsh romance (under the influence of T. Gwynn Jones to whom he wrote a tribute (GCC, pp. 155–8)); Welsh Nonconformity and Anglo-Catholicism; the realities and despair of war; hope and salvation arising from his Christianity; and, to a lesser extent, Marxism-inspired communism. As Densil Morgan points out, his writing from the 1930s is typical of British poetry of the time in its concerns with mechanisation, unemployment and political turmoil.[52] In the course of Gwenallt's life, modernity began a journey which at the end of the century resulted in 'an atomized, individualistic post-modernism in which transcendence has disappeared and the only values are transitory'.[53] In this respect, Gwenallt's work is distinctly Welsh in that as much as Gwenallt saw of the growth of twentieth-century modernity and postmodernity is viewed through the lens of a small nation shaped spiritually by long and still active cultural and faith traditions.[54] Thus, in *Ysgubau'r Awen* (1939), as in later collections such as *Gwreiddiau* (Roots) (1959), 'spiritual experience, theological conviction, poetic sensibility and the dreadful consciousness of God's holiness meet'.[55] His work is also distinctively Welsh in the way in which it is rooted in events from his family's past; in Welsh historical events, myths, locations and archaeology; and in concern with the survival of the Welsh language.

In this regard, 'Rhydcymerau', published in *Eples* (Leaven) (1951), is a significant poem, dependent upon contrast, unexpected juxtaposition and a complex time structure. The first contrast is between the anonymous, authoritative third-person pronoun at the outset of the poem – 'Plannwyd egin coed y Trydydd Rhyfel' (They have planted the saplings / to be trees of the third war) (GCC, p. 148; WP, p. 254) – and a particular Welsh community near Rhydcymerau, on the land of Esgeir-ceir and the fields of Tir-bach, which we learn later in the poem used to be farmed by the poet-narrator's uncle Dafydd. An important difference between the Welsh poem and Conran's English translation is that Conran's version introduces the saplings in the third line of the poem, while the Welsh poem itself introduces them much more emphatically in the first line. Moreover, in the Welsh version, the identification of the land and the fields come before the wider location of 'ger Rhydcymerau' (near Rhydcymerau) which stresses the particular identity of the farm fields that have been ploughed and planted with trees.

In linking the planting of saplings with the prospect of a third world war, the poem projects the reader into an ominous future. It then looks backward to the time of the poet-narrator's grandparents. Here the poem contrasts two types of memory: the poet-narrator's personal memory of his grandmother and the familial memories of his grandfather whom he never knew. The discussion of both of them suggests how overlapping generations bring into the present of the new generation the influence of previous centuries. The poet-narrator's grandmother is associated with nineteenth-century puritan Wales while the grandfather seemed as if he'd just strayed in from the eighteenth century ('Crwydryn o'r ddeunawfed ganrif ydoedd ef') (GCC, p. 148; WP, p. 254). The lines describing the difference in their characters in the Welsh text are much more carefully balanced than in Conran's translation, and the balance establishes a more emphatic contrast between them. Thus, the line describing the puritan nature of the grandmother reads: 'Darn o Gymru Biwritanaidd y ganrif ddiwethaf ydoedd hi' (A bit of the puritan Wales she was of last century) (GCC, p. 148; WP, p. 254). In this stanza, the poem introduces a traditional Welsh community based on the Welsh language (the grandmother speaks 'Cymraeg Pantycelyn, the Welsh of Pantycelyn'), religion, poetry and the land. Long before the introduction of contraception, they have a large family, and it is noteworthy that only the success of the men is mentioned; they became 'poets, deacons, and Sunday School teachers', reflecting the status and the importance of the church in this community.

With the third verse, the poem moves to the poet-narrator's parents' time when Uncle Dafydd used to farm Tir-bach. The Welsh-language community of the grandparents has survived into this generation. As well as working the land, Dafydd is a poet who is recognised locally, while his eldest son becomes both a poet and a Calvinist Methodist minister. Across these two generations, Gwenallt's poem provides a glimpse of a Welsh-speaking community established around religion, family and the land. It highlights how in this community, and in the sense of community itself, it is impossible to separate these different elements, encapsulated in the image of Dafydd composing poetry while watching his sheep. The extent of this interdependence, especially in terms of the role of the Welsh language, is further evident in the way in which Dafydd's poetry is written in Welsh forms such as *cynghanedd, englynion* and eight-line stanzas of eight–seven measure. The detail underscores the solid nature of what once existed. But the small piece of information that the poet-narrator no longer lives there and only visits during the summer holidays suggests that the community is no longer as intact and as sustainable as it once was.

The last stanza of 'Rhydcymerau' projects the reader into a future that is beyond that in which the poem opens. The saplings which were planted then have now grown and the community has disappeared: 'Coed lle y bu cymdogaeth, / Fforest lle bu ffermydd' (Trees where neighbourhood was, / And a forest that once was farmland) (GCC, p. 149; WP, p. 255). The introduction of 'cymdogaeth' (neighbourhood) is especially powerful. In Welsh, it has a stronger resonance than simply 'neighbourhood', suggestive of a community based on interaction, which is not necessarily true of a 'neighbourhood', and where individuals recognise the value of each other. The destruction of the community, the church, families, poetry and the farming that once existed marks not only the end of a rural village but the disappearance of a Welsh-language intelligentsia that provided a particular kind of leadership: 'Ysgyberdau beirdd, blaenoriaid, gweinidogion ac athrawon / Ysgol Sul' (The bones of poets, deacons, ministers, and teachers of Sunday School / Bleach in the sun) (GCC, p. 149; WP, p. 255). The poem seems to ask, can these bones live again?

SHOCKING TRUTHS

The conflation of religion, pacifism and radicalism in Gwenallt's work is distinctly Welsh. As Ned Thomas says, from the start when Welsh Nonconformity engaged with the ordinary people of Wales in ways which the established church, associated with the landlord class, failed to do, it was 'a courageous and radical force', and in Wales 'religion and rebelliousness are compatible'.[56] Like Waldo's work, Gwenallt's poetry relies upon imagery, but some of that imagery is more impassioned and much more disturbing. As a Christian pacifist, he captures the mood of the late 1930s and the prospect of another war in the following line from 'Y Gristionogaeth': 'Awr y finegar a'r fynwent, oes dwym y ffagl a'r ystanc' (GCC, p. 73) (The hour of vinegar and the tomb, the scorched hour of the torch and the stake).[57] Indeed, such uncompromisingly raw images characterise his poetry from this decade. 'Ar Gyfeiliorn'[58] is one of his most shocking poems in this respect. It was first published in *Heddiw*, 1 August 1936, under the title 'Heddiw', and Morgan notes that the editor, Aneirin Talfan Davies, said that 'his heart *leaped up* when he first read it, and how he was *stunned by the rawness of its style; it was like a scalpel dissecting the fatty tissues of our complacent pietism*'.[59] It is one of the most powerful Christian pacifist poems in Welsh from the 1930s and a challenge for an English translator is to maintain 'the rawness of its style' and its rending of the 'complacent pietism' which worried many pacifists at this time.

The poem is typical of Gwenallt's work in the way in which it disturbingly links the heavy industries of south Wales with the trenches: 'Mae lludw yng ngenau'r genhedlaeth, a chrawn ei bron yn ei phoer' (The generation's mouth contains dust, and chest's pus in its spit) (GCC, p. 72; PT, p. 149). Occasionally, Morgan's translation of the poem better conveys the energy of the Welsh than Patrick Thomas's translation. He translates 'lludw' more literally as 'ash', whereas Thomas opts for 'dust': 'This generation has ash in its mouth, its spittle is full of pus.'[60] But overall Thomas's translation better fuses the impact of unemployment in south Wales in the 1930s with the fallout from war:

> Dynion yn y Deheudir heb ddiod na bwyd na ffag,
> A balchder eu bro dan domennydd ysgrap, ysindrins, yslag:
> Y canél mewn pentrefi'n sefyllian, heb ryd na symud na sŵn,
> A'r llygod boliog yn llarpio cyrff y cathod a'r cŵn. (GCC, p. 72)

> Men in South Wales without a drink or food or a fag,
> And the pride of their district under heaps of scrap,
> cinders and slag:
> The canal stagnant in villages, without shout or movement or sound
> And the pot-bellied rats ripping up the bodies of
> dogs and cats. (PT, p. 149)

Both translations capture the figurative nature of Gwenallt's writing although Thomas translates 'tin-droi', as 'loiters', but 'arsing around' might better capture Gwenallt's deliberate coarseness.

In several respects, 'Pechod' ('Sin') may best reflect the mood of Wales, and the UK generally, in the 1930s. It opens with an invitation to consider what is revealed when we are stripped naked, reminding us of how Myrddin Tomos in *Plasau'r Brenin* was stripped in his induction to prison, not only of his clothes but his entire identity. Here, we are encouraged to consider what remains when with our clothes we discard our respectability and wisdom ('Mantell parchusrwydd a gwybodaeth ddoeth', GCC, 103). Controversially, and uncompromisingly, we are told that we are stripped back to the origins of life: 'Mae'r llaid cyntefig yn ein deunydd tlawd' (The primitive mud is in our poor matter) (GCC, p. 103; PT, p. 147).

As one might expect of a poem entitled 'Pechod', it is a dark Welsh pacifist poem, treading a narrow line between the human race with primitive origins, the beast's slime in its veins, and, as it also says, '[y] ddawns anwareiddiedig' (the savage dance in our feet (GCC. p. 103; PT, p. 147), and humanity redeemed by Christ's blood. Its imagery is as suggestive of the apocalypse as of hope. War is seen as a manifestation of what is described as these 'primitive', pre-Christian origins and of 'Llysnafedd bwystfil yn ein mêr a'n gwaed' (the beast's slime in our marrow and our blood) (GCC, p. 103; PT, p. 147).

The image of war in the poem combines 'technology', 'craft' and 'skill': 'Mae saeth y bwa rhwng ein bys a'n bawd' (The bow's arrow is between our finger and thumb) (GCC, p. 103; PT, p. 147). Historians and philosophers have stressed how war has been driven by technological development. Grayling, for example, describes how the 'self bow', made from a single length of sapling, gave way to the composite bow, 'a laminate of horn, wood and sinew, capable of storing far more energy when drawn, and therefore delivering far greater power across greater distances'.[61] In terms of war, conquest and empire, the later combination of the composite bow and the chariot produced what has been described as 'one of the most extraordinary episodes in world history'.[62]

The imagery in this poem conjures up the Welsh archers, mentioned earlier, who acquired such a formidable reputation that when they were captured their enemies amputated their index fingers. But it also suggests, with Gwenallt's typical disquiet, that the bow and arrow is a natural extension of the human hand. While wars change in format and technology, the poem suggests that there is a primitiveness to war that does not change. It underscores the ironic contrast between the sophistication and accumulated learning, skill and knowledge that goes into the manufacture and use of weapons and the primitive instinct that drives, and is revealed by, war. The bow and arrow suggest how weapons are developed for both hunting and war and how, in war, hunting and bloodlust are combined with actions that to the absolute pacifist are anti-human.

'Pechod' closes with a powerful and violent image which is not only characteristic of Gwenallt but recalls the forcefulness of much Welsh pacifist writing mentioned earlier: 'Fel bleiddiaid codwn ni ein ffroenau fry / Gan udo am y gwaed a'n prynodd ni' (We raise our nostrils up like wolves / Baying for the Blood that redeemed us) (GCC, p. 103; PT, p. 147). In this image, the human race is not only compared with wolves but become wolves, reflecting the primitiveness which drives human beings to war and to kill each other. It is a disturbing image with a thin line between human beings as wolves baying for redeeming blood and baying for blood *per se*. The way in which it suggests something that is not quite right is conveyed in the Welsh language in the way the penultimate line appears to lead to alliteration, 'ffr/fr', but then avoids it. The history of humankind is perceived as entangled with the blood of war, hunting, killing and the blood of salvation.

THE AMBIVALENCE OF THE CROSS

In 'Cymru', Gwenallt associates himself, as a Christian pacifist, with what he sees as the special spiritual history of Wales rooted in the Age of the Saints. The saints are mentioned before the Holy Spirit, the crucifixion and the resurrection, prioritising their importance to Welsh Christian faith. Embracing not only an external but an inner sense of peace is seen as an important part of this tradition: 'A bu'r Ysbryd Glân yn nythu, / Fel colomen, yn dy goed' (And the Holy Spirit nested, / Like a dove, in your trees) (GCC, p. 70; PT, p. 98). The poem presents an alternative to the political and religious turmoil in Europe in the 1930s. It looks back to rural, pre-industrial Wales, when the earth was tilled by horse-drawn ploughs, but trade soon followed with the invention of boats and sailing ships. The mention of trade suggests the beginnings not only of international commerce but religious conflict, something that the poem more than hints at when the ship's holds are said to be 'laden with / The merchandise of Calvary' (Ac yn llwythog tan eu byrddau / Farsiandiaeth Calfari) (PT, p. 98; GCC, p. 70).

However, the point is made in 'Cymru' that, in the middle of its forests, the Welsh poets found 'pren y groes' (the Wood of the Cross) (GCC, p. 70). Gwenallt's poetry readily recognises the ambivalence of the cross, as a signifier both of redemption and of torture and execution. As a symbol of agony and bravely borne suffering, the cross provided succour for hundreds of thousands of soldiers called to war. Here it is an emblem of pain and suffering. But the reality of Christ's crucifixion, not just the pain but the shouts of pain, disrupts any romanticising of battle and of death on the battlefield: 'Gri Ei aberth, llef Ei loes' (The Cry of His sacrifice, His shout of pain) (GCC, p. 70; PT, p. 98). Throughout this poem, there is a psychological desire for peacefulness implicitly linked to the image of the Virgin mother and child in Christian art. This is reinforced by the poem's cyclical structure from the reference in the second verse to the Holy Spirit nesting like a dove in the trees, an image of profound peacefulness, to the final image of Wales gathering its saints as a hen gathers its chicks under its wings: 'Ac fe'u cesgli dan d'adenydd / Fel y cywion dan yr iâr' (GCC, p. 71).

Both 'Cymru' and 'Pechod' invite comparison with the poem, 'Y Lleianod' (The nuns). It brings us back again to Britain in the 1930s agonising not only over the prospect of another war but of invasion. 'Y Lleianod' begins with the arrival of nuns and the founding of Cistercian communities in mid-Cardiganshire and north-east Wales, a very different kind of invasion from that which was expected in the 1930s. The nuns are compared with doves, associated with the introduction of peace and peacefulness into what is described as 'ein drycinog oes' (our stormy age) (GCC, p. 106; PT, p. 146), a reference to the political turmoil of the inter-war years. Once again, trees and forests figure prominently in this poem, but the allusions to the cross and the crucifixion are less overt. The poem stands in contrast to 'Pechod' and 'Cymru' by referring to the 'Tree of Life':

Pan dreio'r ddrycin a phan edwo'r gwynt
A dod o'r sudd i'r bôn a'r dail i'r brig,
Codwch o'r goedwig fel y gwnaethoch gynt.

When the storm ebbs and the wind dies down
And the sap comes to the trunk and the leaves to the branches,
You'll rise up from the forest as before. (GCC, p. 106; PT, p. 146).

It is a poem of hope in which the natural, almost pagan, image of rebirth in the rising sap is interwoven with the resurrection of Christ, echoing how the resurrection in 'Cymru' is envisaged as the spiritual spring of Wales. While the feeble forest of our 'stormy age' (coedwig fusgrell) (GCC, p. 106) is an image of dwindling hope in the midst of political turmoil, at the core of the poem is the return of the vibrancy of the forest. As in the title of Waldo's collection *Dail Pren*, the head of leaves becomes a strong spiritual signifier in which Christ's heart rejoices, 'yn llawenychu' (GCC, p. 106). Like the sap rising through the trees, the poem builds to an image of doves rising up from the forest as before, culminating this time in an image of a crown of leaves, replacing as it were the crown of thorns.

POST-SECOND WORLD WAR

Among the most ambitious and disturbing of Gwenallt's poems are those written after the Second World War. As mentioned in the discussion of *Plasau'r Brenin*, Gwenallt was brought up in the area of Wales that produced a number of prominent hymn writers. Gwenallt's poem 'Pantycelyn', addresses one of the most famous of them:

I wladwyr, a gadwynid wrth y pridd,
Fel ychen wrth y dres, drwy gydol oes,
Cenaist, yn eu tafodiaith, gân y ffydd
A glywit ar ddigangenbren y groes. (GCC, p. 108)

You sang to countrymen, chained to the earth
Like oxen all their lives,
In their own dialect, the song of faith
You heard on the branchless tree of the Cross. (PT, p. 143)

A product of Gwenallt's reflections on his Christian faith, the emphasis on Nonconformist preachers addressing ordinary people in their own language brings to the fore an aspect of the 1930s which we mentioned in Chapter 1, the extent to which Hitler's rise to power in Germany was closely linked to his capacity to address, and engage with, his people. The pre-Christian Celts are 'chained' and work like oxen with little reward, and one might think of the German people 'chained' to the Treaty of Versailles with little prospect of socio-economic or cultural growth. Thus, there is an implicit link, again typical of Gwenallt's capacity to shock, between the itinerant Nonconformist ministers and Hitler in their ability to inspire an audience, giving them the prospect of a brighter future through their rhetorical skills and their charisma as speakers.

If this reading seems to overstretch the poem, it is important to remember that Gwenallt's imagination did extend to Germany between and after the wars, as exemplified in one of the most original poems from the collection *Eples* (Leaven) written between 1943 and 1951, 'Plant Yr Almaen' (Germany's Children). The first half of the poem concerns starvation and famine:

> Y mae Rahel o hyd yn yr Almaen
> Yn wylo yn wanllyd a di-stŵr;
> Trugarocach ydoedd cleddyf Herod
> Na'r newyn ar y Rhein, yn y Ruhr. (GCC, p. 184)

> In Germany Rachel still
> Weakly, silently weeps:
> Herod's sword was more merciful
> Than the famine on the Rhine, on the Ruhr. (PT, p. 123)

The second part of the poem weaves images of death –– biers, graves, funerals – with the crucifixion. The new world ushered in by the Second World War is encapsulated in one of Gwenallt's most devastating images. The number of children killed in the war is suggested by the smallness of the coffins.

The poem makes an important contribution to post-war pacifist thinking by highlighting the impact of the war upon the enemy country and in the way in which the meanings of 'war', 'victory' and 'defeat' are evasive. For example, the ending of military hostilities does not necessarily mean the end of the 'war' because its impact, as this poem stresses, is immeasurable. Thus, 'victory' is not necessarily a cause for celebration even when war is embarked upon for what are perceived as just reasons:

Mae tosturi'r Crist ar Ei groesbren
  Yn ffrydio o'i ystlys a'i draed
Pob angladd yn ddraen yn Ei benglog,
  Pob bedd yn ddiferyn o waed. (GCC, p. 184)

The crucified Christ's pity
  Streams from His side and his feet;
Every funeral is a thorn in His skull,
  Every grave a drop of blood. (PT, p. 123)

'Y Meirwon' (The Dead) takes a distinctively Welsh approach to war in that it ostensibly concerns those who have been killed in the steel and coal industries of south Wales, as indeed was Gwenallt's own father. But throughout the poem, the language and imagery allude to the two world wars through references to sacrifice, gas, coughing blood and suffering; to the fact that many have died before their time; and to widows who have to live on 'arian y gwaed' (blood money). One of the most compelling comparisons is in the allusion to how both war and labour in the heavy industries and in mining bring out the 'primitiveness' in men: 'Trôi tanchwa a llif-pwll ni yn anwariad, dro, / Yn ymladd â phwerau catastroffig, cyntefig, cas' (Explosion and flood changed us often into savages / Fighting catastrophic and devilish powers) (GCC, p. 139; WP, p. 252). Approaching the wars through allusion in a poem about the steel industry revitalises the horrors of war to which readers familiar with twentieth-century war reporting might have become desensitised. But in an understandably Welsh line of thought, the poem emphasises how heavy industry, coal works and war are bound up with capitalism and how each has been responsible for the development of the other:

Ni freuddwydiais y cawn glywed am ddau o'r cyfoedion hyn
  Yn chwydu eu hysgyfaint i fwced yn fudr goch. (GCC, p. 139).

I never dreamed that I'd hear of two of my friends
  Coughing up their lungs dirty red into a bucket. (PT, p. 135)

In the 1930s, as we discussed in Chapter 1, there was anxiety among some Welsh pacifists as to whether pacifism could extend its reach to be sufficiently meaningful to those suffering poverty and economic deprivation in industrial as well as rural Wales. Gwenallt's poetry pre-dates that question, as it were, by revealing the roots of Welsh pacifism in industrial Wales in the comparable sufferings Welsh people there had to endure in peace and war. The reference to sudden, chemical-induced and lingering death, 'yr angau llychlyd, myglyd, meddw' (the dusty, choking, drunk death) (GCC, p. 139; PT, p. 135), brings not only industrial deaths to mind, but, for example, the impact of the nuclear bombs dropped on Japan; the blitz on Swansea and London; the heavy bombing of German cities such as Dresden; and the first use of gas in the First World War. But through the interweaving of heavy industry and war, and the impact of death on so many Welsh families and communities, the poem introduces a further distinctive feature of Welsh pacifism; the 'long-memory' of men experiencing premature, violent deaths through what, like the war, could be seen as capitalist endeavour. This is encapsulated in the poignant image of the flowers laid on a grave on Palm Sunday: 'O rosynnau silicotig a lili mor welw â'r nwy' (Of silicotic roses and lilies as white as gas) (GCC, p. 140; PT, p. 136). The final part of the poem conflates the values of family, neighbourhood and community which were so important for Gwenallt, Waldo and George Davies as well as the Christian concept of suffering, which here is given a humanist perspective:

> Ac nid oes a erys heddiw ar waelod y cof
> Ond teulu a chymdogaeth, aberth a dioddefaint dyn. (GCC, p. 140)

> Today what remains at the back of the memory
> Is family and neighbourhood, the sacrifice and suffering of man.
> (PT, p. 136)

'Colomennod' (Pigeons) is also a poem which like 'Y Meirwon' can be read as an indictment of the impact of industrial employment conditions on the working man. But in focusing on how workers in their leisure activities attained a degree of spiritual fulfilment and peacefulness denied them by their work, it recalls George Davies's pacifist essays which emphasise the importance of individual spiritual attainment and criticise the mechanistic nature of industrial and factory employment:

> Amgylchynent yn yr wybr y pileri mwg
> Gan roi lliw ar y llwydni crwm;
> Talpiau o degwch ynghanol y tawch;
> Llun yr Ysbryd Glân uwch y cwm. (GCC, p. 144)

In the sky they'd surround the pillars of smoke
 Giving colour to the crooked greyness;
Masses of beauty amidst the mist;
 The Holy Spirit's picture above the Valley. (PT, p. 134)

In its image of the release of the pigeons as a 'white cloud', 'ei gwmwl gwyn', the poem associates them with doves, signifying, in turn, external and inner peace. The pigeons are linked, like the implied dove, with the Holy Spirit and, like the Holy Spirit, turn 'the worker into a living person' (A throi gweithiwr yn berson byw). The poem provides an interesting comparison with 'Colomennod' in T. E. Nicholas's *Llygad y Drws* and Menna Elfyn's 'Colomennod Cwm', entitled 'Pigeons in Ebbw Vale' in the English version of the bilingual text. Elfyn contrasts the mildness of the birds ('Adar trugaredd' / 'Birds of mercy') with the hard world from which they are released and the solace which they offer in a valley riven by unemployment and the closure of the mines.[63]

The innovative ways in which Gwenallt, as a Christian pacifist, writes about war in the years following the Second World War are reinforced by his startling imagery and language. For example, in 'Y Meirwon', 'ar eu beddau bwys / O rosynnau silicotig a lili mor welw â'r nwys' (on their graves a posy / Of silicotic roses and lilies as pale as gas); in the opening of 'Plant Yr Almaen' (Germany's Children), 'Y mae Rahel o hyd yn yr Almaen / Yn wylo yn wanllyd a di-stŵr' (in Germany Rachel still / Weakly, silently weeps) and in 'Colomennod' (Pigeons) 'Amgylchynent yn yr wybr y pileri mwg / Gan roi lliw ar y llwydni crwm' (In the sky they'd surround the pillars of smoke / Giving colour to the crooked greyness) (GCC, pp. 140, 184, 144; PT, pp. 136, 123, 134).

One of his most powerful pacifist poems, relying on the cumulative impact of startling imagery, is 'Trychineb Aber-fan' (Aberfan Disaster).[64] I am of a generation which lived through this disaster and who do not need to be reminded, as Morgan says, that 'Like the Great War and the Holocaust, Aberfan was, in Wales, a defining moment in the way in which a whole generation viewed their existence.'[65] The first part of the poem vividly depicts the tragedy: the landslide, the junior school like a living dam and the eerie silence which followed and the small bodies laid to rest in Bethania. The second part of the poem provides a reflection on these events, shifting its viewpoint to the Holy Land, referring to Herod's killing of the innocents and

Rachel in Ramah shedding tears for Benjamin.[66] The first part of the poem is particularly effective in its imagery which encapsulates the speed, power and immediate aftermath of the tip's movement. There is an allusion to war in the noise which is compared to the screeching of a very low flying jet: 'Ei sŵn oedd fel sgrechain jet wrth ehedeg yn isel iawn' (GCC, p. 288). War and the coalmines are conflated in the way mud and destruction are linked: 'Y mwd / Yn cario'r ffens, yn tywyllu'r ffenestri, yn symud y waliau / Ac yn un pen ohoni yn dringo mor uchel a'r to' (GCC, p. 288). The extensiveness of the destruction, as the mud takes out windows, moves walls and covers houses to the top of their roofs is such that it would bring the blitz to the minds of older Aberfan residents.

This is an appropriate poem with which to conclude a discussion of Gwenallt and Waldo as pacifist poets. In the account of the destruction of the school and the houses, there is a strong sense of the peace (not war and mass destruction) which, as Oliver Richmond says, should be 'at the centre of the human experience'.[67] It is this perspective which conflates the pacifist principles at the heart of both Gwenallt's and Waldo's poetry; bringing together the traditional rural communities of Waldo's work and the juxtaposition of industrial Wales and war in Gwenallt's later work.

5

Unpeaceful Voices: Writing the Home Fronts

> And although I hate war and reject everything that is associated with it, I feel today that my hands are red with blood.
>
> (Pennar Davies, *Diary of a Soul*)

The Second World War and its aftermath presented huge challenges for pacifism, as we discussed in Chapter 1. *Outside the House of Baal* (1965) is a novel written by the north Wales pacifist and conscientious objector Emyr Humphreys whom we introduced in Chapter 1. While Humphreys's *A Toy Epic* concerns pacifism, as we discussed in that chapter, *Outside the House of Baal* is more fully engaged with Welsh Nonconformity and pacifism as developed by the Welsh-language intelligentsia. It is a text troubled by war and its disruption of human motivation, normal social behaviour and peaceful existence which the majority of people crave.

The novel effectively divides the first half of the twentieth century into four periods: pre-First World War, the interwar years, the Second World War and the post-war years. Two of its principal achievements are the way in which the three generations with which it is concerned are closely interconnected throughout, and how, through a labyrinth of often cryptic allusions, it never loses sight of constantly changing and multi-layered social, political and religious Welsh environments.

'CHARISMATIC' MINISTERS

A useful starting point for a discussion of *Outside the House of Baal* as a pacifist text is its engagement with George M. Ll. Davies who, as we have seen, dominated Welsh pacifist thinking during much of the period with which this novel is concerned. Wynn Thomas, who argues that the book is 'a major fictional work of Welsh nonconformity,'[1] has pointed out that aspects of one of its main characters, the Revd J. T. Miles, are 'modelled' on George Davies himself and another controversial Nonconformist minister known as Tom Nefyn (Thomas Williams)[2], of whom Davies was a staunch supporter and defender. All three departed from the orthodox beliefs of their denominations, particularly through their preaching of pacifist ideals and their involvement with 'liberal, socially progressive campaigns'.[3] But 'J.T.', as Humphreys's character is known in the novel, is such an unconventional figure that, at times, he brings Nefyn rather than Davies to mind. Like J.T., Tom Nefyn, was 'a charismatic and complex man, a powerful preacher, and something of an enigma'.[4]

All three ministers brought political ideas into their ministry. Llywelyn points out that 'chapel ministers were expected to be non-political and uncontentious'.[5] But this was not always the case. Indeed, Tom Nefyn became as legendary for his politics as his preaching. His congregation passed a vote condemning the arrest of 164 miners after a labour dispute in December 1925; in 1926, he sent a report to the coal owners about the poor condition of the miners' housing in Tumble, a case also made by George Davies five years later; and during the General Strike and after, he organised collections for the strikers and, as Llywellyn says, donated his own stipend.[6] Like Humphreys's creation, both Davies and Nefyn chose to follow a 'social gospel', which as we discussed in Chapters 1 and 2 became a cornerstone of Welsh pacifism in the 1930s, rather than confine themselves to an evangelical mission. Llywelyn observes that Davies eventually resigned from the Calvinistic Methodist Church because of 'the denomination's treatment of Tom Nefyn and its attitude to the social gospel'.[7] It is the controversy over the social gospel from the point of view of Calvinistic Nonconformists that gradually unfolds through Humphreys's novel which interweaves how the pacifist social gospel was perceived as posing a socialist threat to the existing political and economic order (through its privileging of Christ's social mission over the theology of the cross) and doctrines of salvation.

Although there are similarities between Humphreys's J.T. and George Davies, there are further parallels between J.T. and a ministerial colleague who had a great influence on Davies and is recalled in his recollection for the year 1936 in *Pilgrimage of Peace*, James Morgan Jones, known as 'J.M.'. The extent of the similarity between the two abbreviated names, 'J.M' and 'J.T', is enough to suggest that Humphreys's pacifist minister is at least partly modelled on 'J.M'. George Davies notes that J.M. refused a career in the established church for a life 'among peasants and miners and unemployed men', which brings J.T. to mind. Like J.T., he was a pacifist. Davies wryly observes, 'men who supported the war left him' while 'those who opposed war crowded into his church'.[8] Like J.T, J.M. was deserted by traditional Calvinist Nonconformists when it became known that he was opposed to all kinds of war and that his pacifism extended to class war. The wider pacifism which links the two preachers underlines the novel's concern with the question: why war? It is useful here to remember the philosopher Anthony Grayling's argument:

> If there is one key to the entire question of war, it is *justice*. A fair world would be a far less conflicted one. Inequality and injustice are ripe causes of social unrest within a society; they have analogues in the international sphere which are heady-prompts for conflict.[9]

In their search for a theology of 'fairness' and 'justice', J.T., Tom Nefyn and J.M. departed from some of the central premises of Calvinistic Nonconformity, particularly the doctrine of election. While the Calvinist Nonconformist church upheld election, J.M., like J.T., took the view, as George Davies says, that election 'plunges through vice and crime' and extends to all 'witnesses of His salvation through grace – His election not ours' (PP, p. 62). In essence, this is the theology of J.T., who maintains that 'there is none other name under heaven given among men, whereby we must be saved', insisting, 'neither is there salvation in any other' (OTHB, p. 95). In particular, J.T., like J.M., argues against the Calvinist concept of original sin: 'the idea of total corruption flowing with the seed from father to son is primitive and barbaric and it leads in the end to making us morally impotent' (OTHB, p. 299). Tom Nefyn, as Thomas points out, may have provided Humphreys with source material for a minister who loses his stipend for his political preaching. But J.M. draws attention to how Keir Hardie had his stipend withdrawn for specifically preaching pacifism.

DEBATES AND CONTROVERSIES

J.T.'s life in the novel charts not only the history of Nonconformity but of Welsh pacifism. In looking back to Davies, Tom Nefyn and James Morgan Jones, Humphreys is not simply modelling a character on them, but recreating the wider environment of Welsh pacifism in which preachers took sides against the authorities, and often against each other. Davies staunchly defended Nefyn when he was called before the Calvinistic Methodists' ruling body in 1927 and suspended from the ministry, and Humphreys's novel draws on the debates and controversies in which ministers became involved, including Davies's articles and essays and Nefyn's articles in *Y Cymro* (The Welshman), and those involving pacifist academics and writers in magazines such as *Y Llenor.* In fact, *Outside the House of Baal* opens with J.T.'s father dismantling a watch, which is redolent of W. J. Gruffydd's 'Y Tro Olaf' (The Last Time) based on the dismantling of a grandfather clock to which we referred in Chapter 1, and the debates and discussions in Humphreys's novel are of the kind which Gruffydd published as the editor of *Y Llenor* with which Humphreys must have been familiar.

Wynn Thomas points out that episodes in the novel also provide fictional equivalents to Davies's visit to the Oberammergau Peace Conference (1926) and to his role as unofficial peace envoy between Britain and Ireland.[10] In fact, Davies's discussion of the Oberammergau conference opens the reflection, 'Peace by Reconciliation', in *Pilgrimage of Peace* dated 1930. Once again, this suggests that *Pilgrimage of Peace* was an important influence on *Outside the House of Baal* for the reflection goes on to discuss what proves a key aspect of the novel. At Oberammergau, Davies argued that the

> first resort, no less than the last sanction was Faith – faith that the power of Love, as seen in its fullness in the life and death of Jesus Christ was the power that . . . could 'break down the dividing-wall of the differences that were between us and so make peace'. (PP, p. 44)

This anticipates J.T., who says of himself that he tries to preach from 'a testament of Love': 'God is a God of Love . . . Love God. Love one another. Love your neighbour. Love your enemy' (OTHB, p. 290). Davies preaches: 'When you and I come to great darkness, when our world is falling to pieces . . . then there is nothing less than that terrific, unreasonable love of God in Christ that can meet our need' (PP, p. 37). He goes on to talk of the 'disastrous disintegration of nationality, class, party, sect, into still smaller units of antagonism and hostility' (PP, p. 44). In essence, this is the social vision of *Outside the House of Baal.*

A further aspect of Humphreys's novel which closely reflects *Pilgrimage of Peace* is J.T.'s belief that if the factionalism and hostility within the church are to be repaired it must rebuild its 'foundations' in a deeper sense of spirituality. Both texts argue that 'war, for all its magnitude, was but one symptom of a deep-seated social disease and disintegration' (PP, p. 46). Within this context, J.T.'s life is motivated by the conviction which *Pilgrimage of Peace* attributes to J.M. in support of this mission: 'The same quest, the same age-long dream, the reconciling of the whole life of man, spiritual, intellectual, economic, on the pattern of Christ and on the lives of the Apostles and the Prophets' (PP, p. 59). Davies rarely lets pass an opportunity to criticise a church that in his view 'went war-mad',[11] and his defence of Nefyn is no exception. His attacks on how the church failed to speak out against the First World War provide examples of how Davies developed the forceful register which characterised the voice of pacifism and dissent in inter-war Wales. In his defence of Nefyn, he draws a distinction between what he calls 'the reserve of sagacious apostleship, dealing tenderly with scruple and fearfulness and fine sensibility of conscience' and 'intellectual cowardice'.[12] Arguing that the church must 'admit honestly that our doctrines are 'filthy rags', like Humphreys's J.T., he believed that the church should be 'thankful for every help to erect a theological home worthier of our moral and religious experience'.[13] The combination of scathing criticism and aspiration here characterises J.T.'s outspokenness and reflects his personality. But in *Outside the House of Baal*, Humphreys goes further and recreates some of the more important debates among pacifist theologians between the wars.[14] Davies, Nefyn and Humphreys's J.T. share reliance on the teachings of Christ and, as Davies says in his defence of Nefyn, they aspire to 'a more perfect obedience' to Christ.[15]

Thus, Humphreys is not simply using aspects of the life and experiences of George Davies, Tom Nefyn and J.M. in creating J.T., a similar thorn in the side of his denomination between the wars. The novel provides a sense of the debates around pacifism and war during this period; of a Welsh-language intelligentsia in which theologians of the day played prominent roles; and of the sacrifices which were made at all levels of the church and society because of pacifist and socially progressive ideals. It is not only the individuals themselves who are important to the novel but the relationship between them as members of a liberal, interwar intelligentsia.

Of the many ways in which Davies and his *Pilgrimage of Peace* influenced this novel, one of the most important was his involvement in the Quaker educational settlement in the Rhondda Valleys in 1933. As Humphreys's novel demonstrates, the south Wales industrial environment into which the Quakers came in 1926, as Llywelyn says, was one of 'anger, exploitation, bitterness and poverty'.[16] Through J.T.'s life and work, it also highlights the central division in pacifist social thinking at the time between an international brotherhood, inspired by the League of Nations, and commitment to more localised centres and projects for which Davies argued in his essays.[17]

Humphreys's novel follows *Pilgrimage of Peace* in exploring how Nonconformity and pacifism were pieces, albeit important ones, in a larger jigsaw of Welsh life in the first half of the twentieth century, which included science, unemployment, socialism, Marxism and the Welsh-language. If the novel were not held together by the interplay of image, allusion and theological and political debate, one cannot help but suspect that all its different pieces would spiral out of control. The range of the subject matter is matched by its depth but coloured throughout by the mood introduced in its opening pages.

LLOYD GEORGE AND GERMANY

Wynn Thomas points out that J.T., as a First World War pacifist, 'courageously heckles a politician (clearly modelled on Lloyd George) who is delivering a fiery recruitment address from the Eisteddfod platform', as did Lloyd George himself.[18] Elsewhere in the novel, 'D. Ll. George' is compared to O. M. Edwards, the chief inspector of schools for Wales, who is said to have higher and more elevated ideals for Wales (OTHB, p. 122). The comparison between them is a pointed one because Edwards, as Gwynfor Evans reminds us, contributed extensively to the Welsh language and Welsh culture. A prominent member of the Welsh-language intelligentsia which eventually turned against Lloyd George, he was active in the Liberal nationalist movement Cymru Fydd; founder and editor of *Cymru* to which many Welsh-language speakers were indebted; and founder also of *Cymru'r Plant* for children.[19]

In implying that the orator is Lloyd George, the novel invokes one of the great controversies in Welsh pacifism, how Lloyd George changed from a well-known Welsh pacifist to a Welsh war leader. This scene in the novel is particularly pertinent because, as Price maintains, 'before and after conscription was introduced in 1916, Lloyd George made considerable use of his gift of oratory, his wife's personal prestige and every contact he could muster to lead and sustain the war effort in Wales'.[20] Price goes on to point out how 'he ordered the authorities to issue huge propaganda posters in Welsh and was ruthless in his condemnation of many erstwhile friends who were conscientious objectors, being particularly condemnatory of the diehard absolutionists who refused to do any kind of state service'.[21] As suggested in Chapter 1, a result of this, from a political perspective, was that among many intellectuals, radicals and pacifists his reputation in Wales was seriously damaged.[22] As the casualties of war mounted, there was increasing opposition to his premiership.[23] In his address, Humphreys's orator uses arguments with which Lloyd George was associated, appealing to the Welsh nation to come forward to protect small nations, such as Belgium, and to emerge from the 'sheltered valley' in which people have lived for generations (OTHB, pp. 151–2). This is ironic from a pacifist point of view because, as we have seen, Waldo and Gwenallt associated their pacifism with values which had been nurtured in small, rural communities.

The speaker motivates the crowd through his sophisticated oratory and well-orchestrated performance, reminding us (as T. Gwynn Jones recalled in the 1920s) how 'the undeniable effect of the sermons of many preachers must have been due to powerful dramatic talent, consciously cultivated in some cases, acting upon the feelings of a highly imaginative people, peculiarly open to the regret for things past and to sentimental appeals generally'.[24] From this perspective, he brings the later German leader Adolf Hitler to mind who displayed, to adapt Jones's words, a similar consciously cultivated dramatic talent which appealed to a people resentful of the Treaty of Versailles and who were susceptible to emotional as much as intellectual argument. In their own ways, each appealed to the kind of mass-mindedness which, as we saw in Chapter 1, George Davies criticised.

However, Humphreys examines the way in which the crowd turn on J.T.. Some of them pursue him outside, accusing him of being a German. Here J.T.'s experience echoes that of Keir Hardie who, when he argued before his constituents in Aberdare that Wales should have remained neutral in the war, was met, as Gwynfor Evans says, by 'hooting' and 'God save our Gracious King'. Afterwards, he was followed to his lodgings by a crowd chanting 'Turn the German out!'[25] While Humphreys's episode is set in the First World War, it anticipates the crowds in Germany in the 1930s who spilled on to the streets after Hitler's speeches and turned their frustration on the Jews. Writing with hindsight, Humphreys suggests that Britain shared with Germany a worrying propensity to encourage racist ideologies among its people and through oratory to appeal to mass consciousness, which he traces back to the First World War.

In Chapter 1, we discussed how some notable pacifists and non-pacifists in the late 1930s believed that peace with Germany was possible. With hindsight, this seems less feasible than it appeared at the time. But J.T.'s experience also highlights the way in which Welsh opinion at the start of the First World War, often at a local level, turned against innocent Germans. This is a shameful aspect of the war which has not been fully explored and in some cases is only even now being acknowledged. For example, when war was declared, Dr Hermann Ethé, who had joined University College of Wales, Aberystwyth in 1875, fell under suspicion in a small town that had never fully accepted him despite his marriage to an English wife and his British passport. On his return from holiday in Germany, a mob formed at Shiloh Chapel which was addressed by two town dignitaries – T. J. Samuel, a local solicitor and prospective mayor, and Dr T. D. Harries, a GP and former mayor – after which, at their instigation, it marched on Dr Ethé's house, intent on forcing the couple to leave the town which they did that night.

The experience which Hermann Ethé suffered overturned the respect which, the historian John Davies argues, the Welsh traditionally had for Germany:

> There were many in Wales who held Germany in high regard. Labour supporters admired the German socialist party – the largest in the world; the country was extolled as the birthplace of the Protestant Reformation; its theologians and its linguistic scholars were deeply respected; Heine and other German romantic poets were greatly esteemed; every choir in Wales knew of the works of Handel, Bach and Mendelssohn.[26]

Humphreys's depiction of the crowd turning on J.T. reflects a major theme which developed in Welsh pacifism from 1914 onwards; how enthusiasm for war was stirred up by politicians such as Lloyd George, and by British propaganda which cast the Germans as the destroyers of civilisation. *Y Wawr*, the anti-war journal to which leading pacifists at the University College of Wales, Aberystwyth, such as Thomas Parry-Williams and T. Gwynn Jones contributed, revealed the more macabre aspects of British anti-German propaganda, 'lurid fables of German atrocities and war-time destruction, the mutilated children, the margarine factory sustained by prisoners' corpses and so on'.[27] Grayling observes that 'the propaganda technique of encouraging pro-war sentiment in one's own country by claiming that the enemy commits atrocities . . . is to make going to war against a supposed such enemy more acceptable'.[28] *Y Wawr* exposed how such alleged events constituted an important part of British war strategy in creating an anti-German public mood, an issue raised in *Outside the House of Baal* when the theological college principal takes J.T. to task for preaching pacifism:

> The principal's voice rose angrily.
> – Have you no sense of honour? Little Belgian children with their hands severed at the wrists!
>
> He struck his wrist several times with his stiffened index finger.
> – Promises broken. Villages burnt. Old men shot. Young women raped. Germany is a mad dog, Miles. It must be put down. There is nothing else to say.
>
> The Principal was waving his arm. (OTHB, p. 141)

The Principal's argument is based on assertion rather than evidence and anticipates the way in which not only First World War politicians but Hitler and other Nazi orators appealed to emotion rather than reason in performances accompanied, as in the Principal's case here, with dramatic hand gestures.

As a pacifist text, Humphreys's novel piles irony upon irony. The accusation that J.T. is a German, as an allusion to what happened to a German academic in Aberystwyth, is deeply ironic when considered in the light of that real event's own ironies. Most strikingly, that a professor of German should have been forced out of his post in a university college which had had such an important role in bringing pacifists together. It is also ironic that one of the crowd who turn on J.T. is a 'fisherman' reminding us of Christ calling two of his disciples, who were fishing at the Sea of Galilee, to become fishers of men (Matthew 4:18–19). But a particularly disturbing element of this scene in the novel is the way in which the police officer who is present is complicit in, and to some extent orchestrates, what happens to J.T..

Lloyd George's role in whipping up the emotions of the crowd is in itself ironic because he was himself a victim of similar mob violence. Price describes how

> his militant anti-war, anti-imperialist stance . . . led him to be verbally and physically attacked, in his own patch at Cricieth and at Bangor and most revealingly in the lion's den of Joseph Chamberlain's imperialistic Birmingham, from where he had to escape a baying mob, disguised as a policeman.[29]

Although there is a suggestion that the orator is Lloyd George his identity is kept elusive. It was not only Lloyd George who motivated the Welsh, especially the rural Welsh, the north Wales quarry men and the south Wales miners, to volunteer for war, but others such as C. B. Stanton. John Davies maintains that, by the end of 1914, 40,000 miners of the south Wales coalfield had joined the armed forces.[30] Indeed, as he goes on to say, quoting Robert Graves, the enthusiasm of Lloyd George and those like C. B. Stanton who followed him, was one of the most important factors in shifting the Welsh focus from pacifism and anti-war-ism, 'persuad[ing] the chapels that the war was a crusade'.[31]

Further ironies are that J.T. is rescued by his friend Griff, a serving soldier, and that when confronted by violence and fearful for his own life, J.T. resorts to violence. Scenarios such as this, often involving loved ones, were devised by tribunals to test the resolve of conscientious objectors. But it also brings to mind how Christ refused to respond with violence to the Roman soldiers who seized him in the Garden of Gethsemane. It was here that his last miracle was purported to have occurred when he healed the ear of Malchus, servant of the Jewish High Priest, after it had been slashed by Peter (Matthew 26:52–4; Mark 14:47; John 18:10–11; Luke 22:49–51). This is a key pacifist text because it shows that Jesus was not concerned with helping himself, but that his mission was to lead people to peace with themselves and with God.

A PACIFIST'S EXPERIENCE

In J.T., Humphreys has invented a character who, like many in Welsh pacifist texts, is haunted by doubt and suffers bouts of despair and depression. Like George Davies, who himself suffered from depression, he becomes obsessive about his causes and his, sometimes very personal, beliefs. In J.T., Humphreys also creates a minister who has a troubled relationship with Christ. In this context, Humphreys is pursuing a theme which occurs in several of his novels, what motivates people to violence. J.T.'s relationship to Christ encourages the reader to ask questions about his state of mind:

> The slaughter, J.T. said. The awful slaughter. It will go on and on. I pray to God to stop it, Lydia. Every hour of the day. Men are doing this to Him. Every bullet that finds flesh, every piece of shrapnel that tears through a body – every time it's a new nail being hammered into the palm of His hand, a new sword being thrust into His side. (OTHB, p. 188)

This is a troubling passage. Although J.T. is talking with, or rather at, his wife, this is an outpouring of rage and frustration rather than a conversation. The sequence of opening short phrases, delivered like the nails he goes on to mention, says as much about his emotional state as the slaughter in the trenches. He appears to verbally grab Lydia and pull her into his soliloquy with an increasing emphasis upon violence: 'finds flesh', 'tears', 'hammered' and 'thrust'. This not only reflects the real violence of the crucifixion and the trenches but recreates them, at a level almost inappropriate for an intimate conversation with his wife, providing insight into the whirlpool of his own imagination. The drama of this episode is continued in their physical responses, 'J.T. stood up and began to pace up and down the confined kitchen', while Lydia sighs and gets up to clear the table. J.T.'s movements here echo those of J.M., described by Davies in *Pilgrimage of Peace*: 'In talking of doctrine and false-doctrine, he would rise from his chair, look me in the eyes, clench his fist like one who is fighting beasts in Ephesus' (PP, p. 62).

Lydia's reaction suggests how weary she has become of J.T.'s emotional outbursts. But he emerges suddenly from this personal despair and appears to return to his pulpit, as Lydia recognises, wishing he could always preach like that:

> To cut, he said, to cut away the moorings. No connection with humanity, no connection with God. Outside the plan. To hold on to your little bit of life like the man who buried his one talent, and not to care about anyone or anything else. That's the temptation. To hug your own little bit

> of life to yourself, and fondle it and hide it and nurse it like a miser with his savings, paying out days like pennies and feeling safe, knowing that you've got thousands more to come. (OTHB, p. 188)

This passage is followed by a disturbing confession and an unexpected shift of focus. First, he admits how in the pulpit he 'keep[s] on seeing faces that put me off. It's funny, they grow big in the pew' (OHTB, pp. 188–9). This provides a worrying insight into how his subconscious interrupts, and disrupts, his conscious mind. Second, continuing to move quickly from one thought to another, he begins to talk to, and eventually with, Lydia. Confessing more quietly to her that he often feels tongue-tied in the pulpit, he moves unexpectedly to tell her that he loves her and proposes to her before inviting her to make love with him. But this is a novel of interruption and his attempt to make love with her is interrupted by her reservations about the time and place and then by the news that her sister Kate has seriously damaged her eye.

The novel appears to set out to be deliberately unsettling and all the characters in the book are restless and/or troubled. J.T. summarises this when he says of doubt, and this is certainly a narrative about doubt: 'Doubts are part and parcel of faith' (OTHB, p. 287). Indeed, interruption and disruption characterise J.T. as a Christian pacifist. But it is not only at a personal, and solipsistic, level as we see here. Although his pacifist ideals are frequently articulated in a personal way, like George Davies's writings and speeches, they challenge the thinking and theology of others. This is brought out, for example, in his argument on a bus with the Rev. T. Machno Jones who preaches a gospel of sin and consequence. In his theology, war, famine, plague and death are the consequences of sin. Much of what he says recalls the Book of Ezekiel in the Old Testament, the first half of which is characterised by vehement attacks on social sins (Ezekiel, 16, 20, 23). Although Ezekiel's tone softens in the latter half of the Book, he remains more judge than priest, acting out of duty rather than love and a sense of fellowship. J.T.'s theology, like George Davies's, contradicts this Calvinist outlook, for, as we have seen, he tries to preach from 'a testament of Love'. In this regard, J.T.'s thinking echoes that of the Peace Pledge Union and pacifist, Welsh-language poets such as Waldo and Gwenallt.

The psychoanalytic critic Julia Kristeva maintains in a discussion of the concept of 'original sin' that it creates a human being who 'is always already evil, even if free will gives it responsibility for sin' and 'turns human beings into a *massa damnata*'.[32] As discussed in Chapter 1, the Welsh pacifist and Welsh cultural historian Iorwerth Peate suggests, in his essay 'Anghydffurfiaeth A'r Trefi' (1944), that it is not possible to be a pacifist and believe in hereditary sin because the gospel was addressed to people as individual persons.[33] In the theological debates and quarrels in *Outside the House of Baal*, there is what Kristeva describes, in a discussion of Augustine's writings, as a 'seesawing between the excesses of the flesh and the stern though merciful demands of absolute judgement'.[34]

The novel creates a dialogue between J.T.'s idealism and his wife's 'realism'. When J.T. and Lydia move into a rural cottage, he appears to think in terms of the idealism expressed by Waldo's and Gwenallt's poetry: 'This is how people should live, he said. In peace. With Love' (OTHB, p. 187). Often in Humphreys's fiction, women are more practical than men and this is the case here. Lydia's response is sharp, 'You wouldn't find many people willing to live in a shack like this,' and the dispute between them highlights how Welsh pacifism, especially in its extended form as a social gospel, was often seen by non-pacifists as 'unrealistic'. Lydia notes what is wrong with the cottage and hammers her complaints like nails into his idealism: 'An earth floor, she said. A rusty grate. Damp higher than the windows' (OTHB, p. 188). Lydia has an important role in the novel's exploration of what motivates people to turn from pacifist ideals. When Lydia and J.T. argue over the strike in which he provides financial support for the strikers at the expense of the needs of his own family, Lydia turns on him: 'I could hit you. I could really. I could hit you' (OTHB, p. 271).

In incidents such as this, Humphreys explores how pacifist ideals can lead to selfish behaviours and how pacifist politics can neglect more immediate family demands. Wynn Thomas observes that in his show of 'solidarity with the striking miners [J.T.] virtually starves his wife and children out of house and home'.[35] But the 'violence' in Lydia's response, given these circumstances, might not appear to be wholly unreasonable. It suggests how being human might necessarily involve, as the New Testament representation of Christ implies, impetuosity and even violence in different circumstances as we saw in the discussion of Glyn Jones in Chapter 2. When the telegram arrives announcing that Griff has been killed, Lydia, grasping a knife, immediately wants to kill the four German prisoners of war working on the farm: 'The devils, Lydia said. I'll kill them. I'll kill them' (OTHB,

p. 204). J.T.'s reaction on hearing the news is the opposite, he drops his knife, 'a section of old scythe blade', and it sinks into the damp soil (OTHB, pp. 207–8). But as this image reminds us that we all return to the soil, Griff's death arouses the racism and national prejudice created by the war. Observing the prisoners of war sheltering from the rain, Tomi Moch spits out, 'Bloody Germans' (OTHB, p. 208).

A MILITARY MIND

Like the earlier novel *A Toy Epic*, which we discussed in Chapter 1, *Outside the House of Baal* explores the social attitudes and discourses that create the mentality that turns ordinary people into soldiers. In his free time, under his mother's watchful eye for his father's return, J. T.'s son Vernon draws a castle, covering its battlements with tiny men and flags. The size of the soldiers and the flags suggest that they have less value individually than collectively, signified also by the arrows which fill the air. As was noted in the discussion of Gwenallt's poetry in Chapter 3, the bow and arrow became one of the first weapons that could be used for indiscriminate killing. While Vernon is drawing a battle scene, Ronnie, in the absence of his father, is reading about war in *The Boy's Own Paper*. On its pink cover, signifying the British empire, Tommies with fixed bayonets are leaping into a German trench. The German soldiers are cringing in abject fear; from a pacifist perspective, we would have sympathy for them, but from a militaristic perspective they might be seen, unlike the Tommies, as cowards. But in the wider context of the novel, the reader is encouraged to ask whether the Tommies are courageous or foolhardy. Elsewhere in the novel, as a stretcher-bearer, J.T. takes it on himself to rescue a wounded soldier whom, at the time, he cannot identify with certainty as a Turkish or German officer. His fellow soldier, who is killed in the rescue, warns him before they go that this is an act of madness. But it is not clear whether J.T. is foolhardy, brave or irresponsible.

The domestic scene reflects perspectives on pacifism which can be traced back to the period following the Boer War which were articulated by writers and cultural commentators such as William Clark. Vernon's drawing and Ronnie's reading reflect the way in which pacifism became interested, in Clark's words, in 'other phases of war and the war-spirit, which are not so often considered as are the horrors of the battlefield'.[36] Of these, one of the most important was, as pacifist thinking between the wars stressed, how war 'plunges man into the very abyss of brute force, from which he struggles to emerge, and from which he must emerge if he is to fulfil the designs of his Creator'.[37] In particular, the relationship between Lydia and her children embodies the ideal in pacifism that 'Nature herself has compelled man to develop a warmer affection for his offspring than has been the case in the lower forms of life'.[38] However, the access which she allows them to materials about war in their leisure time undermines this, as does the hint of tension in the relationship between the children and their father's Christian pacifism. Vernon's drawing, Ronnie's reading and events like J.T.'s dash with the stretcher take us back to the title of the novel, the significance of which – especially in relation to the pacifism in the novel – has been generally overlooked. The House of Baal in the novel refers to a public house, but in the Bible it is the temple of the god Ba'al in Samaria. Ba'al worship, which was learned from the agricultural Canaanites, was perceived as a degradation of Yhwh and the exaltation of symbols of the reproductive powers of nature. Jehu turned the temple into the site of the massacre of all of Ba'al's worshippers. Believing that it was Yhwh's will that this Canaanite religion be eliminated he built an altar to attract Ba'al worshippers to this site where he had them slaughtered and the temple destroyed (1 Kings 16:32; 2 Kings 10:1–11). In Old Testament terms, the incident suggests that sinners rush to their own destruction, that sin blinds us to the consequences of our actions and that God deals harshly with sinners. But it is also analogous to how soldiers in the world wars believed that it was their duty to eliminate the enemy and how the enemy was depicted as deserving elimination. The event provides a commentary on the First World War in that soldiers rushed to the trenches, blind to the consequences; the build-up to both world wars involved identifying, stereotyping and targeting enemies as the worshippers of Ba'al were targeted; and that the forces of war, like Vernon's drawing and Jehu's campaign, involve slaughter on a grand scale which does not recognise the value of the individual human being.

Beginning with J.T. as an elderly man sharing a house with his sister-in-law, and moving between J.T.'s present and past, there is a sense in *Outside the House of Baal* of not only a man in the last phase of his life but of a clearly identifiable period of Welsh Nonconformity and Welsh pacifism coming to an end. It is a phase of Welsh pacifism which had its roots, as we have seen, in the nineteenth century; emerged as an anti-war movement focused on conscription and conscientious objection; and transformed itself into a wider social gospel in the 1930s. It is associated, as we saw in Chapter 1, with a particular Welsh-language intelligentsia who contributed tirelessly to Welsh pacifist thinking through much of the first two-thirds of the twentieth century. Written around the perspectives of a pacifist and conscientious objector, the novel draws not only on the experience of George Davies and other pacifist ministers but of Emyr Humphreys as a conscientious objector himself as well as the war experiences of his father. It explores the complexity of being a pacifist and the personal moral and psychological dilemmas which torment someone choosing that path.

Outside the House of Baal engages with different aspects of Welsh cultural life and the impact of war on Welsh thought and behaviour. Read alongside the other pacifist texts discussed in this book, it highlights the impact of war on the psychology of Wales and how the wars were perceived on the Home Fronts from different perspectives. It is a text rooted in the changing nature of war, Nonconformity and pacifism itself. But it is also concerned with the way in which war influenced the thinking of ordinary people; made individuals strangers to each other and even to the ones with whom they had the closest relationships; enticed people to assume social and psychological masks; and encouraged the privileging of mass consciousness over individual subjectivity. Moreover, Humphreys's novel recognises how war, as Gwenallt realised, involves the return of repressed primitive instincts and the expression of repressed violence.

Conflicting Worlds

6

Post-Pacifism: Peace and War

And life has times, minutes of heaven, when
The soul forsakes the present, for a while.
(William Thomas, 'The Storm')

Whether they are fully conscious of the fact or not, a number of Welsh authors who are concerned with peace as a major theme in their writing betray the influence of the distinctive Welsh pacifist heritage. This chapter contrasts two important works that employ themes and concepts which have been developed by Welsh, and especially Welsh-language, pacifists throughout the twentieth century. *War Voices* (1995) by Tony Curtis, an established poet who was born in west Wales but has spent much of his life in the Cardiff area, is an important collection of poetry which has yet to receive the critical attention it deserves. Although the poems are in English, the book is distinctly Welsh in its frame of reference and outlook. *The Life of Rebecca Jones* is an English translation by Lloyd Jones of Angharad Price's Welsh-language novel *O! Tyn y Gorchudd* (O! Pull Aside the Veil) (2002), which won the National Eisteddfod Prose Medal in the year in which it was published and the Welsh Language Book of the Year Award in 2003. The novel is rooted in what Oliver Richmond called the 'private transcript of everyday history', in which 'a positive peace becomes visible as located in everyday life'.[1] Although a much shorter work than *Outside the House of Baal*, it spans an even longer period of time. As the narrator says towards the end of her imagined life, 'I was given a long life. It has spanned almost the whole of the twentieth century and has been full of experience'[2] (Cefais innau fywyd hir. Rhychwantodd yr ugeinfed ganrif, bron).[3] There is limited reference to 'public' history, and the narrative suggests that it may be less important to the inhabitants of Maesglasau than family events, including domestic achievements, illnesses and misfortunes, and the rhythms of rural life. In affirming the importance of 'everyday' life, the book's chronology moves backward and forward through the lives of the Jones family members, for the most part Rebecca's brothers and sisters.

These texts might be said to be about the multi-voices of peace and war. In them, individual voices are manifestations of personalised, subjective experiences, establishing a dialectic between the voices of different social groups, cultural contexts and generations. This can best be appreciated through the way in which the language pulls the reader 'centripetally', but also 'centrifugally', towards the margins and a multiplicity of different voices.

TONY CURTIS, *WAR VOICES* (1995)

War Voices is an expansion of a group of poems originally published in *The Last Candles* (1989),[4] which, like Humphreys's *Outside the House of Baal*, looks back over the twentieth century. Questioning what we mean in talking of 'two world wars', given the number of wars which have occurred subsequently across the world, it has a much broader frame of reference than Humphreys's novel, and includes Flanders, Bosnia, Russia, Suez, India, Ireland, Vietnam and the Cold War. The voices to which the title refers come from the poet's own memories, a poet-narrator and people involved in different wars at different times in different parts of the world. McConkey says of artists that 'deeply hidden and continuously present within the artist's mind, there is a kind of memory bank composed of images of other works of art and past experiences'.[5] *War Voices* suggests a poet whose mind is a memory box of images of war derived from paintings, reading and the media.

Two recurring themes are how memories of military conflict are preserved and how they, in turn, stimulate further memories. Many of the poems are based on allusions to the periods and cultural contexts in which they are set. For example, the first poem, 'From the City that Shone', describes how, after bathing in a tin bath outside a derelict convent school in Flanders, a soldier rises from the water like a classical god with 'arms outstretched'. We are reminded of the part played by Graeco-Roman culture in the late nineteenth- and early twentieth-century English education system, and how the role of team-building sports like cricket – the soap is 'diving in the slip' – provided a framework for talk about honour, courage and patriotism in war.[6]

War Voices is different from some of the collections of Welsh-language poems considered earlier in that it is more wide-ranging geographically and less explicitly religious. However, although *War Voices* excludes the experience of pacifists and conscientious objectors during the world wars, it pursues some of the themes of Welsh, pacifist writing of the first half of the century, such as friendship, family, community and home, in a variety of different contexts. Jane Aaron and Wynn Thomas's juxtaposition of Curtis's work with pacifist poetry inspired by the Greenham peace camp, which we noted in Chapter 1, does not consider the complex nature of Curtis's position in relation to the Welsh pacifist tradition, nor his subconscious interest in war and the military. Looking back to his childhood in the 1950s, he remembers:

> the war lived on powerfully in the imagination of boys – I deployed Dinky armoured columns over the carpets, cartwheeled my Spitfire through clouds of bedclothes on summer's nights absurdly light long after bedtime. Donner und Blitzen, Stuka, Hitler, he only had one . . . Belsen.[7]

Ahead of him lay the hindsight with which he would look back on this very young Curtis differently. As a post-war schoolboy he was conditioned, as the older Curtis was to realise, to see those who enlisted and those who opted out on the grounds of conscience in particular ways. In a poem in which he sought to make light of his years in the grammar school, he reflects on how he thought of some of his teachers as 'classroom NCO's from some distant war of tears', and others as among those who 'missed the show, or dodged the chance to fight'.[8]

In this creative essay, Curtis admits that *War Voices* was inspired by 'illustrated books on the First World War' and 'the marvellous twenty-six-episode BBC TV series in 1984' [originally broadcast in 1964].[9] But what he doesn't mention is that, at the time he was writing at least some of these poems, he was also working on his introduction to the work of the Cardiff poet and playwright Dannie Abse. It is a book which reveals the complexity of Curtis's relationship to pacifism and his interest in war. Not simply criticism, it is, at times, a deeply personal engagement with Abse's work. While this approach may upset some scholarly purists, it makes for an especially interesting book and one which has as much to say about Curtis as about Abse. As the similarities between them, and between Curtis and Welsh pacifist writers generally, emerge, a complex picture forms of Curtis himself as a troubled writer whose motivation is summarised in what is almost an aside: 'Our living challenges us to make sense of life: absurd though it may at times seem, we have no choice but to "Hunt the Thimble".'[10]

From the evidence of his study of Abse and his own poetry, in some respects, Curtis's engagement with the world is more in line with Glyn Jones than, say, Waldo, because he worries, like Jones, about death and decomposition, and as he says, 'we have to confront the world while we are in possession of that knowledge'.[11] While pacifism is about choosing to be a pacifist and living by that decision, Curtis's work is more concerned with what takes away choice. But as he twists and turns with Abse, others step inside the ring. Abse's work soon returns the reader to the *shoah*, and what almost brought pacifism to its knees. As Curtis says, bringing to mind Iorwerth Peate's approach to the post-war European mind which we discussed in Chapter 1, 'That image of war, of pogroms, touches the collective subconscious of Europe, and so it should.' [12] In Curtis's writing about Abse, there is a suggestion that he would never cast out George Davies, as Emyr Humphreys once hinted in his notebooks that he might, for his 'saintly qualities of forgiveness and celebration'.[13] But Curtis finds himself at one with Abse as a writer who 'recognises the legitimacy, the purity of anger'.[14] In fact, Abse is the ghost at Curtis's writing desk: 'Once more the argument leads back to individual responsibility. This writer addresses himself time and time again to that question.'[15] When Curtis puts his cards on the table, they seem to come from a pacifist deck – writers fail 'creatively and morally' if they cannot redeem the 'gross error' of 'aiding the cause that sent millions . . . to the death camps and the gas chambers' – but Abse is admired for reminding us of 'the depths in our shared heart of darkness'.[16]

Curtis's poetry frequently returns to delusions, blocked escape routes and the impossibility of protecting ourselves against pain and loss. He believes that Abse's 'Tenants of the House' has 'a sad relevance for us still' in that 'so many masks have been worn that the human face may no longer recognise itself'.[17] There is a dark side to Curtis that, despite his obvious abhorrence of war, must make us as wary of his work as he is at times of Abse's. But there is one line in his book on Abse that appears to be so overwhelmingly an observation from his own soul (rather than simply a comment on Abse) that it cries out to us to trace the pacific, if not the pacifist, element in his work: 'and love is the only way to touch another.'[18]

THE MEANING OF PEACE

There is a particular emphasis throughout *War Voices* on the Welsh pacifist concepts we discussed in relation to Waldo, 'personalism' and 'adnabod'. But *War Voices* is aligned with Welsh pacifist literature also in its emphasis upon ordinary lives and is informed by the pacifist conviction articulated by George M. Ll. Davies: 'It is the meek who seem to us to have most truly inherited the earth, and not those who talked and acted "lebensraum". The men we love are often very different from the men we admire for their achievements.'[19] *War Voices* brings us back to Curtis's very revealing line about love – and to the fact that it is more than simply a collection of anti-war poems; at its heart, to employ George Davies's words, is the 'need and opportunity for reconciliation into peace' (PP, p. 88). But the range of reference to war in *War Voices* is linked to a sceptical strain which runs throughout the collection and counter to its search for peace. Curtis certainly cannot be accused, as Densil Morgan suggested some pacifists in the 1930s were, of 'an incapacity to comprehend the disturbing, the irrational and the demonic'.[20]

War Voices is sandwiched between opening and closing poems concerned with the First and Second World Wars respectively. The first poem introduces the reader to how, throughout the collection as a whole, the horrors of battle are often, as here, kept at a distance and only introduced subtly. However, there are a few poems that bring the violence and aftermath of war to the fore more shockingly but, usually, briefly. For example, in 'Brady's Glass', there are 'Faint grey ghosts fallen / in a dirt road ditch with awkward limbs / and bloated bellies, backs arched in pain' (WV, p. 25). Here *War Voices* looks back to anti-war poetry of the First World War and the challenge of providing enough detail to make its opposition to war persuasive without appearing to indulge the violence. But, more often, one or two words are enough to bring to mind horrors which other authors might have exploited in more detail. The poet appears to want to re-sensitise readers who have been desensitised by over-graphic depictions of war and violence in the media.

The numerous allusions to the First World War in 'From the City that Shone' keeps it ever present: in the references to it being 'too risky' to sing in the bath; to the Taube in the sky (which refers to a pre-First World War monoplane named after the German word for 'dove', which given the aircraft's use in the war proved ironic); to the guns that are due to start up; to the soap thrown like a grenade; and to the dog-rose each man places in his tunic. The poem introduces the perspective suggested by the title of the first section, 'Through fields of white crosses', an image which has a pacifist association, suggesting the white, as opposed to red, poppy. Because there are many graves, the image stresses how war devalues the importance of the individual in contrast to the way in which 'personalism' values the individual.

In focusing on the camaraderie between the two soldiers, this poem recalls the way 'adnabod' and personalism are developed in Welsh-language poetry. The relationship between the narrator and his comrade 'John' is subtly stressed when John is said to have playfully 'lobbed the soap / grenade-like at my head', and how it is a relationship based on concern for each other when the poet narrator says, 'I drew fresh water for him and passed the soap' (WV, p. 9). These simple details suggest a camaraderie which goes beyond what the military encourages among its troops and embraces something closer to what we have in the poetry of Waldo and Gwenallt. The concern of one soldier for another as a fellow human being is interwoven with a renewed sense of the intensity of ordinary life.

The final poem, based on a photograph of the Women's Land Army, reveals that one of the women is the narrator's mother, and this stimulates a memory of his father. It echoes the first poem in the way in which it emphasises camaraderie, this time among the women on the Home Front; the importance of ordinary things, like hair perms and make-up; and the intensity of nature, evident in the 'delicate blue flowers' of the flax. Like 'From the City that Shone', it is concerned with 'displacement', in this case the movement of women from England to Wales. War, too, is ever present in the background, in the final image of the Sunderland flying boat and the allusions to the trenches: 'wading into a field of water' and 'eyes weeping as the smoke blew back' (WV, p. 79).

The poem appears to share Waldo's concern over the land army ploughing up the countryside of west Wales for the war effort. The cryptic reference to the man with his head on his mother's shoulder suggests that he might be a conscientious objector who, like George

Davies and Emyr Humphreys, was sent to work on farms in west Wales as a non-combatant. The farmer in the photograph, 'not really knowing about Hitler', reminds us of how Lloyd George, in his campaigning speeches in the First World War, urged an end to the sheltered character of rural Wales. Changes in how land is farmed is a motif in 'In McDonough County', which describes the combine-based farming 'chewing down the rows, ruling the farms' geometry' (WV, p. 78). This poem, although not set in Wales, would remind a Welsh readership of how war changed the official attitude to Welsh farming. As we have seen from a 1930s issue of *The Welsh Outlook*, a concept of agricultural development emerged between the wars which overlooked the life supported by the rural landscape, signified here by references to crickets, foxes and racoons. Again, war is ever present in the background through the comparison of the silos to 'silver missiles'; in the reference to the silo that, like a left-over bomb in England and Wales, suddenly explodes; and in the description of how the poet-narrator is woken by 'a low, wide rumbling', reminiscent of a bomber (WV, p. 78).

Poems which compare wars with their aftermath pursue the question posed in 'From the City that Shone': what does all this mean? In 'Belgium: Coffee', the poet-narrator is taking a flight as a civilian in which he recalls flying over the continent during the war. He recollects the ill-fitting uniforms, the drowned horses, the trucks that are ditched and burned, the ragged flotilla of rescue boats, the dregs of an army and the dog-fights. Now the war seems an increasingly distant scrapbook of memories as the plane passes over rich, flat countryside, villages and neat ploughed fields which signify an 'everyday' sense of peacefuness. His recollections are interrupted by the drinks trolley which brings together the two experiences in the final image of spilled coffee 'hot and sticky on my leg', which in the war would probably have been blood.

'What does all this mean?' is the question implied but left unasked at the end of the poem 'Reg Webb', which reflects on the veteran's life in a way in which *War Voices*, as a whole, reviews a century of war. The fact that he is named enhances the reader's sense of interest in him as a person; the personalism or 'adnabod' which pervades Welsh pacifist writing. Reg Webb's wartime career, when he 'corkscrewed merchantmen / through icy shoals of Atlantic U-boats', is contrasted with his life after the war when 'he piloted the fat oil hulks' to the Milford terminal (WV, p. 71). His career as a peacetime skipper throws his wartime experiences into dark relief. As the account of his life moves beyond the war, beyond his retirement, 'pottering / with the roses and bulbs' (WV, p. 71), beyond illness and his death, the poem asks in effect, when was life most meaningful to him? The answer lies in the responsibility which he showed towards others. In describing how he becomes very ill, the poem employs naval imagery which brings not only his life on ships but the Second World War itself to mind: 'awash with bile', 'bilges leaking', 'becalmed in the straits of morphine', 'the port of his front room and tv', and, in relation to his cremation, 'fire in the hold, and a hard stoke / for one last evasive action, making smoke' (WV, p. 71). At the end of everything, his life seems to have been at its most valuable when he worked with others in a society in which peace promoted social and economic growth and in those periods in his life when he himself enjoyed an inner peace.

'Pictures in a School Hall' takes us back to a theme of the 1930s, which we have seen in Emyr Humphreys's novel *A Toy Epic*; the way in which school halls and vestibules commemorated sporting achievements alongside death in war. In the years following the First World War, the distinction between the two became blurred. In this poem, the photographs of students who have been part of sports teams are compared to 'tombstones' and a teacher to a cavalry officer. The poem interlinks the complacency of the period with that of young men who responded to the call to enlist. This, in turn, is contrasted with the long view: 'And out of these games came a war, more wars' (WV, p. 60). In this respect, the poem takes us back to the Welsh pacifist writing of George Davies, who saw the school system as inhibiting and repressing true personal development, reflected here in the description of the 'stifled, polished hall'.

In 'William Orpen & Yvonne Aubicq in the Rue Dannon', the fragility of life, which makes it the more precious, is suggested by butterflies. Through their delicacy and colour, they inspire peace, which is made evident in the way William gently brushes the butterflies off his tunic. The interjection of a memory of the Somme in baking August heat introduces an intensity of colour which turns it into an impressionist painting, a genre where, as the art critic McConkey says, there is 'the continuous accumulation of small sensations in front of nature':[21] 'dazzling white', 'blood-red poppies', a 'blue flower', 'white butterflies', and fields of white crosses. But the memory contrasts the value of colour, nature and flowers with the horror of war, which is woven through the poem in the ruined buildings, the 'torn bodies', the 'green limbs under shell-hole water', the white crosses, butterflies 'slamming' against the car's windscreen, the torn trunk of a tree, and the explosion of a loose shell.

Acknowledging the butterfly as a symbol of peace, encourages William to recognise the value of individual as well as collective beauty. The exploration of 'personalism' in relation to war begins with the contrast between 'William Orpen & Yvonne Aubicq in the Rue Dannon' and the first poem, 'From the City that Shone'. The juxtaposition of the two poems highlights the emotional difference in the relationship between the poet-narrator and John in the first poem, and between William and Yvonne in the second poem. 'William Orpen & Yvonne Aubicq in the Rue Dannon' is based on a type of painting which McConkey says became common in the Edwardian era, 'the picture within the picture, drawing together sexual and cerebral desires'.[22] The poem opens with William waking in his bed, draped by his model, Yvonne. She is the object of his gaze, reflecting how, as his model, she is turned into an object in the gaze of other spectators. In effect, as McConkey says, the artist, like the poet in this collection of war voices, 'unwittingly partook of a shared memory' and the 'power to translate life into a work of art' which the spectator, or the reader in Curtis's case, then reworks.[23]

Two lines suggest that William may be using Yvonne for her attractiveness and social status: 'The mayor's beautiful daughter lies in his bed. / He is having a good war' (WV, p. 11). These lines raise the question, is *she* having a good war? When she is betrayed by him, the poem effectively asks, who is betraying who? Whereas 'personalism' brings people, as the two soldiers in the first poem, together, this poem stresses how people are together and distant at the same time. Distance is the key trope, evident in William dreaming of 'lobsters moving behind glass' in the Savoy, the landscape which stretches for miles, and the way that Yvonne, as Orpen's model, is removed from him. The way in which she half-covers herself in his studio contrasts with her nakedness before the firing squad. Her nakedness, in his bed and at her execution asks the question whether either of them ever stands fully revealed in this poem. William's painting, we are told, will soon be complete. But this poem is made up of fragments of a story, and nothing is complete. Whereas personalism is based on a desire for a more complete understanding of others, indifference, reserve, ambivalence and hidden motivations characterise how William and Yvonne relate to each other.

In 'The Front', no one is named and this reinforces the overall mood of the poem, as does the contrasting use of the first person to describe an attempt to rescue someone, and the third person to emphasise the enemy: 'their fire' and 'they did not let up' (WV, p. 13). The poem is about an act of courage which is also an act of 'personalism', evident in what the poet-narrator says: 'I have you, / It's alright / I said' (WV, p. 13). It is written in a style that is clipped and sparse but also effective, with no more than three syllables to a line. The repetition of the first person and the emphasis on assurance underlie the sense of human concern in contrast to the other type of contact in this poem: 'He took a bullet' and 'Taking bullets all the while' (WV, p. 13). As in *War Voices* as a whole, 'intimacy' and 'distance' stand in sharp contrast to each other: 'His face was wet against my neck' and 'He died against me' (WV, p. 13). Not only is the poem about 'brawdoliaeth', to use Waldo's word, it constitutes the spine of the text, from the act of running to a wounded man, to the carrying of a corpse, to the poem's concluding lines: 'my brother / my other skin' (WV, p. 13). There are small but crucial changes in the language of the poem, from 'a bullet' to 'bullets' and from 'I carried him' to 'I wore him' (WV, p. 13). The ambiguity of the last line very deliberately contrasts the two attitudes to humanity: one, about getting inside another person's emotional skin, is about saving a life, and the other, which can reduce the skin of an individual being to a pelt, is based on the disposability of the individual life.

Personalism in these poems, as in Welsh pacifist thinking in the first two-thirds of the twentieth century, often emerges in an environment in which the value of human life is difficult to uphold. In 'Incident on a hospital train from Calcutta, 1944', the poet-narrator remembers how he 'unwrapped / a dirty, days-old girl, too weak for cries' (WV, p. 18). Such an image is one which has been seen many times on television programmes and in charity advertisements seeking donations to support relief projects in Developing countries. The strength of poems, such as this one, which incorporate familiar images in new contexts, lies not simply in one or two vivid images but in their recognition of the value of another life, evident in this poem in what is suggested or can be imagined rather than what has been explicitly described: the feelings of the mother who hands over her child; the nurses who leave the child because of her fever; and the seriously wounded soldier who offers the poet-narrator consoling words. There is a contrast between the soldier who looks up at the narrator and offers consolation and the voice of the poet-narrator which, although sympathetic, betrays the way in which war inhibits extended shows of humanity, all evident in the way in which the 'mother turned into the smoke and steam'; in the nurse's fear that 'that child would have emptied half our beds'; and in the description of the soldier who offers the poet consolation as 'the corporal whose arms had gone' (WV, p. 18). The matter-of-fact tone is not devoid of compassion but it is a voice subdued by the poet-narrator's own 'constant jolting of pain' and, in his words, his need to put the horror of war 'out of our reach' (WV, p. 18).

'Home Front' blurs the distinction between the fronts, juxtaposing the experience of a war widow with the death of her husband on a torpedoed freighter. How he constituted an important part of her life is contrasted with the way he is seen collectively as one of the 'men overboard', sinking 'into the anonymous dark' (WV, p. 29). His death is personalised by a final memory of his wife's penchant for collecting coins. The 'Home Front' is marked by a fear of German invasion, to which tribunal panels often referred in testing the resolve of conscientious objectors. In this poem, the widow without her husband to support her would gas her children. Her dilemma, which is an individual one but not unique to herself, is compared with the personal dimension of the constitutional crisis caused by the abdication of 'the love-lost king'. Like many pacifist texts, the poem acquires Welsh perspectives through its geography, the image of the bombardment of the Welsh coastline, the parachutes that 'flower in the Vale' and the Welsh ports 'at the edge of night' (WV, p. 29), an image which alludes to the blackout and the end of the nation. The poem contrasts seven 'polished shillings' in her hands with the hours of cleaning work that she has had to do to earn them. The coins encapsulate the sense of empire, the colonialism, the militarism and the sense of nationhood which lead to war and betray the individuals who are caught up in these grand narratives.

The horror of war, as in many Welsh pacifist texts, is conveyed in images that contrast the hostilities of war to the wonder of nature or describe nature in terms of war imagery. In 'Home Front', the torpedoed freighter is said to have 'reared and plunged like a whale' (WV, p. 29); in 'The Captain's Diary', the wind from the Irish Sea 'cuts through tweed like a bayonet' (WV, p. 28) and in 'Brady's Glass', about the American Civil War, the fruit is bruised 'grey and blue' (WV, p. 25). In 'Manoeuvres on Kinder Scout', the poet-narrator recalls 'the wind scouring my ears like shells' (WV, p. 76) and in 'Window seat to Chicago', 'the whaler's prow / Mushrooms out its harpoon / and crashes the dream' (WV, p. 77).

The poems reflect how pacifism became increasingly concerned, in the wake of nuclear weapons, with the preservation of human life, even life itself. 'The World' provides a vision of how the world will end in the case of a nuclear war: two Russian submarines 'from the ocean / retaliate / before they drown' (WV, p. 20). It is described matter-of-factly in lines of four syllables around the single, ominous word 'retaliate', which in a nuclear context has devastating consequences. This is echoed in 'Manoeuvres on Kinder Scout' in lines as 'stark and simple' as the vision the poet-narrator sees in his mind's eye:

> and those cities laid waste
> in a terror of nuclear heat,
> brick and flesh charred peat-black
> in a sear of thick light. (WV, p. 76)

The distinctions between brick and flesh and between light and heat disappear, as does time, in this nuclear instantaneity. The pressing of the nuclear launch button is contrasted with the actions of the older boy who rescues a grouse chick and returns it to the overgrowth of heather, an action initially misunderstood by its mother who becomes a pacifist in her response, 'I'm bigger, take me, I'm bigger' (WV, p. 75). How he holds the bird in his hand stands in contrast to the raised fist of a victorious bomber pilot. It seems that he finds in this nurturing role an inner peacefulness arising from his sense of contact with all living things, whereas the pilot with his raised fist suggests a society that is based on the separation of humankind from other living things and more intent, as a consequence, on war and violence.

The boy's act of kindness recalls the sensitive Iorwerth in Emyr Humphreys's *A Toy Epic*, whom we discussed in Chapter 1. He is very different from J.T.'s sons in *Outside the House of Baal* and the young boy that Curtis himself remembers being, all of whom played out in their homes a subconscious interest in the military determined by the social discourses around war and masculinity. Here we have an example of the kind of pacifism which extends into the way we live our life in terms of an everyday peace which we summarised in Chapter 1 in the words of one of the witnesses in the Imperial War Museum project: 'a horror of violence, disapproving of blood sports, capital punishment, corporal punishment and the whole shooting match'.

ANGHARAD PRICE, *THE LIFE OF REBECCA JONES* (2012)

Lloyd Jones's translation of *O! Tyn y Gorchudd* describes the rural valley in which the book is set, Cwm Maesglasau, as a 'temple to tranquillity', a place of 'tranquillity' and a 'peaceful place' (TLRJ, pp. 9–10). Anticipating the notable Welsh pacifist writers and theologians of the twentieth century, Rebecca, the participant narrator, says: 'I too have sought peace throughout my life' (TLRJ, p. 10). While the English version makes use of the words 'tranquillity' and 'peace', the Welsh version uses only one word 'distaw', quietude, so that Maesglasau is a 'teml i dawelwch', the valley is a site of 'tawelwch' and 'lle distaw' respectively, and Rebecca says, 'Bûm innau'n chwilio tawelwch am lawer o'm hoes' (OTYG, pp. 8–9).

The tranquillity, or 'tawelwch', in the valley is exacerbated by the extent to which life is lived in close contact with, and shaped by, nature, as in the small west Wales communities depicted by Waldo and Gwenallt. This is suggested at the outset of the book in subtle ways; for example, Rachel's mother's wedding dress has 'the same intricate design' as the flowers in the hedgerow, and the horse that draws their wedding cart 'is slowed by the hill's sharp incline' (TLRJ, pp. 12, 13). Like the villages to which Waldo and Gwenallt allude, Maesglasau is a place of community where, on the whole, individuals and different families are recognised and valued: so Rebecca's mother and father are welcomed home by the neighbours; every five months or so a pig is slaughtered at one of the farms and the meat shared among the neighbouring farms; harvest brings the people together to work each other's crops; and sheep shearing is a communal activity undertaken on a rota. From early in the narrative, however, there are hints of hierarchy, division and rivalry which threaten to disrupt the peacefulness which is seemingly at the core of this rural community.

Maesglasau, like the Welsh rural communities on which Waldo and Gwenallt look back, is centred on the chapel and the Bible. The majority of books which the children have to read, apart from the Bible, are books linked to, or are commentaries on, the Bible; and the weekend and the Sabbath are dominated, as Gwenallt suggests in *Plasau'r Brenin* (1936) and W. J. Gruffydd in *Hen Atgofion* (1936), by chapel and Sunday school. But Sunday school is where the children, and Rebecca, discover Welsh-language books and poetry in both English and Welsh.

The novel approaches life at Maesglasau from a feminist perspective. While Rebecca's mother finds, like Rebecca herself, a degree of peace in this traditional Welsh community, it is a hard life. Tradition brings problems as well as familial and communal support, as does the isolation of the valley, and life is especially difficult for women. In the English version of the novel, as Rebecca's mother approaches her new home with her husband, there is a suggestion of the enclosed and confining life she will lead, as there they will 'face the walls of married life' (TLRJ, p. 15). The Welsh version does not talk of facing 'walls' but facing 'stone and mortar', which they will confront together, 'wynebu carreg a mortar eu byw ynghyd' (OTYG, p. 26). The Welsh version is a more accurate suggestion of what unfolds in the novel, as Rebecca and Evan for the most part confront things together and 'carreg a mortar' better suggests the trials and tribulations which family and communal life bring. As Rebecca says of her life, mirroring that of her mother: 'I have felt the rough fist of misfortune and the soft palm of joy' (TLRJ, p. 144); 'Teimlais ddwrn profedigaeth a chledr llawenydd' (OTYG, p. 141). The Welsh version is slightly different and talks of 'bereavement', rather than the 'rough fist of misfortune', which more accurately suggests how Rebecca's family-centred life brings 'joy' (llawenydd) and, with the passage of time, the death of loved ones. The feminist slant of the book, in both the English and Welsh versions, stresses the uncertainty and hardship facing Rebecca as a newly married woman: 'I imagine my mother bracing herself' (TLRJ, p. 15); 'Gwelaf fy mam yn llyncu 'i phoer' (OTYG, p. 26). But perhaps the Welsh-language version, 'Gwelaf', 'I see', rather than 'imagine', has more force and sense of actuality. Rebecca's mother soon discovers that there are things 'expected' of her, as the novel says, but while she is expected at times to help out the men with their additional seasonal tasks, the men do not reciprocate as far as her domestic duties are concerned. At times, the Welsh version stresses that there is a more profound transition between the women across the generations than the English version. While, in the latter, Rebecca reveals that 'I was named Rebecca after my mother and grandmother' (TLRJ, p. 20), the Welsh version avoids 'grandmother', spelling out 'ar ôl fy mam, ar ôl mam fy mam' (OTYG, p. 31). Towards the end of her imagined narrative, Rebecca admits that at one level, she regrets her 'nunnish life in a remote cwm' (TLRJ,

p. 126). The Welsh version, in which she regrets her 'monastic life' (byw'n fynachaidd), emphasises how she would have liked to live nearer the action, 'ymhell o gyffro pob gweithred' (OTYG, p. 125). The peaceful life of the valley is transformed in her eyes by Mair's life, but also by Bob, who becomes a Labour councillor and magistrate, and his wife, who is a Plaid supporter.

For the most part, women in the story are associated with peace. Rebecca's mother is spiritual and chapel-going. Confronted by Evan's grandmother, who makes it clear that she and her two daughters have lived together very well – like the three legs of a milking stool – Rebecca replies as a pacifist might: 'I've never quarrelled with anyone in my life, Catrin Jones, and I'm not going to start now' (TLRJ, p. 17). The Welsh version again is more emphatic: 'Ffraeais i erioed efo neb yn fy mywyd, Catrin Jones, a ddechreua i ddim heddiw' (OTYG, p. 28). But Catrin Jones is not entirely the villain of the piece, for she herself is the victim of tradition. When the new generation arrives, she has to move to a smaller home at the end of the valley, as eventually does Rebecca in the imagined narrative. Rebecca's Aunt Sarah exemplifies the importance of recognising spirituality in others, which is at the heart of the pacifist creed, and this is encapsulated on her gravestone:

> Early was Sara silenced – tranquil, serious
> She fell quiet ere the crowd's applause
> But the spell cast by her life's goodness
> Radiates over her cold resting place. (TLRJ, p. 21)

The Welsh version better suggests the way in which good works and a pacifist demeanour influence the nature of communities. The Welsh word, 'wasgara', placed at the end of the final line, means, 'disperse', 'scatter' or 'sow', and is appropriate to the rural community and to the way in which good deeds sow reciprocal acts of kindness and support.

PEACE, WAR AND LANGUAGE

For Maesglasau, the mid-twentieth century revolves around the way in which the peace of the valley is disrupted, if not destroyed, by the violence of war that comes from the larger world outside. The first indicator is the narrator finding it difficult to believe that such a peaceful place was created by violent volcanic and glacial activity, and there are allusions to war and invasion – for example, in the reference to men coming 'in waves to conquer new lands' (TLRJ, p. 17) – which anticipate the prospect of a Nazi-led German invasion. The disruption, like the phoney war, is slow to develop, which is signified by the distribution of gas masks and reports on the radio. But with the war, a new, foreign language enters Maesglasau through words such as 'German Junker 88', 'American B17 Flying Fortress', 'fortress firestorms' and 'V1 and V2 bombs' (TLRJ, p. 93). In the Welsh version, the foreignness of these words is, of course, more pronounced. There are new words for death in this new kind of warfare which are translated into Welsh: 'firestorms' (tanchwa) and 'hit directly' (uniongyrchol) (TLRJ, p. 93; OTYG, p. 98).

The intervention of war is marked by a short quotation from the Welsh hymnist and translator who was born in Maesglasau, and whose hymn 'O! Pull aside the veil' provided the title of the original Welsh version of the novel, Hugh Jones (1749–1825): 'And for why did they meet in anger, those mighty creatures? The mountains were big enow [*sic*] for them both in our eyes, their sad encounter had no need' (TLRJ, p. 92). The chapter concerned with the impact of the Second World War juxtaposes, and contrasts, the hostilities with the communal events of harvest and sheep shearing. The emphasis is on the disruption of what Richmond calls 'private' history. For example, Gruffydd has to leave his parish in London because his church is destroyed in the blitz; Rebecca's grandmother's cousin, who lives in London, is killed in an air raid; and her daughter Evelyn, who is orphaned, has to stay for a while at the farm.

The emphasis on family and personal history is extended to the arrival of Italian prisoners of war who continue and develop the book's concern with peace; the significance of the human being; the value of being close to nature and/or traditional crafts; the spiritual potential of each individual; and the importance of recognising another person's individuality. The collective term 'prisoner of war' stands in contradistinction to the way in which the personalities of named individuals emerge in this book and with the way in which they are approached as individuals. With the exception of the angry Piero, the Italian prisoners sent to the farm are peaceful people. Angelo, like the Joneses, is a family person who has more feeling for his wife and children than for war (TLRJ, p. 95). Ernesto, too, has something in common with the Joneses; as a carpenter, he is also a practitioner of a traditional craft and, like Angelo, is a peaceful man, 'good-natured with not much fighting in his blood' (TLRJ, p. 97). Unlike the war which is the chronological centre of Rebecca's life, Angelo, for the four months in which he is with her, becomes her spiritual and sexual centre. Their relationship is important to the development of the concept of 'personalism' in the novel, highlighting how an individual can only grow as a spiritual and sexual being in recognising and knowing another: 'They were four months of learning, also. Learning about someone I could laugh with, be solemn and joyous with, in a natural way' (TLRJ, p. 99). But the novel explores the difficulties and complexities which this involves; in Rebecca's case, in the unfortunate circumstances which have brought them together and in the fact that he has a family of his own in Italy: 'Learning also to hide my feelings; to modulate emotions and subdue the body. I learned how to live a lie; keeping a flood of emotions behind a dam of pride, hesitation and anxiety' (TLRJ, p. 99). The irony here is that the way in which she is forced to behave exemplifies a pattern which has dominated her entire life in a traditional, Nonconformist environment controlled by men.

Rebecca positions herself, or rather is positioned, on a cusp of law and desire. At one point, she notices Bob staring at her. Here she is the object of the gaze which defines her in terms of women's roles in Maesglasau. She recognises the significance of the 'law': 'Then I steady myself and return to my work, as befits a woman approaching forty' and 'I bow into the machine and work away' (TLRJ, p. 98). But this is not the last word. Her behaviour and her desires have brought her knowledge; here, for the first time in the novel, she is conscious of performing a role and of the way in which she is more than a role. Bob is aware of this. But his stare suggests that he recognises also what she recognises about sin. According to the psychoanalytic critic Julia Kristeva, the biblical conception of sin, which is what the Joneses have been brought up to know, has always remained close 'to the concrete truth of the sexed and social being'.[24] In Bob's gaze, as the gaze of the 'law', Rebecca's role as moral, as well as life, giver surrenders its surety; as Kristeva says, 'sin is a logical unruliness, an incongruous act of judgement'.[25]

This chapter contrasts two new ways of naming which, in their different ways, make the world anew: the military language which comes with the Second World War and Italian which Rebecca begins to learn. Her relationship with Angelo ironically repeats the pattern of her life as a mother, a mixture of joy and misfortune: 'And this rebirth happened in the summer of 1943. Only to die again . . .' (TLRJ, p. 100). The structure of the Welsh version instigates an effective, heavy rhythm of repetition employing three sentences beginning with the same construction, 'darfu pan . . .' (dying/expiring when . . .): when Mussolini was overthrown and the Italian government surrendered, when the prisoners of war were released, and when Angelo was recalled (OTYG, p. 104).

The way in which Rebecca and Angelo come together is exemplified in the interrelationship between Welsh and Italian words. The words which are listed have significance for Rebecca's life. The list begins with 'ponte/pont/bridge' and 'finestra/ffenest/window', which summarise how Rebecca has spent much of her life in this secluded valley, looking out; building a bridge to others, not least her husband Evan and her blind children, and eventually Angelo himself; and looking for a bridge to her spiritual and sexual self. The latter is reinforced by the position of 'corpo/corff/body' at the centre of the list, while the word that follows, 'credere/credu/believe', signifies the importance of Christian belief to her life and identity. But the most important word of all, in terms of her life and her relationship with Angelo is the final one, 'celare/celu/hide/secret' (TLRJ, p. 99).

Despite the way in which Curtis's *War Voices* betrays an interest in war and a scepticism that wars will ever come to an end, both the texts discussed in this chapter value peace in the way in which it enables communities to prosper and, consciously or unconsciously, embrace many of the ideals of Welsh pacifism in the first two-thirds of the twentieth century. While it might not always be as explicitly concerned with pacifism as some of the other works discussed in this book, Price's novel demonstrates how the 'peace' of Welsh rural communities provided an expansive spiritual experience, but often one that was intellectually limited and limiting, not always benefiting women or allowing them to develop their sexual, spiritual, political and Welsh national aspirations and potential.

7

A Welsh Pacifist Translation of an English Classic . . . an Afterword

> There is a different complex of values embodied in every language . . . and full translation becomes possible only when those intentions become the same.
>
> (Ned Thomas, *The Welsh Extremist*)

This book is conceived as a beginning rather than an ending. As an introduction to a subject that has been overlooked in Welsh studies, it is intended to stimulate further study and debate. It suggests that Welsh writing contributes much to our understanding of pacifism and to what distinguishes Welsh from English pacifism. Although the two cannot be entirely separated, for much of the first half of the twentieth century there was a call to establish Welsh organisations and Welsh branches of the key pacifist movements. This reflected the influence of Welsh-language writers, academics and theologians in pacifist debates in Wales, which in turn was an index of the extent to which pacifism, the Welsh language, nationalism, Nonconformity and the growing consciousness of Wales as a small, independent nation were intricately connected.

Much of this study has revolved around two salient questions: how far did the ideas that impelled Welsh pacifism, such as those promoted by George M. Ll. Davies, Waldo and Gwenallt, permeate both Welsh- and English-language literature? And how far did Welsh pacifism have its origins in a Welsh-language intelligentsia? Such was this interrelationship that Welsh pacifists always had one eye on the future of the Welsh language in the generations to come. Many Welsh-language pacifist writers, such as Tegla Davies, Waldo

Williams and T. Gwynn Jones, wrote works for young readers, as well as texts targeting adults, and in them there are clear suggestions of the importance of peace, inner 'peacefulness' and the peaceful everyday life that people want. However, in the period following the conclusion of the Second World War, there was anxiety among Welsh-language speakers that there was a shortage of original Welsh-language books for young readers. Bell points out that 'in 1951, the Llanrwst National Eisteddfod, realizing the need for "suitable reading in Welsh for our young people", published . . . a fat volume of *Storïau Ias a Chyffro* (Thrilling and Exciting Stories)' written for this readership.[1]

In addition to original stories, the book included two translations which reflected another important development. A number of Welsh pacifist writers undertook translations of works from English editions into Welsh, but these were often intended for older readers, such as Thomas Parry's translation of *Hedda Gabler* (1930) and W. J. Gruffydd's translations, in 1950, of *King Lear* and Sophocles' *Antigone*. Given the post-war concern over the dearth of Welsh-language books for young readers, it is not surprising that the 1950s should witness translations into Welsh of a number of English classics. One of these is particularly important to the themes of this book: a Welsh translation of *Black Beauty* (*Du Del*), published in 1954, by the pacifist John Eilian, the bardic name of John Tudor Jones, who saw the war out as a newspaper correspondent and won a considerable reputation as a translator.[2] The project raises many questions. Why should Eilian have chosen to translate this particular text at this time? Does his translation betray any reasons why, as a pacifist, he should have selected this novel? Are his pacifist convictions reflected in the translation and, particularly, in the way in which he has adapted this particular English text? What insights does this translation provide into the nature of Welsh pacifism in the middle of the twentieth century and especially after the Second World War?

Published in 1877, *Black Beauty* was intended for a young adult audience, although it soon acquired a wider appeal. Eilian's translation and adaptation finds in Sewell's work, no doubt through the influence of many abridged English versions for children, ideas and themes that pervade Welsh pacifist writing in the first half of the twentieth century, such as respect for others, reverence for life generally, and the rejection of violence, abuse and cruelty. It is no news that in *Du Del* the relationship between horses and between humans and horses are analogous to relationships between people. It should be equally unsurprising that this Welsh translation of *Black Beauty* is so attuned to ideas in Welsh pacifism, such as 'personalism' and 'adnabod', as Sewell herself was born into a Quaker family and, although she eventually left the Society of Friends to join the Church of England, she remained active in evangelical circles.

Eilian's Welsh in *Du Del* captures the plain, simple narrative voice of the original English text. But in both the Welsh and the original nineteenth-century text, the pacifist voice reflects the forcefulness which characterises the conviction of religious dissenters. The critic Peter Hollindale could be writing for many Welsh pacifists when he says of Sewell's Quaker upbringing, 'to be pacific is not to be passive'.[3] But her original novel also anticipates Welsh pacifism in its emphasis upon pragmatic argument as much as spirituality and idealism. *Du Del* respects the way in which Sewell's novel, as Hollindale maintains, achieves a 'balancing of individual voices with a common moral idiom'.[4] One might add here, 'as Welsh pacifist novels of the 1930s tended to do', but there is more to this than Hollindale suggests.

Du Del follows the way in which Sewell's novel, as Horst Dölvers says, 'revolves around a small number of traditional values and moral attitudes' and, as in much Welsh pacifist writing, the way in which 'utterances . . . are index signs beyond their conventional communicative sign content: they characterise their speakers as by themselves "good", "gentle", "kind", "honest" and inclined to be "loving"'.[5] This aspect of pacifist writing is evident, for example, in George Davies's reflections on people in his essays and prison letters; the way Victor sees others in *Eunice Fleet*; and the way individuals are judged in Gwenallt's *Plasau'r Brenin*. It is a motif in Glyn Jones's short fiction where in some of his stories, as we have seen, it is developed negatively into an uncompromising judgementalism that inhibits the development of positive attitudes towards others. A translation into Welsh of this particular classic would have appealed to pacifists at this time, seeing themselves, and being seen, as presenting anti-war arguments and a critique of the codes of human behaviour legitimated by the cruelty, violence and horror of the Second World War. As has been so often pointed out, *Black Beauty* was 'the last great first-person narrative in the listen-to-my-life style'[6] and this was a style that had been revitalised in twentieth-century experiential writing about war.

As an abridged version of the novel, Eilian's translation omits details and aspects of the original book while subtly shifting the focus of the narrative to an even more overt pacifist perspective. This is evident in the second chapter of *Du Del*, 'Yr Helfa' (The Hunt). The running down of a small hare by huntsmen and hounds involves, as in the original novel, the destruction of an agricultural environment. While Sewell may have had in mind the destruction of the agrarian south by the industrial north in the American Civil War, which occurred less than a decade before she started work on the book, the scene would have had a particular resonance for Welsh pacifists, recalling the destruction of rural communities in west Wales to serve the war effort. But the response of the other horses to the arrival of the huntsmen and the indifference to their fields also echoes the way in which small nations in the 1930s and 1940s were overrun and destroyed. The idyllic life which Du Del enjoys with his mother is analogous to the external and internal peacefulness which human families desire above all else within their communities. But it is interrupted by violence, as were the Welsh rural communities in Waldo's and Gwenallt's poetry, and the peaceful cwm Maesglasau in Angharad Price's *O! Tyn y Gorchudd*.

Du Del's first experience of violence comes from the plough boy, Dic, who attacks the horses with sticks and stones to make them run, and the second experience comes in witnessing a hunt for the first time. Both these events, anticipating the greater violence that is to come later in the novel with the account of the Crimean War, reflect the Darwinian-based argument that, as Grayling summarises, 'war is the outcome of a natural propensity in humans'.[7] This chapter appears to have been adapted to emphasise what happens in this episode from a pacifist perspective. The hunt begins with the sound of noise in the distance, as might a cavalry charge, and closes with the death of the squire's son. The original chapter is pared down to highlight three events which would have resonance for Welsh pacifists in the 1930s and 1940s in addition to the destruction of the field: the panic of the hare which tries to escape through the wall but fails; the desperate attempts of the pursuing hunt to cross and get out of the stream; and the death of the young huntsman. The original text in which the body of the hare, torn apart by the dogs, is held up may have been deemed too harrowing for young readers. But in any event, the image of the bewildered hare – 'fe driodd yr ysgyfarnog fynd trwodd, ond methu' (p. 10) – encapsulates the confusion and sense of terror generated in Europe in the 1930s and 1940s.

The chapter closes with Du Del's mother pondering why men want to go to a hunt in which they and their horses can be killed and fields destroyed ('Cael eu briwo y maen' hw', a difetha'u ceffylau, a rhwygo'r caeau') (p. 12). The pacifist perspective and anti-war analogy are emphasised in the last sentence, expressing the puzzlement of the horses as to why anyone should do this ('Ond ceffylau wyt ti a fi, heb allu deall y pethau hyn') (p. 12). In *Du Del*, the young horse's introduction to the bridle, rein and saddle, which are essential to the separation of mother and foal, follows the episode of the hunt, and has a symbolic as well as a functional meaning. It hardly needs pointing out that this episode lends itself to reading through a framework provided by psychoanalytic semiotics, for Du Del's breaking in is associated, like much of the violence in the book, with men. But, additionally, it is analogous to the 'breaking in' of soldiers, Eilian's narrative having been translated and abridged so as to juxtapose more sharply the connection between masculinity and violence.

The later chapter 'Stori Capten' is similarly pared down to emphasise pacifist themes which would have resonance for readers in the 1950s. This chapter is given over to the story of an officer's horse which was taken to the Crimean War at the height of tensions between Russia and Turkey. The Crimean War is very relevant to pacifist and anti-war perspectives because it provides a notable example, anticipating the use of the press in the First World War, of public opinion being shaped by forces beyond its control. Initially *The Times* argued for peace, but it came to see itself leading the nation to war at a time when the government was reluctant to do so. During the Crimean War, *The Times* increased its circulation beyond that of all its rivals and became Britain's most powerful and influential newspaper.

Capten's preparation, journey to the Crimea and hours of standing are analogous to the experiences of troops in the First and Second World Wars. One strain in the story, concerning the officer himself, celebrates courage and heroism. As on First World War Welsh-language recruiting posters which called for 'Dynion Dewr' (brave men) to enlist, Capten describes his master as 'meistr dewr' (p. 62), which is evident in his continuing on foot in order to encourage his men after he has been thrown from his horse ('Wrthi'n calonogi ei frodyr i fynd ymlaen') (p. 62). But the use of the Welsh word 'frodyr' (brothers) to describe the troops has a special resonance for Welsh pacifism, suggesting the concept of 'brawdoliaeth' (brotherhood). Here, Capten's officer is depicted like the war heroes of *The Boy's Own Paper* and other comics which we mentioned in Chapter 1 in the discussion of militarism and cultural discourse. But another theme in Capten's story undercuts the focus on courage in the sense that in running beside his cavalry, which overtakes him, the officer may be seen as a symbol of futility. This is reinforced by the retelling of the familiar story of the Crimean War in which hundreds of cavalry soldiers were massacred by cannon fire. In this version, the sound of the cannons recalls how the hunt in the earlier chapter is announced by the sound of hooves and a bugle, and the death of the officer mirrors the death of the squire's young son in the earlier chapter.

These parallels and echoes recall the sense of Du Del's mother's bewilderment over why men should hunt mentioned earlier. In Sewell's text, Black Beauty comments upon the futility of the charge. Unlike the famous observation in Tennyson's poem, 'The Charge of the Light Brigade' – 'Theirs not to reason why' – the horses in *Black Beauty* do question it. But Eilian's *Du Del* omits the conversation between Black Beauty and Capten in Sewell's original novel and relies on an implied questioning which emerges from a comparison of the Crimean War with the hunt earlier in the book which the horses certainly do question. In *Du Del*, the horror of war is conveyed in a muted but effective way in the reference to the number of men and horses that Capten has seen killed ('imi weled lladd llawer gŵr llawer march', pp. 61–2) and the overwhelming sound and light from the guns: 'Yr oedd y gynnau mawr yn rhuo ar bob tu, ac fe gwympodd llawer dyn' (p. 62). In the wake of the Second World War, this image would have had resonance for those who had recently had experience of fire power on a greater scale, aerial bombardment and the dropping of atomic bombs.

Du Del is a version of the original book which has been adapted to emphasise experiences and images which would have had a particular resonance in the 1950s for Welsh people with experience of the overturning of rural communities, the invasion of small nations by their powerful neighbours and the horror of war. In its later chapters, *Du Del* closely follows Sewell's interest in how economic and commercial interests can encourage cruelty and how profit can override respect for the value and quality of another life – themes that were central to the work of George Davies, Iorwerth Peate, Waldo and Gwenallt in the 1930s and 1940s. Eilian's abridged version brings into much sharper focus the contrast between the economically driven environment in the latter half of the book, which brings Du Del to his knees, and the peaceful rural life he lives at the beginning of the novel, which is analogous to the Welsh rural communities in which Welsh pacifist ideals had their roots.

A further motif that would have had a special resonance for Welsh pacifists is the way in which Du Del is repeatedly inspected and judged on whether he is fit for purpose. In writing her original text, Sewell may well have had in mind not only horse fairs but markets in which black slaves were sold. In the 1920s and 1930s, it would have been impossible to read these scenes without thinking of the importance of eugenics to Nazi-led Germany and Hitler's emphasis on pure breeding in *Mein Kampf*.

The way in which this abridged text brings salient images into juxtaposition highlights pacifist themes which point towards alternative ways of living where the emphasis is no longer upon violence, cruelty and killing. Eilian, in effect, recasts the narrative so that it is haunted by acts of kindness, sympathy and generosity. What is impressive is the level of detail which is analogous to war: the breaking in of horses as analogous to the breaking in of soldiers; the body of Ginger in a cart redolent of the recovery of the war dead; and the cruelty meted out to cab horses as indicative of a world rooted in an acceptance of interpersonal violence. The blinkers which the horses are made to wear so that they can only see ahead are analogous to the wider failure in society to look, as pacifism does, from different perspectives. *Du Del* encourages its young readership to realise that they are still having to live with violence, cruelty and war and, therefore, continue to have challenges to face.

The way in which writing for children can provide opportunities to reflect on war, violence and peace has a long tradition in world literature, which was seized upon by the Bloomsbury pacifists Roger Fry and Winifred Gill in their Omega workshops (1913–19) where they promoted children's writing and children's art in two exhibitions in 1917 and 1919. The events and experiences of *Du Del* are analogous to the world in which its readers live and will continue to live. It is a world where war did not end with the Crimean War any more than it ended with the conclusion of the Second World War. *Du Del* returns its readers to an important premise which encapsulates the importance of studying the part which pacifism has played, and continues to play, in Welsh culture. It is interestingly summarised by Grayling: 'Meanwhile we are still having to live with war, and therefore have a battle to fight: to prevent it whenever possible, to limit it if not, to press for humanitarian restraint when it happens, to hold war makers to account, to argue and educate against it always.'[8] His perspective is one which he himself, as discussed in Chapter 1, has labelled 'realist' and 'pessimist'. But even if we still have to live with war, pacifism has a purpose and crucial role, as do the texts discussed in this study, and that is to 'argue and educate against it always'.

In her writings, Virginia Woolf conceived of war not simply as a product of external events but of inner turmoil and psychological conditioning, an argument which, as we have seen, had an important influence on Emyr Humphreys's *A Toy Epic* and *Outside the House of Baal*. In both their works, this is supplanted by exploring peace, to borrow the words of David Cadman and Scherto Gill, 'not as something that is imposed from outside, but as a shared human aspiration, rooted in [what they see as] our innate peacefulness, and our relationship with others and within our communities and societies'.[9] They betray no knowledge of the Welsh pacifists discussed in this book, but what they say encapsulates exactly the mode of being found in, or sought in, many Welsh pacifist texts including, of course, Eilian's translation of *Black Beauty*. Welsh pacifist texts have a further importance in that they ultimately promote a peaceful, if not prayerful, mode of being which extends from the inside out and which, if supported with appropriate external structures, supplants aggression and violence.

Notes

1: Mapping Welsh Pacifism

1 Daniel Hughes, 'Translator's foreword', in T. E. Nicholas, *Prison Sonnets*, trans. Daniel Hughes, Dewi Emrys, Eric Davies and Wil Ifan, Preface by Dr Iorwerth Peate (London: W. Griffiths & Co., 1948).

2 R. S. White, *Pacifism and English Literature: Minstrels of Peace* (Basingstoke: Palgrave Macmillan, 2008), p. 6.

3 David Cadman and Scherto Gill, 'Introduction', in David Cadman and Scherto Gill (eds), *Peacefulness: Being Peace and Making Peace* (Reykjavik: Spirit of Humanity Press, 2017), p. 8.

4 George M. Ll. Davies, *Pilgrimage of Peace* (London: The Fellowship of Reconciliation, 1950), p. 25. Subsequent references to this work are abbreviated as 'PP' and page numbers are given in parentheses in the text.

5 M. Wynn Thomas, '*Outside the House of Baal*: the evolution of a major novel', in Sam Adams (ed.), *Seeing Wales Whole: Essays on the Literature of Wales. In Honour of Meic Stephens* (Cardiff: University of Wales Press, 1998), p. 125 (pp. 121–43).

6 George M. Ll. Davies, *Essays Towards Peace* (London: Sheppard Press, 1946), p. 66. Subsequent references to this work are abbreviated as 'ETP' and page numbers are given in parentheses in the text.

7 Ned Thomas, *The Welsh Extremist* (Talybont: Y Lolfa, [1973]; rpt 1991 with a new concluding chapter), p. 35.

8 David Gee, *Spectacle, Reality, Resistance: Confronting a Culture of Militarism* (London: Forces Watch, 2014), p. 10.

9 Gee, *Spectacle, Reality, Resistance*, pp. 10–11.

10 Gee, *Spectacle, Reality, Resistance*, pp. 22–3.

11 Peace Pledge Union, 2018, Online. Available at *www.ppu.org.uk* (accessed 3 August 2018).

12 George M. Ll. Davies, *Religion and the Quest for Peace* (London: The Peace Pledge Union, 1942), p. 8. Subsequent references to this pamphlet are abbreviated as 'RQP' and page numbers are given in parentheses in the text.

13 Gee, *Spectacle, Reality, Resistance*, p. 12.
14 Gee, *Spectacle, Reality, Resistance*, p. 12.
15 Gee, *Spectacle, Reality, Resistance*, p. 13.
16 K. O. Morgan, 'Peace Movements in Wales, 1899–1945', *Welsh History Review*, 10/3 (June 1981), 400 (398–430).
17 K. O. Morgan, 'Peace Movements in Wales, 1899–1945', 400.
18 Jen Llywelyn, *Pilgrim of Peace: A Life of George M. Ll. Davies* (Talybont: Y Lolfa, 2016), p. 117.
19 Llywelyn, *Pilgrim of Peace*, p. 124.
20 The Welsh-language version has the title *Y Tri Llais* (The Three Voices) which may have been suggested by Dylan Thomas's *Under Milk Wood: A Play for Voices*, especially since the Welsh-language text, like Thomas's work, makes use of dream sequences.
21 Linden Peach, *The Fiction of Emyr Humphreys: Contemporary Critical Perspectives* (Cardiff: University of Wales Press, 2011), p. 32.
22 Emyr Humphreys, *A Toy Epic* ([1958]; rpt Bridgend: Seren Books, 1989), p. 23. Subsequent references to this edition, edited and introduced by M. Wynn Thomas, are abbreviated as 'ATE' and page numbers are given in parentheses in the text.
23 Joanna Bourke, *Wounding the World: How Military Violence and War-Play Invade Our Lives* (London: Virago, 2014), p. 228.
24 Lyn Smith, *Voices Against War, A Century of Protest* (Harmondsworth: Penguin, 2009), p. 71.
25 '"Now they have all gone," said Louis . . . I am left standing by the wall among the flowers. It is very early, before lessons. Flower after flower is specked on the depths of green. The petals are harlequins"' (Virginia Woolf, *The Waves*, ed. Michael Herbert and Susan Sellars (Cambridge: Cambridge University Press, 2011), p. 7).
26 Virginia Woolf, 'Thoughts on peace in an air raid', in *The Essays of Virginia Woolf*, vol. 6, ed. Stuart N. Clarke (London: The Hogarth Press, 2011), p. 244 (pp. 242–8).
27 Adam Riches, *When the Comics Went to War* (Edinburgh: Mainstream Publishing, 2009), p. 128.
28 Riches, *When the Comics Went to War*, p. 22. *The Boy's Own Paper* was published by the Religious Tract Society from 1879 to 1939; by Lutterworth Press, 1939–63; by Purnell & Sons Ltd, 1963–5; and BPC Publishing Ltd, 1965–7. It ran for a total of 2,511 issues, making it one of the longest-running story papers published in the UK.
29 Riches, *When the Comics Went to War*, p. 23.
30 Riches, *When the Comics Went to War*, p. 25.
31 Oliver P. Richmond, *Peace: A Very Short Introduction* (Oxford: Oxford University Press, 2014), p. 1.
32 Richmond, *Peace*, p. 1.
33 Thomas, 'Outside the House of Baal: the evolution of a major novel', p. 122.
34 Cadman and Gill, *Peacefulness*, p. 9.
35 C. E. Raven, *The Starting Point of Pacifism* (London: Peace Pledge Union, 1940), p. 9.

36 Catrin Stevens, *Iorwerth C. Peate* (Cardiff: University of Wales Press, 1986), p. 37.
37 Iorwerth C. Peate, *Ym Mhob Pen . . . Ysgrifau* (Llandysul: Gwasg Gomer, 1948), p. 56.
38 Peate. *Ym Mhob Pen*, p. 56.
39 Thomas, *The Welsh Extremist*, p. 12.
40 See, for example, Gwynfor Evans's book-length study of this subject, *Heddychiaeth Gristnogol yng Nghymru* (Llangollen: Cymdeithas y Cymrod yng Nghymru, 1991).
41 Morgan, 'Peace Movements in Wales', p. 398.
42 Emyr Price, *David Lloyd George* (Cardiff: University of Wales Press, 2006), pp. 200, 202.
43 Biography of T. Gwynn Jones, National Library of Wales, NLW, 2001, Online. Available at *http://yba.llgc.org.uk/en/s2-JONE-GWY-1871.html* (accessed 3 August 2018).
44 *The Grail*, Magazine of the Calvinistic Methodist Theological College, Aberystwyth, 4/12 (1911).
45 T. Gwynn Jones, 'The Heart of a Man', *The Grail*, 4/12 (1911), 58 (55–8).
46 Sian Rhiannon Evans, 'The true "Gymraes": images of women in women's nineteenth-century Welsh periodicals', in Angela V. John (ed.), *Our Mothers' Land: Chapters in Welsh Women's History 1830–1939* (Cardiff: University of Wales Press, 1991), p. 86 (pp. 69–91).
47 Letter to the Prime Minister and others, Papers of Mrs Gwladys Thoday, Bangor University Archive.
48 John Davies, *A History of Wales* (Harmondsworth: Penguin, [1990]; revised and updated 2007), p. 629.
49 'Y Tro Olaf' is an intriguing creative essay which in some respects anticipates T. Rowland Hughes's *O Law i Law* (1943). It is constructed out of the experience of cleaning, oiling and reassembling a grandfather clock. Since, this only needs to be done every twenty-five years, the next time it needs to be done the responsibility will fall to someone else. See, T. J. Morgan, *W. J. Gruffydd* (Cardiff: University of Wales, Press, 1970), p. 54.
50 *Eples, Cyfrol o Farddoniaeth (1951), Gwreiddiau, Cyfrol o Farddoniaeth (1959) and Y Coed* (1969).
51 *Baledi'r Ddeunawfed Ganrif* (1935), a caustic study of eighteenth-century, popular literature; *Hanes Llenyddiaeth Gymraeg hyd 1900* (1944) and a major edition of the work of the medieval Welsh poet Dafydd ap Gwilym, *Gwaith Dafydd ap Gwilym* (1952).
52 Angharad Price, Biography of Sir T. H. Parry-Williams, NLW, 2014, Online. Available at *http://yba.llgc.org.uk/en/s10-PARR-HER-1887.html* (accessed 3 August 2018). The works published in this period include *Olion* (1935), *Lloffion* (1942), *O'r Pedwar Gwynt* (1944), *Ugain o Gerddi* (1949), *Myfyrdodau* (1957) and *Pensynnu* (1966).
53 Hughes published a novel a year, around Christmastime, from 1943 until his early death in 1947, several of which have been translated posthumously into English. Katherine Williams ('Kate Roberts'), Biography of Thomas Rowland Hughes, NLW, 2001, Online. Available at *http://yba.llgc.org.uk/en/s2-HUGH-ROW-1903.html* (accessed 3 August 2018). *O Law i Law* (1943), his

most innovative and most accomplished work, was followed by *William Jones* (1944), *Yr Ogof* (1945), *Chwalfa* (1946) and *Y Cychwyn* (1947).

54 Davies, *A History of Wales*, p. 629.

55 Llywelyn, *Pilgrim of Peace*, p. 258.

56 R. Gerallt Jones, 'Like foolish boys: some thoughts on the poetry of two cousins', in Sam Adams (ed.), *Seeing Wales Whole*, pp. 105–6 (pp. 102–20).

57 T. Gwynn Jones, *Thomas Huws Davies, O.B.E. (1882–1940)* (London: The Honourable Society of Cymmrodorion, 1941), p. 19.

58 Davies, *A History of Wales*, pp. 494–5.

59 Russell Davies, '"Do not go gentle into that good night"? Women and suicide in Carmarthenshire', in Angela V. John (ed.), *Our Mothers' Land*, p. 100 (pp. 93–108).

60 Evans, *Heddychiaeth Gristnogol*, p. 46.

61 Price, *David Lloyd George*, p. 198.

62 H. Idris Bell, 'The Twentieth Century', appendix to Thomas Parry, *A History of Welsh Literature*, trans. Idris Bell (Oxford: Clarendon Press, 1955), p. 408 (pp. 374–501).

63 They include R. T. Jenkins, W. J. Gruffydd, Professor Cyril Brett, Professor of English at University College Cardiff, D. Gwilym James, a friend of Peate's in Aberystwyth, Gwyn Jones who became Professor of English at University College, Cardiff, Professor David Williams, John Griffiths from the BBC, Kate Roberts, before she moved to the Rhondda, Tom Bassett, publisher of *Y Llenor* and a conscientious objector during the war, and Sir Cyril Fox of Yr Amgueddfa Genedlaethol (Donahaye, *The Greatest Need*, p. 83).

64 Iorwerth Peate, *Rhwng Dau Fyd* (Between Two Worlds) (Aberystwyth: Cambrian News, 1976), p. 88.

65 Jasmine Donahaye, *The Greatest Need: The Creative Life and Troubled Times of Lily Tobias, a Welsh Jew in Palestine* (Dinas Powys: Honno, 2015), p. 58.

66 M. Wynn Thomas, 'From Walt to Waldo: Whitman's Welsh admirers', *Walt Whitman Quarterly Review*, 10/2 (1992), 63 (61–73).

67 James Nicholas, *Waldo Williams* (Cardiff: University of Wales Press, 1975), p. 12.

68 Nicholas, *Waldo Williams*, p. 12.

69 Thomas, 'From Walt to Waldo', p. 65.

70 Nicholas, *Waldo Williams*, p. 12.

71 Bell, 'The Twentieth Century', p. 422.

72 Heloise Brown, *'The Truest Form of Patriotism': Pacifist Feminism in Britain, 1870–1902* (Manchester: Manchester University Press, 2003), pp. 14–15.

73 Brown, *'The Truest Form of Patriotism'*, pp. 16–17.

74 Brown, *'The Truest Form of Patriotism'*, p. 18.

75 Llywelyn, *Pilgrim of Peace*, p. 135

76 Morgan, 'Peace Movements in Wales', p. 414.

77 Llion Wigley, Biography of Merfyn Lloyd Turner, NLW, 2001, Online. Available at *http://yba.llgc.org.uk/en/s10-TURN-LLO-1915.html* (accessed 3 August 2018).

78 Wigley, Merfyn Lloyd Turner, *http://yba.llgc.org.uk/en/s10-TURN-LLO-1915.html*.

79 Price, Biography of Sir T. H. Parry-Williams.

80 Derec Llwyd Morgan, Biography of Thomas Parry, NLW, 2009, Online. Available at *http://yba.llgc.org.uk/en/s6-PARR-THO-1904.html* (accessed 3 August 2018).
81 Morgan, 'Peace Movements in Wales', p. 422.
82 Morgan, 'Peace Movements in Wales', p. 423.
83 Gwynfor Evans, *Land of My Fathers: 2000 Years of Welsh History* ([1974]; English version, Talybont: Y Lolfa, 1992), p. 439.
84 Davies, *A History of Wales*, p. 511.
85 Bell, 'The Twentieth Century', p. 395.
86 Davies, *A History of Wales*, p. 496. The Independent Labour Party was formed by Keir Hardie in 1893.
87 Davies, *A History of Wales*, p. 501.
88 Davies, *A History of Wales*, p. 501.
89 Morgan, 'Peace Movements in Wales', p. 416.
90 Davies, *A History of Wales*, p. 499.
91 Davies, *A History of Wales*, p. 500.
92 Bell, 'The Twentieth Century', p. 388.
93 Thomas, *The Welsh Extremist*, p. 133.
94 R. Ruck (trans.), *T. Rowland Hughes, William Jones* (Aberystwyth: Gwasg Aberystwyth, 1953). The book was originally published in Welsh in 1944.
95 Ruck, *T. Rowland Hughes, William Jones*, p. 111.
96 Davies, *A History of Wales*, p. 495.
97 Morgan, 'Peace Movements in Wales, p. 416.
98 Jasmine Donahaye, 'Introduction', in Lily Tobias, *Eunice Fleet* ([1933]; rpt. Dinas Powys: Honno, 2004), p. xii. Subsequent references to this novel are abbreviated as 'EF' and page numbers are incorporated in parentheses in the text.
99 Morgan, 'Peace Movements in Wales', pp. 415–16.
100 Bell, 'The Twentieth Century', p. 422. A detailed and nuanced account of the opposition to, and the support of, the war in the south Wales industrial belt is provided in Aled Eirug, *The Opposition to the Great War in Wales 1914–1918* (Cardiff: University of Wales Press, 2018). He also attributes importance to the influence of the Russian revolution (pp. 99–104).
101 See, for example, Stephen Knight, *A Hundred Years of Fiction* (Cardiff: University of Wales Press, 2004); H. Gustav Klaus (ed.), *The Socialist Novel in Britain* (Brighton: Harvester, 1982) and Raymond Williams, *The Welsh Industrial Novel* (Cardiff: University of Wales Press, 1979).
102 Llywelyn, *Pilgrim of Peace*, p. 257.
103 Emyr Humphreys, *Outside the House of Baal* ([1965]; rpt. London: J. M. Dent & Sons Ltd., 1988), pp. 332–4. Subsequent references to this edition are abbreviated as 'OTHB' and page numbers are given in parentheses in the text.
104 Peate, *Ym Mhob Pen*, p. 23.
105 Peate, *Ym Mhob Pen*, p. 23.
106 The National Eisteddfod was nominated for the Nobel Peace Prize in 2004.
107 Peate, *Ym Mhob Pen*, p. 24.
108 D. Densil Morgan, *The Span of the Cross* (Cardiff: University of Wales Press, 2011), p. 161.
109 Morgan, *The Span of the Cross*, p. 160.

110 Morgan, *The Span of the Cross*, p. 159.
111 A. C. Grayling, *War: An Enquiry* (New Haven and London: Yale University Press, 2017), p. 145.
112 Grayling, *War*, p. 146.
113 Morgan, *The Span of the Cross*, p. 161.
114 Morgan, *The Span of the Cross*, pp. 160–1.
115 Morgan, *The Span of the Cross*, p. 234.
116 Meic Stephens (trans.), *For the Sake of Wales: The Memoirs of Gwynfor Evans* ([1996]; Cardiff: Welsh Academic Press, 2001), p. 234.
117 Gee, *Spectacle, Reality, Resistance*, p. 10.
118 Gee, *Spectacle, Reality, Resistance*, p. 10.
119 Davies, *A History of Wales*, p. 579.
120 Ian Kershaw, *Hitler* (Harmondsworth: Penguin Books, 1998), p. 265.
121 *Documents concerning German–Polish Relations and the Outbreak of Hostilities between Great Britain and Germany on September 3, 1939* (London: H.M. Stationery Office, 1939), p. 92.
122 *Documents concerning German–Polish Relations*, p. 102.
123 *Documents concerning German–Polish Relations*, p. 104.
124 Bell, *The Twentieth Century*, p. 385.
125 Bell, *The Twentieth Century*, p. 390.
126 T. Gwynn Jones, *Caniadau* (Abertawe: Hughes a'i Fab (Cyhoeddwyr), 1978), p. 112.
127 T. Gwynn Jones, 'Argoed', trans. Anthony Conran, in Anthony Conran (trans.), *The Penguin Book of Welsh Verse* (Harmondsworth: Penguin, 1967), p. 235. Subsequent references this book are abbreviated as 'WP' and page numbers are given in parentheses in the text.
128 Gwilym Arthur Jones, Biography of E. Morgan Humphreys, NLW, 2001, Online. Available at *http://yba.llgc.org.uk/en/s2-HUMP-MOR-1882.html* (accessed 3 August 2018).
129 Thomas, *The Welsh Extremist*, p. 11.
130 Thomas, *The Welsh Extremist*, p. 12.
131 *The Welsh Outlook* (July 1925), Editorial, 1.
132 Thomas, *The Welsh Extremist*, p. 12.
133 Morgan, 'Peace Movements in Wales', pp. 423–4.
134 Stevens, *Iorwerth C. Peate*, p. 51.
135 Stevens, *Iorwerth C. Peate*, p. 51.
136 *A Great Welshman: Symposium of Tributes to Dr. T. Gwynn Jones* (Cardiff: The Welsh Committee of the Communist Party; South Wales Bookshop Ltd), p. 16. Although no date is given, two of the contributions are dated 1944.
137 *A Great Welshman: Symposium of Tributes to Dr. T. Gwynn Jones.*
138 Revd J. Vyrnwy Morgan, *The Philosophy of Welsh History* (London: John Lane, The Bodley Head, 1914), p. 118.
139 Morgan, *The Philosophy of Welsh History*, p. 11.
140 Thomas, *The Welsh Extremist*, p. 13.
141 M. Wynn Thomas, *In the Shadow of the Pulpit: Literature and Nonconformist Wales* (Cardiff: University of Wales Press, 2010), p. 258.
142 Davies, *A History of Wales*, p. 631.
143 Thomas, *In the Shadow of the Pulpit*, p. 258.
144 Davies, *A History of Wales*, p. 630.

145 Meic Stephens, Obituary of Gwynfor Evans, *Independent*, 21 April 2005 [Online]. Available at *https://www.independent.co.uk/news/obituaries/gwynfor-evans-49* (accessed 3 August 2018).
146 Morgan, 'Peace Movements in Wales', p. 425.
147 Morgan, 'Peace Movements in Wales', p. 425
148 Morgan, 'Peace Movements in Wales', p. 427.
149 Morgan, 'Peace Movements in Wales', p. 428.
150 Price, *David Lloyd George*, p. 205.
151 Llywelyn, *Pilgrim of Peace*, p. 256.
152 Evans, *Heddychiaeth Gristnogol*, p. 43.
153 Stevens, *Iorwerth C. Peate*, p. 37.
154 Peate, *Ym Mhob Pen*, pp. 77–9.
155 Peate, *Ym Mhob Pen*, p. 76.
156 Peate, *Ym Mhob Pen*, p. 76.
157 Peate, *Ym Mhob Pen*, p. 76.
158 Peate, *Ym Mhob Pen*, p.50.
159 Peate, *Ym Mhob Pen*, p. 72.
160 Peate, *Ym Mhob Pen*, p. 56.
161 Stephens, *For the Sake of Wales*, p. 235.
162 Stephens, *For the Sake of Wales*, pp. 235–6.
163 By 1962, chapel affiliation was down in the Presbyterian Church of Wales (to 131,000), the Congregationalists (to 125,000), the Baptists (to 90,000) and Methodists (to 16,500). See Morgan, *The Span of the Cross*, p. 212.
164 Emyr Humphreys, *The Shop* (Bridgend: Seren, 2005), pp. 86–7.
165 Humphreys, *The Shop*, p. 86.
166 White, *Pacifism and English Literature*, p. 18.
167 Stephens, *For the Sake of Wales*, p. 234.
168 Kathleen Lonsdale, *Removing the Causes of War*, Swarthmore Lecture, Society of Friends, 1953 (London: George Allen & Unwin Ltd, 1953), pp. 16–17.
169 Grayling, *War: An Enquiry*, p. 235.
170 Lonsdale, *Removing the Causes of War*, p. 16.
171 Lonsdale, *Removing the Causes of War*, p. 16.
172 Emyr Humphreys, *Unconditional Surrender* (Bridgend: Seren, [1996], rpt 1997), p. 156.
173 Lonsdale, *Removing the Causes of War*, p. 17.
174 Joseph Cohen 'Conversations with Dannie Abse' in *The Poetry of Dannie Abse: Critical Essays and Reminiscences*, ed. Joseph Cohen (London: Robson Books, 1983), p. 173.
175 Lonsdale, *Removing the Causes of War*, p. 18.
176 Evans, *Heddychiaeth Gristnogol*, p. 42.
177 Evans, *Heddychiaeth Gristnogol*, p. 42.
178 Evans, *Heddychiaeth Gristnogol*, p. 42.
179 Jane Aaron and M. Wynn Thomas, '"Pulling you through changes": Welsh writing in English before, between and after two referenda', in M. Wynn Thomas (ed.), *Welsh Writing in English* (Cardiff: University of Wales Press, 2003), p. 290, [278–309].
180 Richmond, *Peace*, p. 3.
181 Aaron and Thomas, 'Pulling you through changes', p. 290.

182 White, *Pacifism and English Literature*, p. 6.
183 Richmond, *Peace*, p. 4.
184 Richmond, *Peace*, p. 9.
185 Thomas, *The Welsh Extremist*, p. 15.
186 Thomas, *The Welsh Extremist*, p. 15.
187 Thomas, *The Welsh Extremist*, p. 16.
188 Thomas, *The Welsh Extremist*, p. 17.
189 Thomas, *The Welsh Extremist*, p. 19.
190 Thomas, *The Welsh Extremist*, pp. 17–18.
191 Thomas, *The Welsh Extremist*, p. 17.
192 Thomas, *The Welsh Extremist*, p. 18.
193 Thomas, *The Welsh Extremist*, p. 17.
194 Thomas, *The Welsh Extremist*, p. 17.

2: Disruptive Bibles

1 M. Wynn Thomas, '*Outside the House of Baal*: the evolution of a major novel', in Sam Adams (ed.), *Seeing Wales Whole: Essays on the Literature of Wales. In Honour of Meic Stephens* (Cardiff: University of Wales Press, 1998), p. 126.
2 George M. Ll. Davies, *Pilgrimage of Peace* (London: The Fellowship of Reconciliation, 1950), pp. 64–5. Subsequent references to this work are abbreviated as 'PP' and page numbers are given in parentheses in the text.
3 K. O. Morgan, 'Peace Movements in Wales, 1899–1945', *Welsh History Review*, 10/3 (June 1981), 409–10 (398–430).
4 Morgan, 'Peace Movements in Wales', 410.
5 George M. Ll. Davies, *Essays Towards Peace* (London: Sheppard Press, 1946), p. 65. Subsequent references to this work are abbreviated as 'ETP' and page numbers are given in parentheses in the text.
6 George M. Ll. Davies, *Religion and the Quest for Peace* (London: The Peace Pledge Union, 1942), p. 7. Subsequent references to this work are abbreviated as 'RQP' and page numbers are given in parentheses in the text.
7 David Gee, *Spectacle, Reality, Resistance: Confronting a Culture of Militarism* (London: Forces Watch, 2014), p. 13.
8 Gee, *Spectacle, Reality, Resistance*, p. 14.
9 Gee, *Spectacle, Reality, Resistance*, p. 14.
10 Jen Llywelyn, *Pilgrim of Peace: A Life of George M. Ll. Davies* (Talybont: Y Lolfa, 2016), p. 81.
11 Llywelyn, *Pilgrim of Peace*, p. 81.
12 Revd John Ellis Meredith, Biography of George M. Ll. Davies, NLW, 2001, Online. Available at *http://yba.llgc.org.uk/en/s2-DAVI-LLO-1880.html* (accessed 3 August 2018).
13 Llywelyn, *Pilgrim of Peace*, p. 42.
14 Llywelyn, *Pilgrim of Peace*, p. 202.
15 David Schmitt, 'Sermons', Concordia theology, Online, 2011. Available at *https://concordiatheology.org>sermon-structs* (accessed 3 August 2018).
16 T. Gwynn Jones, *The Culture and Tradition of Wales* (Wrexham: Urdd y Derynas, 1927), p. 20.

17 Virginia Woolf, 'Thoughts on peace in an air raid', in *The Essays of Virginia Woolf*, vol. 6, ed. Stuart N. Clarke (London: The Hogarth Press, 2011), p. 243.
18 Llywelyn, *Pilgrim of Peace*, p. 80.
19 Woolf, 'Thoughts on peace in an air raid', p. 243.
20 C. E. Raven, *The Starting Point of Pacifism* (London: Peace Pledge Union, 1940), p. 5.
21 Raven, *The Starting Point of Pacifism*, p. 5.
22 T. Gwynn Jones, *The Culture and Tradition of Wales*, p. 22.
23 'Pennar' is the *nom-de-plume* of William Thomas Davies (1911–96).
24 Herbert Hughes, 'Introduction', in Pennar Davies, *Diary of a Soul*, trans. Herbert Hughes (Talybont: Y Lolfa, 2011), p. 16.
25 Davies, *Diary of a Soul*, p. 23.
26 Davies, *Diary of a Soul*, p. 65.
27 Davies, *Diary of a Soul*, p. 85.
28 Davies, *Diary of a Soul*, p. 75.
29 Davies, *Diary of a Soul*, p. 202.
30 *Storïau'r Tir Glas* (Stories of the Green Land) (1936), *Storïau'r Tir Coch* (Stories of the Red Land) (1941) and *Storïau'r Tir Du* (Stories of the Black Land) (1949).
31 Hywel Teifi Edwards, Biography of D. J. Williams, NLW, 2001, Online. Available at *http://yba.llgc.org.uk/en/s2-WILL-JOH-1885.html* (accessed 3 August 2018).
32 Glyn Jones, *The Dragon Has Two Tongues* (Cardiff: University of Wales Press, 2001), p. 31. See also Tony Brown, 'Introduction', *The Collected Stories of Glyn Jones* (Cardiff: University of Wales Press, 1999), xli–xlii. Subsequent references to this edition of Jones's stories are abbreviated as 'GJCS' and page numbers are given in parentheses in the text.
33 R. Ruck (trans.), *T. Rowland Hughes, William Jones* (Aberystwyth: Gwasg Aberystwyth, 1953), p. 74.
34 Jack Zipes, 'Preface', in Tina Pippin and George Aichele (eds), *Violence, Utopia and the Kingdom of God: Fantasy and Ideology in the Bible* (London and New York: Routledge, 1998), (ix–xii).
35 Julia Kristeva, *Powers of Horror: An Essay on Abjection* (New York: Columbia University Press, 1982), p. 3.
36 Kristeva, *Powers of Horror*, p. 3.
37 Kristeva, *Powers of Horror*, p. 1.
38 Kristeva, *Powers of Horror*, p. 127.
39 Kristeva, *Powers of Horror*, p. 127.
40 Kristeva, *Powers of Horror*, p. 3.
41 George Aichele, 'Jesus' violence', in Pippin and Aichele (eds), *Violence, Utopia and the Kingdom of God*, pp. 84–7 (pp. 72–91).

3: Prison(s)

1 T. E. Nicholas, *Llygad y Drws: Sonedau'r Carchar* (Aberystwyth: Gwasg Aberystwyth, 1940) and *Canu'r Carchar* (Ysgrifennwyd yng Ngharcharau Abertawe a Brixton) (Llandysul: Gwasg Gomer, 1943). Subsequent references to this latter selection are abbreviated as 'CC' and page numbers are

incorporated in parentheses in the text. T. E. Nicholas, *Prison Sonnets*, trans. Daniel Hughes, Dewi Emrys, Eric Davies and Wil Ifan, Preface by Iorwerth Peate and Translator's Foreword by Daniel Hughes (London: W. Griffiths & Co., 1948). Subsequent references to this edition are abbreviated as 'PS' and page numbers are incorporated in parentheses in the text.

2 K. O. Morgan, 'Peace Movements in Wales, 1899–1945', *Welsh History Review*, 10/3 (June 1981), 423 (398–430).

3 Bell, 'The Twentieth Century', appendix to Thomas Parry, *A History of Welsh Literature* trans. Idris Bell (Oxford: Clarendon Press, 1955), p. 423.

4 W. Clark Gilpin, 'The Letter from Prison in Christian History and Theology', University of Chicago Divinity School, Online, 2003, p. 1. Available at *https://divinity.uchicago.edu>webforum* (accessed 3 August 2018).

5 Merfyn Turner, *A Pretty Sort of Prison* (London and Dunmow: Pall Mall Press, 1964), p. 7.

6 Turner, *A Pretty Sort of Prison*, pp. 7–8.

7 Jen Llywelyn, *Pilgrim of Peace: A Life of George M. Ll. Davies* (Talybont: Y Lolfa, 2016), p. 124.

8 Llywelyn, *Pilgrim of Peace*, p. 106.

9 Llywelyn, *Pilgrim of Peace*, p. 118.

10 George M. Ll. Davies, *Essays Towards Peace* (London: Sheppard Press, 1946), p. 52. Subsequent references are abbreviated as 'ETP' and page numbers are given in parentheses in the text.

11 Llywelyn, *Pilgrim of Peace*, p. 124.

12 Llywelyn, *Pilgrim of Peace*, p. 124.

13 *The Welsh Outlook* (November 1939), 287.

14 Dyfnallt Morgan, *D. Gwenallt Jones* (Cardiff: University of Wales Press, 1972), p. 10.

15 Ned Thomas, *The Welsh Extremist* (Talybont: Y Lolfa, [1973]; rpt 1991 with a new concluding chapter), p. 50.

16 D. Gwenallt Jones, *Plasau'r Brenin* (Llandysul: Gwasg Gomer, 1934), p. 62. Subsequent references to this edition are abbreviated as 'PB' and are given in parentheses in the text.

17 D. Densil Morgan, 'Gwenallt: Poet of Flesh and Spirit', in Donald Allchin, D. Densil Morgan and Patrick Thomas, *Sensuous Glory: The Poetic Vision of D. Gwenallt Jones* (Norwich: Canterbury Press, 2000), p. 65 (pp. 43–89).

18 Dyfnallt Morgan, *D. Gwenallt Jones* (Cardiff: University of Wales Press, 1972), p. 7.

19 Morgan, *D. Gwenallt Jones*, p. 8.

20 Bell, 'The Twentieth Century', p. 414.

21 Morgan, *D. Gwenallt Jones*, p. 5.

22 D. J. Williams, *The Old Farmhouse*, trans. Waldo Williams (London: George G. Harrap & Co. Ltd, 1961), pp. 140 and 143. As mentioned in Chapter 1, this was originally published in Welsh as *Hen Dŷ Ffarm* (Aberystwyth: Gwasg Aberystwyth, 1953).

23 Thomas, *The Welsh Extremist*, p. 52.

24 Morgan, *D. Gwenallt Jones*, p. 19.

25 Emyr Humphreys, *Outside the House of Baal* ([1965]; rpt. London: J. M. Dent & Sons Ltd, 1988), p. 112.

26 Morgan, *D. Gwenallt Jones*, pp. 22, 224.

27 Lily Tobias, *Eunice Fleet* ([1933]; Dinas Powys: Honno, 2004). References to this edition are abbreviated as 'EF' and page numbers are incorporated in parentheses in the text.
28 Jasmine Donahaye, *The Greatest Need: The Creative Life and Troubled Times of Lily Tobias, a Welsh Jew in Palestine* (Dinas Powys: Honno, 2015), p. 155.
29 Julia Kristeva, *Powers of Horror: An Essay on Abjection* (New York: Columbia University Press, 1982), pp. 36–7.
30 Donahaye, *The Greatest Need*, p. 155.
31 Donahaye, *The Greatest Need*, p. 156.

4: The Spirit of Pacifism: Waldo Williams and D. Gwenallt Jones

1 References to Waldo's poetry in Welsh are to Waldo Williams, *Dail Pren* (Llandysul: Gwasg Gomer, 2010). They are abbreviated as 'DP' and page references are given in parentheses in the text. References to Waldo's poetry in English are to Anthony Conran (trans.), *Waldo Williams, 1904–1971* (Llandysul: Gwasg Gomer/Gomer Press, 1997). They are abbreviated as 'WW' and page numbers are given in parentheses in the text.
2 Alan Llwyd, *Stori Waldo Williams: Bardd Heddwch/The Story of Waldo Williams: Poet of Peace* (Llandybïe: Barddas, bilingual text, 2010), p. 25.
3 Llwyd, *Stori Waldo Williams*, p. 21.
4 Llwyd, *Stori Waldo Williams*, p. 177.
5 H. Idris Bell, 'The Twentieth Century', appendix to Thomas Parry, *A History of Welsh Literature* trans. Idris Bell (Oxford: Clarendon Press, 1955), p. 396.
6 Bell, 'The Twentieth Century', p. 398.
7 Bell, 'The Twentieth Century', p. 398.
8 Llwyd, *Stori Waldo Williams*, p. 63.
9 Rowan Williams, 'Waldo Williams – Poetry and Peacemaking', Annual Lecture to the Waldo Williams Society, 23 March 2012, Pisgah Congregationalist Chapel, Pembrokeshire. Available at *aoc2013.brix.fatbeehive.com*.
10 Llwyd, *Stori Waldo Williams*, p. 99.
11 David Cadman and Scherto Gill (eds), *Peacefulness: Being Peace and Making Peace* (Reykjavik: Spirit of Humanities Press, 2017), p. 34.
12 C. E. Raven, *The Starting Point of Pacifism* (London: Peace Pledge Union, 1940), p. 21.
13 Kenneth McConkey, *Memory and Desire: Painting in Britain and Ireland at the Turn of the Twentieth Century* (Aldershot: Ashgate, 2002), p. 148.
14 Ned Thomas, *The Welsh Extremist* (Talybont: Y Lolfa, [1973]; rpt 1991 with a new concluding chapter), p. 50.
15 Thomas, *The Welsh Extremist*, p. 50.
16 Russell Davies, '"Do not go gentle into that good night"? Women and suicide in Carmarthenshire', in Angela V. John (ed.), *Our Mothers' Land: Chapters in Welsh Women's History 1830–1939* (Cardiff: University of Wales Press, 1991), p. 100.
17 W. J. Gruffydd, *Hen Atgofion* (Aberystwyth: Gwasg Aberystwyth, 1942); D. Parry-Jones, *Welsh Country Characters* (London and New York: B. T. Batsford Ltd., 1952).

18 S. Baring-Gould, *In Dewisland* (London: Methuen, 1904), p. 1.
19 T. Gwynn Jones, *The Culture and Tradition of Wales* (Wrexham: Urdd y Deyrnas, 1927), p. 14.
20 Jones, *The Culture and Tradition of Wales*, p. 15.
21 Llwyd, *Stori Waldo Williams*, p. 55.
22 George M. Ll. Davies, *Essays Towards Peace* (London: Sheppard Press, 1946), p. 10.
23 Siwan Richards, 'Waldo: Rhai o'i Eiriau Mawr', in J. E. Caerwyn Williams (ed.), *Ysgrifau Beirniadol XXIII* (Dinbych, 1997), pp. 241–62, quoted in Jason Walford Davies 'Pa Wyrth Hen eu Perthynas? Waldo Williams a 'Chymdeithasiad Geiriau', in Damian Walford Davies and Jason Walford Davies (eds), *Cof ac Arwydd: Ysgrifau Newydd ar Waldo Williams* (Llandybïe: Cyhoeddiadau Barddas, 2006), pp. 163–4 (pp. 163–211).
24 J. Walford Davies, 'Pa Wyrth Hen eu Perthynas', p. 163.
25 J. Walford Davies, 'Pa Wyrth Hen eu Perthynas', p. 179.
26 Thomas, *The Welsh Extremist*, pp. 51–2.
27 C. Bryner Jones, 'Some Welsh Rural Problems', *The Welsh Outloook*, vol. xvii, no. 11 (November 1930), 301.
28 Jones, 'Some Welsh Rural Problems', 302.
29 Jones, 'Some Welsh Rural Problems', 302.
30 Llwyd, *Stori Waldo Williams*, p. 77.
31 Llwyd, *Stori Waldo Williams*, pp. 74–5.
32 Rowan Williams omits this reference from his translation.
33 Rowan Williams, 'Between two fields', in Damian Walford Davies (ed.), *Cartographies of Culture: New Geographies of Welsh Writing in English* (Cardiff: University of Wales Press, 2012), p. 173.
34 Walford Davies, *Cartographies of Culture*, p. 190.
35 Walford Davies, *Cartographies of Culture*, p. 190.
36 Walford Davies, *Cartographies of Culture*, pp. 191–2.
37 Walford Davies, *Cartographies of Culture*, p. 176.
38 Walford Davies, *Cartographies of Culture*, p. 180.
39 James Nicholas, *Waldo Williams* (Cardiff: University of Wales Press, 1975), p. 70.
40 Nicholas, *Waldo Williams*, p. 39.
41 Rowan Williams, 'Between two fields', p. 173.
42 Llwyd, *Stori Waldo Williams*, p. 71.
43 Raven, *The Starting Point of Pacifism*, p. 5.
44 Alan Llwyd and Robert Rhys, *Waldo Williams: Cerddi 1922–1970* (Llandysul: Gwasg Gomer, 2014), p. 392.
45 Llwyd and Rhys, *Waldo Williams*, p. 392.
46 Llwyd and Rhys, *Waldo Williams*, p. 392.
47 Nicholas, *Waldo Williams*, p. 15. This poem could be seen as an overtly pacifist version of Lynette Roberts's war-time poem 'Swansea Raid'.
48 Nicholas, *Waldo Williams*, p. 44.
49 C. James (ed.), *Cerddi Gwenallt: Y Casgliad Cyflawn* (Llandysul: Gwasg Gomer, 2001), p. 129. Subsequent references to this work are abbreviated as 'GCC' and page numbers are given in parentheses in the text.
50 Bell, 'The Twentieth Century', p. 417.

51 In his lecture, *Folklore and Myth in the Mabinogion* (1950) delivered to Amgueddfa Genedlaethol National Museum of Wales ([1950]; London: Amgueddfa Genedlaethol/Read Books Ltd, 2011).
52 Morgan, 'Gwenallt: Poet of Flesh and Spirit', p. 58.
53 Morgan, 'Gwenallt: Poet of Flesh and Spirit', p. 88.
54 Morgan, 'Gwenallt: Poet of Flesh and Spirit', p. 58.
55 Morgan, 'Gwenallt: Poet of Flesh and Spirit', p. 76.
56 Morgan, 'Gwenallt: Poet of Flesh and Spirit', pp. 55, 54.
57 Morgan, 'Gwenallt: Poet of Flesh and Spirit', p. 58.
58 This title has been translated by Dyfnallt Morgan as 'Adrift'; Dyfnallt Morgan, *D. Gwenallt Jones* (Cardiff: University of Wales Press, 1972), p. 14. Patrick Thomas translates it as 'Astray', which perhaps has a slightly stronger biblical and religious connotation. Thomas, '[Translation of] Selected poems of Gwenallt', in Donald Aitchin, D. Densil Morgan and Patrick Thomas, *Sensuous Glory*, p. 149 (pp. 91–150). All subsequent references to Thomas's translations are abbreviated as 'PT' and page numbers are given in parentheses in the text.
59 Dyfnallt Morgan, *D. Gwenallt Jones* (Cardiff: University of Wales Press, 1972), p. 15.
60 Morgan, *D. Gwenallt Jones*, p. 15.
61 A. C. Grayling, *War: An Enquiry* (New Haven and London: Yale University Press, 2017), p. 23.
62 Grayling, *War: An Enquiry*, p. 22.
63 Menna Elfyn, 'Colomennod Cwm'/'Pigeons in Ebbw Vale', in *Perfect Blemish/Perffaith Nam/New and Selected Poems 1995–2007/Dau Ddetholiad & Cherddi Newydd 1995–2007* (Hexham: Bloodaxe Books Ltd, 2007), pp. 66, 67. The co-location of iron ore and coal in the south Wales valley of Ebbw Vale fed the largest steel mill in Europe before its closure in 1965.
64 At 9.15 on the morning of 21 October 1966 a coal tip engulfed a junior school in Aberfan killing 116 children and 28 adults.
65 Morgan, 'Gwenallt: Poet of Flesh and Spirit', p. 86.
66 Morgan, 'Gwenallt: Poet of Flesh and Spirit', pp. 85–7.
67 Oliver P. Richmond, *Peace: A Very Short Introduction* (Oxford: Oxford University Press, 2014), p. 1.

5: Unpeaceful Voices

1 M. Wynn Thomas, *In the Shadow of the Pulpit: Literature and Nonconformist Wales* (Cardiff: University of Wales Press, 2010), p. 318. References to the novel in this chapter are to Emyr Humphreys, *Outside the House of Baal* ([1965]; rpt. London: J. M. Dent & Sons Ltd, 1988) and page numbers are given in parentheses in the text.
2 Thomas, *In the Shadow of the Pulpit*, pp. 314–16.
3 Thomas, *In the Shadow of the Pulpit*, p. 315.
4 Jen Llywelyn, *Pilgrim of Peace: A Life of George M. Ll. Davies* (Talybont: Y Lolfa, 2016), p. 215.
5 Llywelyn, *Pilgrim of Peace*, p. 215.
6 Llywelyn, *Pilgrim of Peace*, p. 216.
7 Llywelyn, *Pilgrim of Peace*, p. 217.

8 George M. Ll. Davies, *Pilgrimage of Peace* (London: The Fellowship of Reconciliation, 1950), p. 63. All subsequent references to this work are abbreviated as 'PP' and pages numbers are given in parentheses in the text.
9 A. C. Grayling, *War: An Enquiry* (New Haven and London: Yale University Press, 2017), p. 234.
10 Thomas, *In the Shadow of the Pulpit*, p. 315.
11 George M. Ll. Davies, 'Presbyterian Law – And Grace', *The Welsh Outlook*, vol. xvii, no. 11 (November 1930), 293.
12 Davies, 'Presbyterian Law', 294.
13 Davies, 'Presbyterian Law', 294.
14 Davies, 'Presbyterian Law', 293–5.
15 Davies, 'Presbyterian Law', 294.
16 Llywelyn, *Pilgrim of Peace,* p. 220.
17 George M. Ll. Davies, *Essays Towards Peace* (London: Sheppard Press, 1946), pp. 97ff.
18 Thomas, *In the Shadow of the Pulpit*, p. 314.
19 Gwynfor Evans, *Land of My Fathers: 2000 Years of Welsh History* ([1974]; English version, Talybont: Y Lolfa, 1992), p. 424.
20 Emyr Price, *David Lloyd George* (Cardiff: University of Wales Press, 2006), p. 198.
21 Price, *David Lloyd George*, p. 199.
22 Price, *David Lloyd George*, p. 200.
23 Price, *David Lloyd George*, p. 200.
24 T. Gwynn Jones, *The Culture and Tradition of Wales* (Wrexham: Urdd y Deyrnas, 1927), p. 18.
25 Evans, *Land of My Fathers*, p. 431.
26 John Davies, *A History of Wales* (Harmondsworth: Penguin, [1990]; revised and updated 2007), p. 495.
27 K. O. Morgan, 'Peace Movements in Wales', *Welsh History Review*, 10/3 (June 1981), 409 (398–430).
28 Grayling, *War: An Enquiry*, p. 124.
29 Price, *David Lloyd George*, p. 186.
30 Davies, *A History of Wales,* p. 495.
31 Davies, *A History of Wales*, p. 497.
32 Julia Kristeva, *Powers of Horror: An Essay on Abjection* (New York: Columbia University Press, 1982), p. 125.
33 Iorwerth Peate, *Ym Mhob Pen* (Llandysul: Gwasg Gomer, 1948), p. 56.
34 Kristeva, *Powers of Horror*, p. 125,
35 Thomas, *In the Shadow of the Pulpit*, p. 314.
36 William Clark, 'The Curse of Militarism', *The Young Man* [Magazine] (1901), 145 [pp. 145–9].
37 Clark, 'The Curse of Militarism', p. 145.
38 Clark, 'The Curse of Militarism', p. 146.

6: Post-Pacifism: Peace and War

1 Oliver P. Richmond, *Peace: A Very Short Introduction* (Oxford: Oxford University Press, 2014), pp. 9–10.

2 Angharad Price, *The Life of Rebecca Jones*, trans. Lloyd Jones (London: MacLehose Press, 2010), p. 144. Subsequent references to this edition are abbreviated as 'TLRJ' and page numbers are given in parentheses in the text.
3 Angharad Price, *O! Tyn y Gorchudd* (Llandysul: Gwasg Gomer, 2002), p. 141. Subsequent references are abbreviated as 'OTYG' and page numbers are given in parentheses in the text.
4 Tony Curtis, *The Last Candles* (Bridgend: Seren, 1989). Poems reprinted in *War Voices* are in the third section of the book: 'Poles', 'Kalavyrta', 'Window seat to Chicago', 'At Ochrid Lake', 'From the City that Shone', 'The Last Candles', 'Friedhof', and 'Home Front'.
5 Kenneth McConkey, *Memory and Desire: Painting in Britain and Ireland at the Turn of the Twentieth Century* (Aldershot: Ashgate, 2002), p. 17.
6 Tony Curtis, *War Voices* (Bridgend: Seren, 1995), p. 9. Subsequent references are abbreviated as 'WV' and page numbers are given in parentheses in the text.
7 Tony Curtis, 'Killing John Jones: a Writer Looks Back', in Sam Adams (ed.), *Seeing Wales Whole* (Cardiff: University of Wales Press, 1998), p. 146.
8 Curtis, 'Killing John Jones: a Writer Looks Back', p. 158.
9 Curtis, 'Killing John Jones: a Writer Looks Back', p. 161.
10 Tony Curtis, *Dannie Abse* (Cardiff: University of Wales Press, 1985), p. 94.
11 Curtis, *Dannie Abse*, p. 92.
12 Curtis, *Dannie Abse*, p. 88.
13 Curtis, *Dannie Abse*, p. 86.
14 Curtis, *Dannie Abse*, p. 86.
15 Curtis, *Dannie Abse*, p. 84.
16 Curtis, *Dannie Abse*, pp. 82, 83.
17 Curtis, *Dannie Abse*, pp. 72, 73.
18 Curtis, *Dannie Abse*, p. 74.
19 George M. Ll. Davies, *Pilgrimage of Peace* (London: The Fellowship of Reconciliation, 1950), pp. 88–9. Subsequent references to this work are abbreviated as 'PP' and page numbers are given in parenthesis in the text.
20 D. Densil Morgan, *The Span of the Cross: Christian Religion and Society in Wales 1914–2000* (Cardiff: University of Wales Press, 2011), p. 161.
21 McConkey, *Memory and Desire*, p. 231.
22 McConkey, *Memory and Desire*, p. 221.
23 McConkey, *Memory and Desire*, p. 221.
24 Julia Kristeva, *Powers of Horror: An Essay on Abjection* (New York: Columbia University Press, 1982), p. 129.
25 Kristeva, *Powers of Horror*, p. 129.

7: A Welsh Pacifist Translation of an English Classic . . . An Afterword

1 Idris Bell, 'The Twentieth Century', appendix to Thomas Parry, *A History of Welsh Literature*, trans. Idris Bell (Oxford: Clarendon Press, 1955), pp. 461–2.
2 John Eilian (trans.), *Du Del* (Glasgow: Collins Clear-Type Press, 1954). Subsequent references to this edition are abbreviated as 'DD', and page references are given in parentheses in the text.

3 Peter Hollindale, 'Plain Speaking: *Black Beauty* as a Quaker Text', *Children's Literature*, 28 (2000), 98.
4 Hollindale, 'Plain Speaking: *Black Beauty* as a Quaker Text', 110.
5 Horst Dölvers, '"Let the Beasts Bear Gentle Minds": Variety and Conflict of Discourses in Anna Sewell's "Black Beauty"', *Arbeiten aus Anglistik und Amerikanistik, Tübingen*, 18/2 (1 January 1993), 206.
6 Hollindale, 'Plain Speaking: *Black Beauty* as a Quaker Text', 110.
7 A. C. Grayling, *War: An Enquiry* (New Haven and London: Yale University Press, 2017), p. 124.
8 Grayling, *War: An Enquiry*, p. 235.
9 David Cadman and Scherto Gill, 'Introduction', in David Cadman and Scherto Gill (eds), *Peacefulness: Being Peace and Making Peace* (Reykjavik: Spirit of Humanity Press, 2017), p. 9.

Select Bibliography

Texts

Brown, T. (ed.), *The Collected Stories Glyn Jones* (Cardiff: University of Wales Press, 1990).

Clark, W., 'The Curse of Militarism', *The Young Man* [Magazine] (1901), 145–9.

Conran, A. (ed. and trans.), *The Penguin Book of Welsh Verse* (Harmondsworth: Penguin, 1967).

Conran, A. (trans.), *Waldo Williams, 1904–1971* (Llandysul: Gwasg Gomer/Gomer Press, 1997).

Curtis, T., 'Killing John Jones: a writer looks back', in Sam Adams (ed.), *Seeing Wales Whole: Essays on the Literature of Wales, in Honour of Meic Stephens* (Cardiff: University of Wales Press, 1998), pp. 144–70.

Curtis, T., *War Voices* (Bridgend: Seren, 1995).

Curtis, T., *The Last Candles* (Bridgend: Seren, 1989).

Davies, G. M. Ll., *Pilgrimage of Peace* (London: The Fellowship of Reconciliation, 1950).

Davies, G. M. Ll., *Essays Towards Peace* (London: Sheppard Press, 1946).

Davies, G. M. Ll., *Profiadau Pellach* (Dinbych: Llyfrau Pawb, Pererindod Heddwch II, 1943).

Davies, G. M. Ll., *Religion and the Quest for Peace* (London: The Peace Pledge Union, 1942).

Davies, G. M. Ll., 'Presbyterian Law – And Grace', *The Welsh Outlook*, vol. xvii, no. 11 (November 1930), 293–6.

Davies, P., *Diary of a Soul*, trans. Herbert Hughes (Talybont: Y Llolfa, 2011).

Edwards, D. I. (ed.) *Cerddi: W. J. Gruffydd: Elerydd* (Caernarfon: Gwasg Gwynedd, 1990).

Eilian, J. (trans.), *Du Del* (Glasgow: Collins Clear-Type Press, 1954).

Emerson, R. W., *Complete Prose Works* (New York: Ward, Locke & Co. Ltd., 1900).

Evans, G., *Land of My Fathers: 2000 Years of Welsh history* (Talybont: Y Lolfa, 1992).

Evans, G., *Heddychiaeth Gristnogol yng Nghymru* (Llandysul: Gwasg Gomer, 1991).

Gruffydd, W. J., *Tomos a Marged* (Llandysul: Gwasg Gomer, 1965).

Gruffydd, W. J., '*Y Bardd*', in Welsh Committee of the Communist Party, *A Great Welshman: Symposium of Tributes to Dr. T. Gwynn Jones* (Cardiff: South Wales Bookshop Ltd, 1944).

Gruffydd, W. J., *Hen Atgofion* (Aberystwyth: Gwasg Aberystwyth, 1942).

Herbert, M. and Sellars, S. (eds), *Virginia Woolf, The Waves* (Cambridge: Cambridge University Press, 2011).

Hughes, T. R., *William Jones* (Llandysul: Gwasg Gomer, 1944).

Humphreys, E. *The Shop* (Bridgend: Seren, 2005).

Humphreys, E., *Unconditional Surrender* (Bridgend: Seren, 1996).

Humphreys, E., *Outside the House of Baal* ([1965]; rev. edn London: J. M. Dent & Sons Ltd, 1988).

Humphreys, E., *A Toy Epic* ([1958]; rpt Bridgend: Seren, 1989).

James C. (ed.), *Cerddi Gwenallt: Y Casgliad Cyflawn* (Llandysul: Gwasg Gomer, 2001).

Jones, D. G., *Plasau'r Brenin* (Llandysul: Gwasg Gomer, 1934).

Jones, G., *The Dragon Has Two Tongues* (Cardiff: University of Wales Press, 2001).

Jones, T. G., *Caniadau* (Abertawe: Hughes a'i Fab (Cyhoeddwyr), 1978).

Jones, T. G., 'Argoed', trans. Anthony Conran, in Anthony Conran (ed.), *The Penguin Book of Welsh Verse* (Harmondsworth: Penguin, 1967).

Jones, T. G., *Folklore and Myth in the Mabinogion* ([1950]; London: Amgueddfa Genedlaethol/Read Books Ltd, 2011).

Jones, T. G., *Thomas Huws Davies, O.B.E. (1882–1940)* (London: The Honourable Society of Cymmrodorion, 1941).

Jones, T. G., *The Culture and Tradition of Wales* (Wrexham: Urdd y Deyrnas, 1927).

Llwyd, A. and Rhys, R. (eds), *Waldo Williams: Cerddi 1922–1970* (Llandysul: Gwasg Gomer, 2014).

Nicholas, T. E., *Prison Sonnets* (London: W. Griffiths & Co, 1948).

Nicholas, T. E., *Canu'r Carchar* ([1942]; rpt Llandysul: Gwasg Gomer, 1943).

Nicholas, T. E., *Llygad y Drws: Sonedau'r Carchar* (Aberystwyth: Gwasg Aberystwyth, 1940).

Nichols, B., *Cry Havoc* (London: Jonathan Cape, 1933).

Parry-Jones, D., *Welsh Country Characters* (London and New York: B. T. Batsford Ltd, 1952).

Peate, I. C., *Rhwng Dau Fyd* (Aberystwyth: Cambrian News, 1976).

Peate, I. C., *Dyfodol Ein Llenyddiaeth* (Llandybïe: Cyfres yr Academi 3, 1962).

Peate, I. C. *Ym Mhob Pen . . . Ysgrifau* (Llandysul: Gwasg Gomer, 1948).

Peate, I. C., *Y Traddodiad Heddwch yng Nghymru* (Pamffledi Heddwchwyr Cymru, 1, 1941).

Price, A. *The Life of Rebecca Jones*, trans. Lloyd Jones (London: MacLehose Press, 2010).

Price, A., *O! Tyn y Gorchudd* (Llandysul: Gwasg Gomer, 2002).

Ruck, R. (trans.), *T. Rowland Hughes, William Jones* (Aberystwyth: Gwasg Aberystwyth, 1953).

Stephens, M. (trans.), *For the Sake of Wales: The Memoirs of Gwynfor Evans* ([1996]; Cardiff: Welsh Academic Press, 2001).

Thomas, P. (ed. and trans.) 'Selected Poems of Gwenallt', in Donald Allchin, D. Densil Morgan and Patrick Thomas, *Sensuous Glory: The Poetic Vision of D. Gwenallt Jones* (Norwich: The Canterbury Press, in partnership with The Centre for the Advanced Study of Religion, University of Bangor, 2000), pp. 91–154.

Tobias, L., *Eunice Fleet* ([1933]; rpt. Dinas Powys: Honno, 2004).

Turner, M. *A Pretty Sort of Prison* (London and Dunmow: Pall Mall Press, 1964).

Williams, D. J. *Hen Dŷ Ffarm* (Aberystwyth: Gwasg Aberystwyth, 1953).

Williams, R. (trans.), '[Waldo Williams] Between two fields', in Damian Walford Davies, *Cartographies of Culture: New Geographies of Welsh Writing in English* (Cardiff: University of Wales Press, 2012), p. 173.

Williams, W., *Dail Pren* (Llandysul: Gwasg Gomer, 2010).

Williams, W. (trans.), *D. J. Williams, The Old Farmhouse* (London: George G. Harrap & Co. Ltd, 1961).

Woolf, V., 'Thoughts on peace in an air raid', in Stuart N. Clarke (ed.), *The Essays of Virginia Woolf*, vol. 6 (London: The Hogarth Press, 2011), pp. 242–8.

Criticism and secondary works

Aaron, J. and Thomas, M. W., '"Pulling you through changes": Welsh writing in English before, between and after two referenda', in M. Wynn Thomas (ed.), *Welsh Writing in English* (Cardiff: University of Wales Press, 2003), pp. 278–309.

Adams, S. (ed.), *Seeing Wales Whole: Essays on the Literature of Wales, in Honour of Meic Stephens* (Cardiff: University of Wales Press, 1998).

Aichele, G., 'Jesus' violence', in Tina Pippin and George Aichele (eds), *Violence, Utopia and the Kingdom of God* (London and New York: Routledge, 1981), pp. 72–91.

Allchin, D., Morgan, D. D. and Thomas, P., *Sensuous Glory: The Poetic Vision of D. Gwenallt Jones* (Norwich: The Canterbury Press, in partnership with The Centre for the Advanced Study of Religion, University of Bangor, 2000).

Barash, D., *Approaches to Peace* (Oxford: Oxford University Press, 2000).

Barlow, R., *Wales and World War One* (Llandysul: Gomer, 2014).

Bell, H. I., 'The Twentieth Century', appendix to Thomas Parry, *A History of Welsh Literature* trans. Idris Bell (Oxford: Clarendon Press, 1955).

Bell, R. G., *Alternative to War* (London: James Clarke & Co. Ltd, 1959).

Brown, H., *The Truest Form of Patriotism: Pacifist Feminism in Britain, 1870–1902* (Manchester: Manchester University Press, 2004).

Bourke, J., *Wounding the World: How Military Violence and War-Play Invade Our Lives* (London: Virago, 2014).

Cadman, D. and Gill, S. (eds.), *Peacefulness: Being Peace and Making Peace* (Reykjavik: Spirit of Humanity Press, 2017).

Chríost, D. M. G., *Welsh Writing, Political Action and Incarceration: Branwen's Starling*, Palgrave Studies in Minority Languages and Communities (Basingstoke: Palgrave Macmillan, 2013).–

Cohen, J., 'Conversations with Dannie Abse', in Joseph Cohen (ed.), *The Poetry of Dannie Abse: Critical Essays and Reminiscences* (London: Robson Books, 1983).

Cragoe, M. and Williams, C. (eds), *Wales and War: Society, Politics and Religion in the Nineteenth and Twentieth Centuries* (Cardiff: University of Wales Press, 2007).

Curtis, T., *Dannie Abse* (Cardiff: University of Wales Press, 1985).

Davies, R., '"Do not go gentle into that good night"? Women and suicide in Carmarthenshire', in Angela V. John (ed.), *Our Mothers' Land: Chapters in Welsh Women's History 1830–1939* (Cardiff: University of Wales Press, 1991), pp. 93–108

Dölvers, H., '"Let the Beasts Bear Gentle Minds". Variety and Conflict of Discourses in Anna Sewell's "Black Beauty"', *Arbeiten aus Anglistik und Amerikanistik, Tübingen*, 18/2 (1 January 1993), 195–216.

Donahaye, J., *The Greatest Need: The Creative Life and Troubled Times of Lily Tobias, a Welsh Jew in Palestine* (Dinas Powys: Honno, 2015).

Eirug, A., *The Opposition to the Great War in Wales 1914–1918* (Cardiff: University of Wales Press, 2018).

Evans, R., *Gwynfor Evans: Portrait of a Patriot* (Talybont: Y Llolfa, 2008).

Evans, S. R., 'The true "Gymraes": images of women in women's nineteenth-century Welsh periodicals', in Angela V. John (ed.), *Our Mothers' Land: Chapters in Welsh Women's History 1830–1939* (Cardiff: University of Wales Press, 1991), pp. 69–91.

Fry, D. *Beyond War* (Oxford: Oxford University Press, 2007).

Gee, D., *Spectacle, Reality, Resistance: Confronting a Culture of Militarism* (London: Forces Watch, 2014).

Gilpin, W. C., 'The Letter from Prison in Christian History and Theology', University of Chicago Divinity School, Online, 2003. Available at *https://divinity.uchicago.edu>webforum* (accessed 3 August 2018).

Grayling, A. C., *War: An Enquiry* (New Haven and London: Yale University Press, 2017).

Hollindale, P., 'Plain Speaking: *Black Beauty* as a Quaker Text', *Children's Literature*, 28 (2000), 95–111.

Hopkins, D., 'Patriots and Pacifists in Wales 1914–1918', *Llafur*, vol. 1, no. 3 (1974), 27–41.

Howard, M., *The Invention of Peace and War* (London: Profile Books, 2000).

Jackson, R., *Fantasy: The Literature of Subversion* (London: Routledge, 1981).

John, A. V. (ed.), *Our Mothers' Land: Chapters in Welsh Women's History 1830–1939* (Cardiff: University of Wales Press, 1991).

Jones, C. Bryner, 'Some Welsh Rural Problems', *The Welsh Outlook*, vol. xvii, no. 11 (November 1930), 301–3.

Jones, G. J., *The Quest for Peace* (Cardiff: University of Wales Press, 1969).

Jones, R. G., 'Like foolish boys: some thoughts on the poetry of two cousins', in Sam Adams (ed.), *Seeing Wales Whole: Essays on the Literature of Wales, in Honour of Meic Stephens* (Cardiff: University of Wales Press, 1998), pp. 102–20.

Kershaw, I., *Hitler* (Harmondsworth: Penguin Books, 1998).

Kristeva, J., *Powers of Horror: An Essay on Abjection* (New York: Columbia University Press, 1982).

Llywelyn, J., *Pilgrim of Peace: A Life of George M. Ll. Davies* (Talybont: Y Lolfa, 2016).

Llwyd, A., *Stori Waldo Williams: Bardd Heddwch/The Story of Waldo Williams: Poet of Peace*, bilingual text (Llandybïe: Barddas, 2010).

Lonsdale, K., *Removing the Causes of War*, Swarthmore Lecture, Society of Friends, 1953 (London: George Allen &Unwin Ltd, 1953).

McConkey, K., *Memory and Desire: Painting in Britain and Ireland at the Turn of the Twentieth Century* (Aldershot: Ashgate, 2002).

Morgan, D. D., *The Span of the Cross: Christian Religion and Society in Wales 1914–2000* (Cardiff: University of Wales Press, 2011).

Morgan, D. D., 'Gwenallt: Poet of Flesh and Spirit', in Donald Allchin, D. Densil Morgan and Patrick Thomas, *Sensuous Glory: The Poetic Vision of D. Gwenallt Jones* (Norwich: The Canterbury Press, in partnership with The Centre for the Advanced Study of Religion, University of Bangor, 2000), pp. 43–89.

Morgan, D. D., 'Tyst ymhlith y Tystion: profiad Cymro yn Almaen Hitler', *Transactions of the Honourable Society of Cymmrodorion*, New Series 6 (1995), 156–66.

Morgan, D. D., *Gwenallt Jones* (Cardiff: University of Wales Press, 1972).

Morgan, K. O., *Revolution to Devolution: Reflections on Welsh Democracy* (Cardiff: University of Wales Press, 2014).

Morgan, K. O., 'Peace Movements in Wales, 1899–1945', *Welsh History Review*, 10/3 (June 1981), 398–430.

Nicholas, J. (ed.), *Waldo* (Llandysul: Gwasg Gomer, 1977).

Nicholas, J., *Waldo Williams* (Cardiff: University of Wales Press, 1975).

Nichols, B., *Cry Havoc* (London: Jonathan Cape, 1933).

Norris, L., *Glyn Jones* (Cardiff: University of Wales Press, 1973).

Peach, L., *The Fiction of Emyr Humphreys: Contemporary Critical Perspectives* (Cardiff: University of Wales Press, 2011).

Pope, R., *Building Jerusalem: Nonconformity, Labour and the Social Question in Wales, 1906–1939* (Cardiff: University of Wales Press,1998).

Price, E., *David Lloyd George* (Cardiff: University of Wales Press, 2006).

Raven, C. E., *The Starting Point of Pacifism* (London: Peace Pledge Union, 1940).

Rhys, R. (ed.), *Waldo Williams* (Swansea: Gwasg Christopher Davies, 1981).

Richards, S., 'Waldo: Rhai o'i Eiriau Mawr', in J. E. Caerwyn Williams (ed.), *Ysgrifau Beirniadol XXIII* (Dinbych, 1997), pp. 241–62.

Riches, A., *When the Comics Went to War* (Edinburgh: Mainstream, 2009).

Richmond, O. P., *Peace: A Very Short Introduction* (Oxford: Oxford University Press, 2014).

Richmond, O. P., *The Transformation of Peace* (London: Palgrave, 2005).

Richmond, O. P., *Maintaining Order, Making Peace* (London: Palgrave, 2002).

Rose, J., *Why War? – Psychoanalysis, Politics, and the Return to Melanie Klein* (Oxford: Blackwell, 1993).

Schmitt, D., 'Sermons', Concordia Theology, Online, 2011. Available at *https://concordiatheology.org>sermon-structs* (accessed 3 August 2018).

Sheppard, H. R. L., *We Say "No": The Plain Man's Guide to Pacifism* (London: John Murray, 1935).

Smith, L., *Voices Against War: A Century of Protest* (Harmondsworth: Penguin, 2010).

Stephens, M., Obituary of Gwynfor Evans, *Independent*, 21 April 2005 (Online). Available at *https://www.independent.co.uk/news/obituaries/gwynfor-evans-495883.html* (accessed 3 August 2018).

Stevens, C., *Iorwerth C. Peate* (Cardiff: University of Wales Press, 1986).

Thomas. G., 'D. Gwenallt Jones (1899–1968)', *Poetry Wales*, 4/3 (Spring, 1969), 5–10.

Thomas, M. W., *In the Shadow of the Pulpit: Literature and Nonconformist Wales* (Cardiff: University of Wales Press, 2010).

Thomas, M. W. (ed.), *Welsh Writing in English* (Cardiff: University of Wales Press, 2003).

Thomas, M. W., *Corresponding Cultures: The Two Literatures of Wales* (Cardiff: University of Wales Press, 1999).

Thomas, M. W. 'Outside the House of Baal: the evolution of a major novel', in Sam Adams (ed.), *Seeing Wales Whole: Essays on the Literature of Wales* (Cardiff: University of Wales Press, 1998), pp. 121–43.

Thomas, M. W., 'From Walt to Waldo: Whitman's Welsh admirers', *Walt Whitman Quarterly Review*, 10/2 (1992), 61–73.

Thomas, N., *Waldo* (Caernarfon: Gwasg Pantycelyn, 1985).

Thomas, N., *The Welsh Extremist: A Culture in Crisis* (London: Victor Gollancz, [1971]; third edn published as *The Welsh Extremist: Modern Welsh Politics, Literature and Society* (Talybont: Y Llolfa, 1991).

Walford Davies, D., *Cartographies of Culture: New Geographies of Welsh Writing in English* (Cardiff: University of Wales Press, 2012).

Walford Davies, D., *Waldo Williams: Rhyddiaith* (Cardiff: University of Wales Press, 2001).

Walford Davies, J., 'Pa Wyrth Hen eu Perthynas?': Waldo Williams a "Chymdeithasiad Geiriau"', in Damian Walford Davies and Jason Walford Davies (eds), *Cof ac Arwydd: Ysgrifau Newydd ar Waldo Williams* (Llandybïe: Cyhoeddiadau Barddas, 2006), pp. 163–211.

Welsh Committee of the Communist Party, *A Great Welshman: Symposium of Tributes to Dr. T. Gwynn Jones* (Cardiff: South Wales Bookshop Ltd, 1944).

White, R. S., *Pacifism and English Literature: Minstrels of Peace* (Basingstoke: Palgrave Macmillan, 2008).

Williams, R., 'Waldo Williams – Poetry and Peacemaking', Annual Lecture to the Waldo Williams Society, 23 March 2012, Pisgah Congregationalist

Chapel, Pembrokeshire. Available at *aoc2013.brix.fatbeehive.com* (accessed 3 August 2018).

Zipes, J., 'Preface', in Tina Pippin and George Aichele (eds), *Violence, Utopia and the Kingdom of God: Fantasy and Ideology in the Bible* (London and New York: Routledge, 1998), pp. ix–xii.

Index

B

C

N

O

P

Y

Z